SHAKESPEARE SURVEY

SHAKESPEARE SURVEY

AN ANNUAL SURVEY OF
SHAKESPEARIAN STUDY & PRODUCTION

I

EDITED BY
ALLARDYCE NICOLL

Issued under the Sponsorship of
THE UNIVERSITY OF BIRMINGHAM
THE SHAKESPEARE MEMORIAL THEATRE
THE SHAKESPEARE BIRTHPLACE TRUST

CAMBRIDGE
AT THE UNIVERSITY PRESS
1970

Published by the Syndics of the Cambridge University Press
Bentley House, 200 Euston Road, London N.W. I
American Branch: 32 East 57th Street, New York, N.Y. 10022

ISBN 0 521 06414 7

First published 1948
Reprinted 1966 1970

Printed in Great Britain
at the University Printing House, Cambridge
(Brooke Crutchley, University Printer)

PREFACE

Shakespeare Survey, sponsored by a university, a theatre and a library rich in documents relating to Elizabethan times, aims at appealing to the scholar, the theatre-worker and the archivist, while at the same time presenting material likely to be of value to a wider public generally interested in Shakespeare. Although produced in Great Britain, it seeks to be international in its scope, and the Advisory Board is working in association with a panel of correspondents representing many of the chief countries of the world. It is believed that a valuable purpose can be served by such a series of volumes devoted to a dramatic author whose appeal is universal and seeking to record international activities connected with the study of his plays and with their representation on the stage.

The Advisory Board hopes that it will be able to print in successive volumes of *Shakespeare Survey* the results of recent research, and that opportunity will be found for the reproduction of documentary material either new or difficult of access. At the same time, care is being taken to avoid such duplication of effort as might occur through inclusion among its contents of information available elsewhere. For this reason, these volumes will not present any exhaustive bibliographical list of contributions to the study of Shakespeare printed during the twelve months preceding the publication of each volume, nor is any attempt being made to prepare a statistical record of performance of the plays whether in Great Britain or elsewhere. In the surveys of current activities the aim will rather be to select for comment and discussion some few items particularly interesting because of the novelty in their critical approach, of the fresh information they have to record or of their innovations in stage concept.

Apart from publishing original contributions to our knowledge and appreciation of Shakespeare, the Advisory Board believes that *Shakespeare Survey* can render one principal immediate service to those interested in the Elizabethan stage. We are approaching the mid-year of our century, and it is time for us to take stock, to inquire what in fact we have accomplished in study and on stage, and, by considering what yet remains to be done, to direct our path for the future. Hence the core of each volume will consist of a series of articles devoted to some particular aspect of Shakespearian study, introduced by a general survey designed to indicate what the past fifty years have contributed to this selected field of investigation. Thus in the present volume a major part of the contents is concerned with the Elizabethan theatre and with the theatrical influence on Shakespeare's writing; the volume indeed might almost have borne as a sub-title "Shakespeare and his Stage". For the second volume, similarly, a special topic has been chosen—"The Problem Plays and the Romances". Through such association of original articles with introductory 'retrospects', the Advisory Board hopes that *Shakespeare Survey* will not only secure unity of conception but will also serve both to assess the main trends in recent Shakespearian scholarship and to stimulate research in the future.

PREFACE

In addition, the present volume introduces the first of a series of articles devoted to an account of those libraries and archives particularly rich in matter relating to Shakespeare and the Elizabethan drama. Dr McManaway's record of the resources of the Folger Shakespeare Library at Washington will be followed by other kindred studies of collections both in this country and abroad. In later volumes it is planned to introduce a further series of related articles dealing with Shakespeare's fortunes during the past fifty years in diverse countries.

The launching of this venture was originally made possible by the support of its three sponsoring bodies, but a considerable improvement on the plans first determined upon has come from a grant generously contributed by the Rockefeller Foundation. To the Syndics of the Cambridge University Press the Advisory Board is indebted both for their co-operation in the production of this volume and for their active assistance in promoting its interests.

February 1948

CONTENTS

Notes are placed at the end of each contribution

CONTRIBUTORS

H. S. BENNETT
Fellow and Librarian, Emmanuel College, Cambridge

GERALD EADES BENTLEY
Professor of English Literature, Princeton University

HARDIN CRAIG
Professor of English Literature, The University of North Carolina

UNA ELLIS-FERMOR
Professor of English, Bedford College, The University of London

LEVI FOX
Director, The Shakespeare Birthplace Trust

CHARLES LANDSTONE
Associate Drama Director, Arts Council of Great Britain

CLIFFORD LEECH
Lecturer in English, The University of Durham

MICHEÁL MACLIAMMÓIR
Director, The Gate Theatre, Dublin

JAMES G. MCMANAWAY
Acting Director, The Folger Shakespeare Library, Washington

GEORGE RYLANDS
Fellow of King's College, Cambridge; University Lecturer in English

I. A. SHAPIRO
Lecturer in English, The University of Birmingham

J. DOVER WILSON
Emeritus Professor of English, The University of Edinburgh

LIST OF ILLUSTRATIONS

LIST OF ILLUSTRATIONS

STUDIES IN THE ELIZABETHAN STAGE
SINCE 1900

BY

ALLARDYCE NICOLL

Of one thing in particular Shakespearian scholarship during the past fifty years may justly be proud: only within the present century have we approached within measurable distance of an understanding of the methods employed in the original production of Elizabethan plays or endeavoured to set these plays, in our imagination, firmly against the background of their theatrical environment. No other field of investigation more characteristically belongs to our own age than this.

1. THE ELIZABETHAN STAGE IN THE NINETEENTH CENTURY

Even in recognizing the truth of this fact, however, we should not close our eyes to the very real achievements made in this direction by the romantic period preceding our own. Fully a hundred and fifty years ago that vigorous investigator, Edmund Malone, had succeeded in defining some of the main features of the theatres in which Shakespeare had worked. Although he possessed no information about the earliest of all professional London playhouses, the Theatre in Shoreditch, and was not sure when the Globe was built, he knew that the actors originally performed in inn-yards, that the home of Shakespeare's company was round or polygonal, that the audience stood in the yard or sat in the galleries, that dramatic action proceeded both on an upper-stage and on a lower and that the plays were graced with few or no scenic embellishments.

Following Malone came numerous other scholars, each intent on unearthing documentary material, each adding his discoveries to the common store: Collier, Cunningham, Halliwell-Phillipps and others thus actively added to the accumulation of knowledge until, by the century's end, men had a very fair general conception of the way in which the Elizabethan stage differed from the kind of theatre made colourful by an Irving and a Tree.

What is even more significant is the fact that, before the nineteenth century had reached its meridian, such accumulated knowledge was being put to practical use. On 16 March 1844, Benjamin Webster, lessee and director of the Haymarket, presented *The Taming of the Shrew* in a doubly novel manner: he not only gave it in the original text—a startling innovation after years of manhandling—he adopted a fresh method of production. There was a painted set of an inn for the 'Induction'; the scene then changed to the interior of a hall, to remain unaltered for the rest of the comedy. The Katherine-Petruchio play-within-the-play was enacted with "two screens and a pair of curtains" as "the whole dramatic apparatus". The comment of *The Times* critic is interesting:

By the mere substitution of one curtain for another [he explained to his readers] change of scene was indicated, and all the entrances and exits are through the centre of the curtain, or round the screens, the place represented being denoted by a printed placard fastened to the curtain. This arrangement, far from being flat and ineffective, tended to give closeness to the action, and by constantly allowing a great deal of stage room, afforded a sort of freedom to all the parties engaged. The audience did not in the least seem to feel the absence of scenery, and though the play lasted three hours and a half, the attention of the house never failed.

This was an interesting experiment, but something even more radical was happening contemporaneously in Germany. Ludwig Tieck, celebrated translator of Shakespeare and romantic enthusiast for all things Elizabethan, characteristically found in the Globe stage material for a theatrical philosophy. The theatre of his own time, he declared, was a theatre of illusion—an *Illusionsbühne*—but the illusion towards which it aspired was false and calculated to destroy the true poetic illusion. Warmly supported by the poet, dramatist and producer Karl Immermann, he argued that the Elizabethan bare open platform stage—the *Raumbühne*—offered far greater opportunities for the achieving of theatrical effect than the picture-frame stage cluttered up with its distracting wings, backcloths and built-up scenes. As a result, Immermann presented a production of *Twelfth Night* in a specially constructed set which, although it professedly aimed at a reproduction of the Shakespearian stage, was strongly reminiscent of the classical-type proscenium of the sixteenth-century Teatro Olimpico at Vicenza—with a long narrow open platform enclosed by a façade broken by four entrance doors and a kind of inner-stage at the rear. Meanwhile, Tieck himself, in 1843, gave a production of *A Midsummer-Night's Dream* at Potsdam, in which various levels, connected by stairs, together with curtained pillars took the place of the usual scenery.

Nor was this by any means all. The ideas of Tieck and Immermann were taken up and considerably expanded some forty years later at Munich. The enthusiastic reformer in this instance was Jocza Savits, a Hungarian director who came to identify himself with the German theatre. In 1889 *King Lear* was given, under his supervision, at the Hoftheater with a built-up setting intended to approximate the Elizabethan forms. A rounded platform jutted out beyond the curtain-line and was provided with steps leading down into the orchestra. Within the proscenium-frame was shown an open stage backed by a façade, which in turn revealed an inner-stage where scenic backcloths could be displayed. From a contemporary illustration of the storm scene it is obvious that Savits sought to bring his action well to the front of the platform.

All of these endeavours are important, and collectively they demonstrate the ancient truth—that however much we may vaunt our modernity we invariably find, often to our dismay and disgust, that our fondly treasured discoveries have been anticipated many decades before our own time. Inspired by knowledge of the principles of Elizabethan production, men were talking about the 'space-stage' already in the forties of the last century.

Yet, significant as were all these experiments, the year 1900 left the world of Shakespearian scholarship, and the world of the theatre, with a lamentably inadequate awareness of the particular methods by which the known principles were applied. Not only were all these experiments isolated efforts, but the basis of detailed information was largely lacking. It was not until near the end of this period, in 1888, that an illustration of an Elizabethan theatre interior was discovered. In that year K. T. Gaedertz issued his *Zur Kenntnis der altenglischen Bühne* with a reproduction of the now familiar 'De Witt' drawing of the Swan (Plate III): the importance of this discovery was immediately recognized and the same year H. B. Wheatley brought it to the attention of English readers. So illuminating is this drawing and so much has it formed the foundation for all recent discussion of the Elizabethan stage that we may indeed well wonder how Malone and Tieck succeeded at all in forming even the vaguest mental image of the theatre that Shakespeare used, and we may assuredly forgive them for any uncertainties in their interpretation of the meagre evidence at their disposal.

2. THE ELIZABETHAN PUBLIC THEATRE AND ITS WAYS

What the past fifty years have accomplished rests partly in the amassing of further information concerning the Elizabethan theatre as a whole, partly in the minuter scrutiny of evidence with the object of determining the precise methods used by the actors of that time and partly in the application of the accumulated knowledge to the discussion of the plays in general, to the elucidation of puzzling elements in their action, and to the interpretation of the dramatic characters. We are thus concerned both with the various contributions to knowledge effected by individual scholars and with the development of an entirely fresh interpretative path pursued by literary critics as a result of these contributions. There is, indeed, hardly any aspect of Shakespearian study, from bibliography to poetic imagery, which has not been influenced by this kind of investigation: concepts of the nature of acting texts determine the conclusions reached by editors; characters are explained by reference to a particular actor's age, height or manner; groups of plays are discussed not in terms of Shakespeare's supposed psychological development, but in those of changing tastes in the audience or of the shifting personnel of his company.

THE LANDMARKS

Obviously, the first thing we have to consider is the physical stage and the conditions appertaining to its performances. In this area of study the period with which we are concerned, 1900–47, is neatly divided in half by the appearance, in 1923, of two utterly diverse contributions to knowledge. The former is C. H. Herford's *Sketch of Recent Shakespearian Investigation*, which so ably and entertainingly surveys the main trends of scholarly study from the nineties of the last century, and which enables us, in this present 'sketch', to pay less attention to the early decades and to stress, in particular, the achievements of 1923–47. The second work consists of the four invaluable red volumes of Sir Edmund Chambers's *The Elizabethan Stage*. Here indeed is a convenient and commodious half-way house on the road of research wherein we may rest and contemplate earlier accomplishments. At the same time, before and after it there stand numerous other lesser resting-places, each marking a lap of the journey. We start, as it were, from a little international camp where scholars English, American, French, and German have set up their tents during the first years of the century. Here is Carl Brodmeier hoisting the flag of the now wholly discredited 'alternation' theory, which assumes that Shakespeare so constructed his plays as to allow an inner-stage scene to follow each scene on the outer-stage—an assumption clearly influenced by nineteenth-century ideas and not yet freed from concepts based on contemplation of the picture-frame conventions. Here is the worthy William Archer, writing a long essay in *The Quarterly Review* for 1908 on "What We Know of the Elizabethan Stage". Here is Achilles with his myrmidons in the person of C. W. Wallace jealously assembling a treasury of new facts concerning the playhouses. Here is the genial G. F. Reynolds breaking new ground by his stimulating, and perhaps not fully appreciated, booklet on *Some Principles of Elizabethan Staging*

(1905). Here is W. S. Godfrey applying himself to an architectural reconstruction of the Fortune. Here is J. T. Murray surveying theatrical activities in the provinces. And, above all, here is W.W. Greg meticulously and brilliantly editing documents essential for any exact study of the Elizabethan theatre.

The second decade of the century is ushered in by the lively series of essays collected together in W. J. Lawrence's *The Elizabethan Playhouse* (1912–13); Lawrence and Archer join forces to prepare the article on the playhouse in *Shakespeare's England* (1916); T. S. Graves discusses the court and the actors (1913); A. H. Thorndike produces his *Shakespeare's Theatre* (1916), and the year following appears J. Q. Adams's important survey, *Shakespearean Playhouses*.

From the appearance in 1923 of Chambers's volumes onwards to our own time contributions to the subject have been no less numerous. There have been fewer discoveries of new documents, but these later investigations have done valuable work in diverse directions—by still more intensive analysis of the source material, by extension of the field of study and, especially, by shifting attention from general discussion to the discussion of particular instances and by further relating the plays to the stages for which they were written. In 1927 comes T. W. Baldwin's *Organization and Personnel of the Shakespearian Company*. The same year sees the publication of the almost symbolic 'Shakespeare Association' volume on *Shakespeare and the Theatre* and the first of Harley Granville-Barker's *Prefaces*. Sir Edmund Chambers completes his great work by the publication of his *William Shakespeare* in 1930, and about the same time a young American scholar, G. E. Bentley, who is later (*The Jacobean and Caroline Stage*, 1941) to carry on Chambers's work, begins to publish some of his first articles on Elizabethan actors. Miss M. C. Bradbrook's *Elizabethan Stage Conditions* comes in 1932; 1935 brings the first true attempt to estimate the quality of the Elizabethan audience (A. C. Sprague's), followed by Alfred Harbage's more detailed study in 1941; in the years immediately following renewed attention is paid to the methods of acting, and, more significantly, to the study of individual theatres—notably the Globe and the Red Bull. In most of these later essays an important trend is the attempt to shift attention from the purely 'Shakespearian' and to throw light on Shakespeare's work as it were by indirection, through the more intensive study of his contemporaries and of the conditions under which they wrote. It is not merely the stage of Shakespeare that concerns the scholars but, more generally, the stage of the Elizabethans.

THE PUBLIC THEATRES

The entire area of ground thus covered clearly separates itself into knowledge of (*a*) the physical appearance of the theatres, (*b*) the personnel engaged in interpreting the plays, (*c*) their methods of work, and (*d*) the demands of the spectators for whom this work was done.

So far as the theatres themselves are concerned, perhaps the most important task accomplished by the earliest workers in the field has been the demonstration that in Shakespeare's time three distinct types of theatrical enterprise have to be accounted for—the public playhouses, the private and the court. Naturally, of these three the first assumes predominant importance if only because of Shakespeare's association with the Lord Chamberlain's men, but increasing attention has come, during the past five decades, to be paid also to the other two, with the realization that this company also possessed a 'private' house, that some of Shakespeare's plays are likely to have been penned for special (court or other) performances and that towards the end of his career he was probably influenced by that typical production of the court stage—the masque.

The general conclusions reached before 1923 regarding the appearance of the public theatres are, of course, put forth in detail by Chambers, and his bibliographical notes amply show how much important evidence we owe to the researchers of the twentieth century. Certain things have now been determined and are accepted without controversy, although, even after all the devoted work applied to this theme, questions still remain.

THE INNER-STAGE

About the platform stage and the gallery above it there is no debate, but as soon as we move from these comfortably assured features of the Elizabethan playhouse trouble begins. A simple, and excellent, example is the question of the inner-stage. We speak familiarly of its existence and of course we know by implication that something of the kind was used by the actors; we even know that it had a technical name. Yet the 'De Witt' drawing shows no central opening in its rear wall, while discussion of certain particular 'study' scenes questions how precisely they could have been played there and still kept in view of the audience. Debate has been lengthy, at times acrimonious, and even yet, with our accumulated store of evidence, we remain in doubt.

This example, however, raises an interesting point. At the beginning of the century, scholars engaged in exploring such subjects tended gladly to take evidence from any and every source: later, when it was recognized that staging at a 'private' playhouse may have been, and probably was, different from staging at a public theatre, the next generation of scholars turned to select evidence only from large groups of plays known to have been performed at the one type of theatre or the other. It is only within the very last few years that this process of selection has been carried to a further level, and in so extending the method of selection the latest studies suggest that perhaps herein lies a possibility of more closely determining the truth. Thus, for instance, G. F. Reynolds essays a new path by confining his attention to dramas which had been specifically written for one particular theatre, the Red Bull: this leads him to interesting and even revolutionary conclusions. Apart from the fact that his investigation forces him to suggest that, in this theatre at least, various three-dimensional, practicable pieces of scenery were either set on the outer-stage throughout a play or were brought in for particular episodes, he puts forward a novel hypothesis regarding the inner-stage. It has frequently been assumed that the 'De Witt' drawing is defective. There must have been an inner-stage, it is argued; therefore the absence of a central opening in the rear wall of the drawing must be due to the fact that the artist omitted to indicate it. Now Reynolds comes forward with the tentatively and cautiously expressed suggestion that the inner-stage of the Red Bull was possibly nothing more than a curtained framework which could, when need arose, be set up towards the back of the outer-stage. Being a careful scholar (and in this tricky realm of research it is only through the exercise of the very greatest care that any valid results can be reached) Reynolds does not present this as an ascertained fact: yet his evidence is strong and, if it comes to be supported by other evidence similarly obtained, not only shall we have to look once more at the 'De Witt' drawing in a new light, but also we shall be compelled to revise some of our fondest theories regarding Elizabethan staging.

THE UPPER-STAGE

This example may be paralleled by another. In 1942 appeared a work by J. C. Adams, entitled *The Globe Playhouse*, in which an effort is made to give similar attention to the theatre owned by Shakespeare's company. Less cautious than Reynolds, more inclined to leap to conclusions perhaps not wholly warranted by the documentary material available and less rigorous in his selective process, Adams advances several views likely to be rejected by further scrutiny of the subject, but one main hypothesis certainly seems justified by the references he employs—that a very considerable alteration was made in the form of the stage, and especially in that of the upper-stage, when the Globe succeeded the Theatre. If this be accepted, then once more a number of previously accepted conclusions will have to be laid aside. Taking Adams's study along with Reynolds's, we shall probably be right if we accept the conclusions that further advance in our knowledge is likely to come only from a series of selective studies and that, even within the realm of the public playhouse, variety of shape and perhaps variety in staging method prevailed. To seek for consistency here is, as Reynolds suggests, to risk taking ourselves off the track.

THE SITE AND SHAPE OF THE GLOBE

In what an uncertain world we move within this playhouse world is illustrated by a further series of arguments in Adams's work. We are still not absolutely sure of the exact site of the Globe, although the lively debate on the subject during the early twenties may be accepted as closing with a decisive victory for W. W. Braines's argument that the theatre stood to the south of Park Street (Maiden Lane). This question of the site may not be of first-class importance, but the shape of the theatre's structure is—and after these many years of study we find Adams dismissing the belief that Shakespeare's theatre was round. It is important to know whether it was round or polygonal, not because the rotundity or the polygonality would make any material difference in the disposition of the audience but because the one shape would necessarily yield a different stage form from the other. I. A. Shapiro's essay in the present issue of *Shakespeare Survey* discusses this problem anew (see pp. 25–37): as he indicates, there is still much to be accomplished in the way of exact and detailed research into certain particular, and relatively important, problems.

THE SIZE OF THE GLOBE

If we desire still a further example akin to those provided by Reynolds and Adams, we may take one point in Harbage's excellent book on *Shakespeare's Audience*. Quite clearly, one thing above all others that we want to know is the number of persons normally attendant at a performance in the Globe Theatre. We are all aware that a production in a small house has an entirely different 'feel' from a production in a large house, and consequently it is essential for us, if we wish to have an imaginative picture of an Elizabethan performance, to determine whether we are to place ourselves amid a great mass of London's citizens or amid a few score of spectators. Although contemporary visitors to London in the sixteenth century had spoken of theatres accommodating 'thousands', some students have sought to deny the accuracy of these contemporary statements.

De Witt's figure of a 3,000 seating capacity, "even though often mistakenly read as the total capacity of the Swan, has met with determined incredulity", and Greg has gone so far as to allow the Fortune a gallery accommodation of only several hundreds. Now comes Harbage, who, concentrating all his attention on this one subject, succeeds, by a series of ingenious cross-checking calculations, in demonstrating conclusively that after all the foreign visitors were right. The Globe Theatre must have held an audience of between two and three thousand. By applying himself to the consideration of a particular question this scholar has provided us with a significant certainty.

THE QUALITY OF THE AUDIENCE

Another excellent service has been rendered by Harbage and others. In earlier volumes the spectators at the public theatres were given short shrift: they were described as noisy, evil-smelling, crude and brutal—until we were almost prepared to shed tears for gentle Shakespeare and to sigh because of the pearls of poetry cast before such swine. The danger of an unscholarly approach to such subjects is well revealed in the impressionistic essay penned by Robert Bridges for the 'Stratford Town' edition of the works.

Shakespeare [he declares] should not be put into the hands of the young without the warning that the foolish things in his plays are for the foolish, the filthy for the filthy, and the brutal for the brutal; and that, if out of veneration for his genius we are led to admire or even tolerate such things, we may be thereby not conforming ourselves to him, but only degrading ourselves to the level of his audience, and learning contamination from those wretched beings who can never be forgiven their share in preventing the greatest poet and dramatist of the world from being the best artist.

Fortunately the application of scholarly method to this subject enables an entirely different picture to emerge. Particularly from Harbage's study, and also from those of Sprague and H. S. Bennett (*Shakespeare's Audience*, 1944), we get a vision, amply based on exact information, of a vigorous, intellectually alert public, anxious to listen to the high-astounding terms of the stage and by no means prepared to waste their entrance-money by making of the auditorium a rowdy arena.

THE ACTORS

In a kindred manner, recent scholarship has caused us to revise our conception of the actors. During earlier periods of study there had been a glimmering awareness that some of the Elizabethan players were sober men of high integrity, excellent in the quality they professed, but the legend of rogues and vagabonds died hard, and only within the past decades have we come to realize that Shakespeare's fellows were no roistering bohemians just one degree removed from jailbirds, but staid, capable, hardworking interpreters of his lines. What is particularly interesting, apart from this, in recent essays, is the endeavour—admittedly a hazardous task yet one well worth while attempting—to relate, as it were, the actors to the plays. Groups within the acting community are examined and their qualities expressed; thus Hillebrand discusses the minor players' roles (1922) and those of the boy players (1927). Interest in these performers and, at the same time, realization of their importance in our consideration of Shakespeare's plays are attested by the ardent search for biographical information such as has been sought for the authors of the time: here G. E. Bentley and M. Denkinger have done especially useful work. Edwin Nungezer publishes a dictionary of the players: individual performers are given attention, as, for example, in Allison Gaw's discussion of John Sinklo's possible connection with Romeo's Apothecary and Bottom's Starveling or in H. D. Gray's assignment of parts to Will Kemp. The way in which such studies impinge upon literary investigation is well shown in Granville-Barker's discussion of "The Casting of *Hamlet*" (1936) or in John Wilcox's suggestion (1941) that the part of Jaques, of no significance in the plot development of *As You Like It*, was an insertion made by Shakespeare when Burbage had grown too old to act Orlando. T. W. Baldwin essays a general study of the Lord Chamberlain's men and J. Engelen ("Die Schauspieler-Oekonomie in Shakespeares Dramen", 1926) endeavours to show how dependent were the dramatists upon the number of actors available. At the same time, attempts are made to explain and draw inferences from the appearance of actors' names in the texts of some of Shakespeare's plays. Thus, in our growing assurance, do we dare to set the door of the dramatist's workshop ajar and to move backstage into the tiring room.

The very latest attempt is to determine the style—formalized or realistic—of Elizabethan histrionic traditions. This new ground, entirely unprospected hitherto, was broken first by Georg Hartmann in 1924; more fruitful results have, however, been obtained only within the last few years. Much yet remains to be done in this field, but Harbage's study of Elizabethan acting (1939), supported by further notes by W. F. McNeir, gives some reason to believe that a formalized method was in common use.

PUBLIC THEATRE ENTERTAINMENT

We now have knowledge, through a long series of investigations, about the accompaniments of the actors. Louis B. Wright and W. J. Lawrence have been indefatigable in gathering information on almost every conceivable aspect of Elizabethan stage entertainment. We now know about variety shows on the stage, the use of animals in plays and juggling tricks: from bagpipes to bells we have before us an array of the actors' properties. Although the subject of Elizabethan stage costume has been inadequately prospected, M. Channing Linthicum's *Costume in the Drama of Shakespeare* (1936) provides us with some useful information on the dress of the time and on references to it in the plays. Most important material is presented in C. R. Baskerville's *The Elizabethan Jig* (1929) and the significance of dramatic song has been analysed by Richmond Noble and others.

Variety entertainment suggests connections with that peculiar form of Italian improvised performance which for convenience is called the *commedia dell' arte*, and to this too attention has been devoted. In Italy itself, in England, and in America the scope of the Italian popular drama has recently been surveyed in a collection of volumes and further work along the same lines is still proceeding: the latest, the third volume of Mario Apollonio's *Storia del teatro italiano*, has indeed just appeared (1946). Many of these works are only indirectly related to the subject of the present survey, but some, such as Kathleen M. Lea's *Italian Popular Comedy* (1934), devote chapters to consideration of the possible influence of the improvised drama upon the actors of Shakespeare's time and upon Shakespeare himself. In addition, various essays have been written with these objects immediately in view. First in the field was M. J. Wolff who published an article on "Shakespeare und die Commedia dell' arte" in 1910. Since then the stage influence on *The Tempest* has been explored by F. Neri, H. D. Gray and others, while Oscar J. Campbell has applied himself to the Italian actors' influence on Shakespeare's earlier comedies. Although the relations between the Renaissance Italian and the Elizabethan stages have not fully been worked out as yet, these studies have considerably added to the background knowledge so essential for an understanding of sixteenth-century English drama.

DOCUMENTARY DISCOVERIES

The general and particular investigations thus undertaken during the present century have been based partly on application of scrutiny to hitherto unconsidered subjects, partly on the reinterpretation of previously known documents and partly on the unearthing of fresh material. Thus, for instance, Henslowe's diary had been used by various scholars of the nineteenth century, but its real service did not come until Greg issued his standard edition (1904–8), a work which has proved a treasury for all succeeding workers. Not only does it throw light on almost every aspect of London's public theatres but it provides one of the very few sources of information concerning the not unimportant subject of playhouse finance. This forms the main theme of Alwin Thaler's entertaining *Shakespeare to Sheridan* (1922).

Among the new discoveries, those of Wallace in the pre-Chambers period and, more recently, those of Hotson have greatly added to our information concerning Shakespeare's theatrical activities. The former, now familiar to all and fully examined by Chambers and others, give intimate facts concerning the building and organization of the Globe Theatre. Hotson's *Shakespeare versus Shallow* (1931) shows Shakespeare in association with Francis Langley, the builder of the Swan Theatre, and, besides the personal interest of the story revealed by the new documents, with its possible bearing on certain topical allusions in *The Merry Wives of Windsor*, there is here the theatrical interest derived from finding proof of the dramatist's association with the playhouse illustrated by De Witt. Since this is the only Elizabethan theatre so illustrated, these documents are of very particular stage value: the link, hitherto lacking, has been provided between Shakespeare and the prime source of information regarding the stage of his time. Of similar value is Chambers's publication (1925) of an original sixteenth-century drawing of a scene in *Titus Andronicus*, particularly significant for its indication of the costumes worn by the characters represented. This drawing is further discussed in the present volume by J. Dover Wilson (see Plate I and pp. 17–22).

To the list of new documents should be added those employed by J. T. Murray in his survey of provincial companies (1910) and those unearthed by C. J. Sisson, in especial (*a*) the material relating to *Keep the Widow Waking*, which indicate playhouse procedure of a kind hitherto unrealized, and (*b*) that presented in "Mr and Mrs Browne of the Boar's Head", giving entertaining pictures of inn-yard performances. Murray's and Sisson's findings have been supplemented by numerous other items relating to provincial and continental tours by London actors. The digging continues and we may perhaps hope that the mines are not wholly exhausted.

ANALYSIS OF PARTICULAR SCENES

Such searches have, of course, been constant ever since the time of Malone, and some scholars, such as Collier, not content with what they could find, did not scruple to invent documentary evidence of their own. What is new within the past few years is the determined attempt, on the part of many students of the Elizabethan drama, to explain in detail the precise manner in which a number of puzzling scenes were likely to have been put on the boards. Just as general essays on "the Elizabethan Public Playhouse" have been giving way to essays on "the Red Bull" or "the Globe", so the general discussion of staging is being supplanted by the particular. This trend starts with intermediate studies such as Lawrence's "*Hamlet* as Shakespeare Staged It" (1926) or Wright's "Elizabethan Sea Drama and Its Staging" (1927), and proceeds to discussion of individual scenes. Thus J. C. Adams examines the bedroom scenes in *Romeo and Juliet* and the banquet scene in *The Tempest*, while J. Dover Wilson sets a controversy gloriously afloat with his interpretation of Hamlet's mouse-trap. All these recent studies display an increasing understanding of Elizabethan stage practice, although all, so far, have been hindered from reaching beyond conjecture by the fact that we do not possess a practicable stage of Elizabethan proportions on which the theories can be worked out.

3. THE PRIVATE AND COURT THEATRES

Compared with all this attention devoted to the work accomplished in the public theatres, relatively little attention has been paid either to the children's companies or to the private playhouses. This, indeed, is a subject which attracted more attention at an earlier period than during the decades immediately past. In 1883 A. Albrecht presented a general survey of *Das englische Kindertheater* and H. Maas was writing on the same topic at the turn of the century. It was, too, at the beginning of our fifty years that Wallace came forward with his array of documents relating both to the private theatres of the children and to those used by the adult actors. Since then, perhaps the most notable contributions have been those of A. Feuillerat on the Blackfriars and those of H. N. Hillebrand on the Whitefriars. Peculiarly enough, however, the one study which endeavours to examine production method (as distinct from 'staging') in any Elizabethan theatre is the short, but illuminating, article by J. Isaacs on the Blackfriars (1933). Here is a path of research which may well yield valuable results, and no doubt Isaacs was right in taking his first steps on the narrower, smoother pavement of the private house than on the broader, rougher roadway of the Globe.

In general, however, the preponderating interest of the Globe and its associates has tended to outweigh that of the indoor houses. It is certainly to be hoped that the concluding volumes of Bentley's survey of the theatre from 1616 to 1642 will provide us with a clearer picture than we now possess of at least those private playhouses that functioned during the seventeenth century.

THE COURT THEATRE

On the closely related court theatres, on the other hand, much information has been accumulated. A wealth of material came to us when A. Feuillerat published his invaluable set of records from the reigns of Edward VI, Mary and Elizabeth. His and Chambers's interpretation of these documents are of prime significance. How significant is shown when we consider the manner in which so recent an edition as R. W. Bond's of Lyly's plays has been outdated. This edition appeared as late as 1902, yet its setting forth of the dramas has been proved utterly wrong by subsequent studies. Bond thought that Lyly's comedies were performed as Shakespeare's were, and he sought so far as he could to divide them into the 'scenes' familiar in the dramas performed by the adult actors. The result was confusion, since in fact the staging method on which Lyly based his action was a modification of the old medieval simultaneous setting. Only against a background of such setting can his dramaturgy be appreciated, and Bond's forgivable failure serves as a prime example of the way in which stage studies are essential for our appreciation of the literary offerings of this richest age of our drama.

In speaking of the court stage, we must, of course, distinguish between (a) performances by court-sponsored children's companies, (b) occasional performances by the public players, and (c) the presentation of that characteristic kind of palace entertainment—the Masque. Little definite information was available concerning the staging of the last of these before the present century. R. Brotanek's *Die englischen Maskenspiele* (1902) and, more thoroughly, P. Reyher's *Les masques anglais* (1909) opened up an entirely new field of investigation. Then came the dissemination of Inigo Jones's designs, preserved mainly at Chatsworth. In 1848, it is is true, Peter Cunningham and J. P. Collier had prepared a short study of this artist's work and *Shakespeare's England* (1916) gave a few specimens of his skill, but real understanding of his aims and accomplishments came only when the most significant of the drawings were reproduced by Percy Simpson and C. F. Bell in 1924. Many of the remainder appear in the present writer's *Stuart Masques and the Renaissance Stage* (1938).

STAGING IN THE RENAISSANCE

The entire subject of Renaissance staging is one that has found exploration only within the past decades, and even yet large areas of it remain uncharted or at least inadequately mapped. Through the efforts of Wilhelm Creizenach, with his *Geschichte der neueren Dramas* (1893–1916) and Karl Manzius, with his *History of Theatrical Art* (1897–1907: English translation, 1903–21), ably supported later by Lily B. Campbell, with her *Scenes and Machines on the English Stage during the Renaissance* (1923), the relationship between the English and the contemporary European theatres was sketched out, and since then succeeding investigators, chiefly German and Italian (among whom Josef Gregor and Corrado Ricci may be specially mentioned) have made available much new material of great interest. Others, such as Gordon Craig, have aided in introducing this material to the attention of English readers. The majority of these, however, have not aimed at any synthesis or at relating theatrical development to current social conditions and dramatic activity. The most revealing and suggestive study is perhaps H. H. Borcherdt's *Der Renaissancestil des Theaters* (1926), but even this leaves much to be desired. How much remains to be done is well indicated by the scope of George Kernodle's excellent and stimulating survey, *From Art to Theatre* (1944).

4. THE ELIZABETHAN THEATRE AND THE DRAMA

Study of Elizabethan theatrical life has had the effect of materially influencing recent textual and critical contributions to the study of Shakespeare. This is a subject that obviously carries us far beyond the theme of the stage itself and it is one that will be discussed in later volumes of *Shakespeare Survey*. At the same time, in order to provide at least a brief indication of background for the present picture some passing reference must be made to it here.

THE TEXTS

Precisely what copy was given to the printers for the Quartos and the Folio has been a subject of debate from the time of Pope onwards and scholars have always been aware that in dealing with dramatic texts the influence of the players must be kept in mind. Only within the twentieth century, however, have bibliographical problems been approached in an exact and scientific manner; only within this time have editors been given a reasonably assured basis on which to work. What arouses our interest particularly in these modern bibliographical endeavours is the way in which successive investigators, from A. W. Pollard through R. B. McKerrow and W. W. Greg to Peter Alexander and G. I. Duthie, have persistently sought to penetrate within the recesses of the tiring house. Bibliographical history, for example, was made when Greg issued his *Two Elizabethan Stage Abridgements* and was expanded when he followed this extra-ordinarily subtle and epoch-making volume with a series of related essays, such as those on "The Evidence of Theatrical Plots for the History of the Elizabethan Stage" (1925) and "Prompt Copies, Private Transcripts and the Playhouse Scrivener" (1925). His invaluable *Elizabethan Dramatic Documents* appeared in 1931. Pursuing Greg's lead, many scholars have contributed their share to the general store of knowledge, while in J. Dover Wilson Shakespeare has found an editor willing and anxious to make use of all that is known concerning the duties of the prompter, the nature of stage copy, actors' parts and methods of abridgement for special purposes. This, naturally, is a sphere of research which cannot be discussed in the scope of this study, yet mention of it is appropriate here. To realize how deeply and how widely these bibliographical investigations have been influenced by study of the stage we need consider only the brilliant essay by F. P. Wilson on "Shakespeare and the 'New Bibliography'" contributed to the Bibliographical Society's *Studies in Retrospect* (1945).

ACT-DIVISION AND LENGTH OF PLAYS

Two special problems have a very direct bearing on larger questions concerned with methods of performance in Elizabethan times. The first relates to act-divisions. One school of thought, led by J. Dover Wilson, believes in the "seamless texture" of dramatic composition: here it is assumed that a play was conceived by Shakespeare as one many-scened whole. Opposed to this is the school that argues for their original composition in five acts. This subject, much debated during the late twenties, has within the last few months received a weighty contribution from America—Baldwin's lengthy work on five-act structure.

Related to this problem is that of the average length of acting texts. The assumption that an ordinary Elizabethan drama ran to about 3,000 lines was challenged by Alfred Hart: he proposed to reduce this figure to some 2,300 lines. Independently Levin L. Schücking reached almost the same figure in his examination of the *Hamlet* text. The question is still under debate, but it may be suggested that—apart from R. C. Bald's theory, which postulates the existence of both short and long plays, the former designed for private performance—a valid answer can come only after the making of practical experiments. Clearly, this answer must depend on how we interpret references to the "two hours' traffic" of the stage and on what we regard as the normal pace of Elizabethan delivery. It is unlikely that Globe performances always ended pat when a hundred and twenty minutes had been recorded by the sand-glass and, apart from that, we do not as yet have any firm concept of how the lines were spoken. Perhaps we may never be able to gain such a concept, but it would seem that, in so far as this latter question is concerned, we need to have at least a series of experiments carried out by actors under reconstructed 'Elizabethan' conditions. At the Old Vic the full-length *Hamlet* took four hours and thirty-two minutes of playing time: recently, on a stage approximating the Elizabethan shape and without sacrificing audibility, the same drama was given within three hours and a half. This suggests that further experimental productions might well cause us to revise our ideas of how the lines were originally delivered and of how many of them were given to the audiences of Elizabeth's day.

CRITICAL STUDIES

If the results of theatrical investigations have impinged with marked effect on textual work, they have made an even greater impress on critical interpretations of scenes and characters. In 1907 George Pierce Baker, later to found the famous Harvard "47 Workshop" and to direct the Yale Department of Drama, both ventures designed to encourage creative theatre activities, issued his *The Development of Shakespeare as a Dramatist*. In this he strove to analyse the plays, not as character studies or as philosophic disquisitions, but as pieces written by a practical actor-author aiming at immediate popular success. A few years later, another American scholar, Brander Matthews, responsible for the establishment of the Theatre Museum at Columbia, brought out a similarly conceived volume, *Shakespeare as a Playwright*. From this time on, criticism of the contents of the First Folio has tended more and more towards treating the plays as plays and not as poems. We are thus led to J. Dover Wilson's declaration that Shakespeare wrote "not books but prompt-books, or, if you will, theatrical scores for the performance of moving pageants of speech, action, and colour, upon a particular stage by a particular troupe of actors for a particular audience". How far the force of this trend of thought has imposed itself on our age is seen nowhere more clearly than in the facts that the *New Cambridge Shakespeare* was launched under the editorship of J. Dover Wilson on the one hand and, on the other, of Sir Arthur Quiller-Couch, whose lectures on Shakespeare's workmanship were among the earliest English theatrically inspired interpretations of the author's dramatic technique.

Fuller examination of the effects of the theatrical impact upon the literary must, naturally, be reserved for a survey devoted to critical studies, but here again it is important, in connection with inquiry into the nature of the Elizabethan stage, to note at least the broad lines of development in this area.

Schücking comes with a thoroughly realist approach. We must, he asserts, consider Shakespeare's plays in the light of the dramatic conditions of his own time, accept the evident inconsistencies in his delineation of character (instead of trying, by devious means, to explain these inconsistencies away) and understand the basically primitive methods he employs. He is followed by the trenchant Elmer Edgar Stoll, a man of split personality who is constantly struggling between two daimons—the one inducing him to argue that problems such as Hamlet's delay do not exist (for, he asserts, the question is as simple as the proposition: no delay, no play) and the other warming him to a fervent admiration for the wonder of Shakespeare. While on the one hand he stresses his belief that we sadly err if we seek for acute psychological analysis in the dramas, on the other he is impelled to take up the cudgels against Schücking and defend the wholeness of Cleopatra's character ("In her inconsistency she is consistent").

These critics, and their many disciples, are arrayed, whatever their differences, against 'Bradleyism'. Bradley's great work on Shakespearian tragedy had sought to interpret the action and the characters of the plays almost as though the former had actually occurred and as though the latter had had real existence. Against such methods the realists have revolted. J. W. Mackail, for example, asserts categorically that we have no more right to consider "the previous relations between Hamlet and Ophelia" or the earlier 'honesty' of Iago "than to invent a life-history of Autolycus' aunts". An argument of this kind seems valid until we recall that these two things, so far from being parallel, exist on two separate planes: Shakespeare does not mention any aunts (at least not in the sense of nice respectable Victorian-like ladies) but he does deal with Hamlet's love and Iago's honesty. Recognition of the narrowness, indeed, of the theatrically realist approach has for some time shown signs of producing a violent reaction. Perhaps Benedetto Croce's strictures went unheeded, but such pleas as that made by Lascelles Abercrombie have had their effect, and during the past year or two there has been a growing demand for something fresh. Typical is the fact that the year 1946 saw the appearance both of N. Orsini's vigorous criticism of the 'realists' and of Kenneth Muir's anxious cry for a "great interpretative book" on Shakespeare which shall escape from the restrictions of their approach.

The same year, 1946, robbed us of the man who above all others seemed likely to offer us such a volume. Through a long series of studies Harley Granville-Barker, ever growing in interpretative power, provided a kind of enhancing mirror of our age. Himself an actor, producer and playwright, he ever sought to unite the theatrical and the literary. His *Prefaces* are masterpieces, and in such an essay as "From *Henry V* to *Hamlet*" (1925) he presented a view of Shakespeare at once based on consideration of the stage background and instinct with imaginative appreciation. His concept of the 'complaisant' Shakespeare, giving the public what it wanted in a collection of plays up to and including *Henry V*, followed by the 'daemonic' Shakespeare almost breaking the theatre's bounds, is a vision which could have come from no man who was not deeply steeped in all the knowledge of the Elizabethan stage that the twentieth century has brought to us.

5. The Needs of the Future

While no doubt Orsini and others are right in pleading for an escape from the too-strict application of the realist approach, whether theatrical or otherwise, the example of Granville-Barker shows that what we need is not less attention to the stage, but more. We are infinitely better supplied with information on this subject than were the readers of Shakespeare a hundred years ago, yet there is so much we have still to learn.

Search for new documents will continue, of course, but the chances of our turning up really exciting fresh material are yearly becoming slimmer and, in any case, these chances are only chances, dependent upon good fortune rather than upon conscious human will. We should like to have a ground-plan of the Globe, a contemporary illustration of *Hamlet*, an eye-witness description of a Shakespearian performance more complete than what Simon Forman has to give us. We may, however, only sigh for these and offer libations to whatever gods rule over scholars' findings.

Within our own command, however, are certain fields of endeavour and these, it may be hoped, we shall decide to pursue.

1. First, the already existent inquiries into particular, as opposed to general, problems have been seen to have yielded matter of prime interest. We need more of these, conducted with the most rigorous selectivity. Each theatre and its plays should have their appropriate volume.

2. Along with this we badly need a series of essays on Elizabethan production methods and acting technique. True, the stage-directions of that time are meagre and have already been examined: yet it may be suggested that still further exploration would not be without results. In the past, they have been studied for what they can say about certain things; the clues they give for an understanding of other things have remained unnoticed. Thus, for example, much might be learned about the groupings of actors on the stage by minute study of such obvious things as directions of entry and exit; the dramatic use of properties has not been adequately explored— nor has the question of gesture. On all these subjects there is still information to be gathered.

3. Much more might be accomplished in the examination of speech rhythms, following the lead of Stoll, J. W. Draper and Granville-Barker, and expanding both on their methods and conclusions.

4. Above all, we badly need to be given the opportunity of relating theory to practice. When we deal with the theatre, we deal with something physical, and no theory can be a substitute for practical demonstration. Many suggestions already put forward and all the suggestions that will come in the future must inevitably remain in the realm of debate unless we have the chance of showing precisely how they serve to explain matters of puzzlement. The scholars, in fact, need a stage of their own, a kind of laboratory for practical experiments.

5. Or rather, they need several stages. One area of investigation that imperiously calls for further attention is that of Renaissance theatrical activity in general and, since here again the practical should aid the theoretic, more than a single 'Elizabethan' stage would be required. We know our Serlios, our Sabbatinis and our Furttenbachs, but these authors do not give us all the story: the narrative is much longer and much more complex than their words would imply, and the diversity of stage forms is considerable. If Shakespeare is being set against the theatrical background of his age, that theatrical background should, in its turn, be set more firmly against the larger background of Renaissance theatre endeavour, in general and in particular.

6. If this could be accomplished, we might well hope for a greater association between the scholarly and histrionic worlds of to-day. At the very start of this fifty-year period, William Poel was engaged in the praiseworthy, and practically valuable, effort to demonstrate in general terms how the plays of Shakespeare were originally presented. Unquestionably, although his own

activities remained rather outside the ordinary theatre world, his influence upon the stage of the first decades of the century was great. We are now turning from the general to the particular and something more exact and more detailed than the platforms Poel used is called for: his makeshift devices will no longer serve. What is demanded at present goes as far beyond his efforts as scholarly research now goes beyond that of 1900. If the means were available, the opinion might be hazarded that just as the actors of the century's earlier decades benefited considerably from Poel's experiments, so to-day's producers would find fresh inspiration from further work along the same lines. Granville-Barker with gracious dignity demonstrated in one way how a union could be effected between the theatrical and the scholarly, but there are other ways, and for these we are waiting.

Perhaps the dream of a practical stage for the trying-out of theories and for demonstrations of established truths may not be realized, for theatres are costly things to build. Yet it would appear as though only something of this sort can aid us towards fuller and further accomplishment in the study of the Elizabethan theatre. Meanwhile, whether the dream is realized or not, we have reason to be proud of what these fifty years have done. Through inquiry into the playhouse wherein he worked Shakespeare has been brought very much nearer to us; what has been lost by the passing of the years, drawing us ever further away from Elizabeth's age, has been amply counterweighted by increasing knowledge of the conditions under which he wrote. The Elizabethan theatre, despite the many things we still want to learn about it, is infinitely nearer to us than it has been to any generation since the beginning of the seventeenth century.

'TITUS ANDRONICUS' ON THE STAGE IN 1595

BY

J. DOVER WILSON

In *The Library* for March 1925 Sir Edmund Chambers drew the attention of scholars, virtually for the first time, to the presence among the manuscripts in the library of the Marquess of Bath at Longleat (*Harley Papers*, vol. 1, f. 159 v.) of a contemporary drawing illustrating an incident in the opening scene of *Titus Andronicus*. The drawing in question was originally on p. 1 of a folded paper giving two leaves. Beneath it stand forty lines of text in manuscript, with what appears to be a dated signature near the foot of the left-hand margin; and on p. 4 is found an endorsement "Henrye Peachams Hande 1595". Sir Edmund published a collotype facsimile of the whole recto of the first leaf in *The Library*, together with a descriptive note entitled "The First Illustration to 'Shakespeare'". But he reproduced the drawing without the text in his *William Shakespeare* (1930), and again when he reprinted *The Library* article in his *Shakespearean Gleanings* (1944). This was somewhat unfortunate, inasmuch as the document is of first-class importance, *The Library* is a specialist journal not so well known as it should be to the ordinary student of Shakespeare, and the drawing presents several puzzling features which can be solved only in relation to the text that accompanies it. Some of these features have been noted by Sir Edmund, and others were first observed by the late J. Quincy Adams, in a valuable note on the document towards the end of his Introduction to a facsimile of the only extant copy of the First Quarto of *Titus Andronicus*, now in the Folger Shakespeare Library in Washington. Neither scholar has, however, been able to decide what is the exact incident the drawing attempts to depict, or to determine its date.

The editor[1] and I believe, therefore, that readers of *Shakespeare Survey*, many of whom may not even be aware hitherto of the manuscript's existence, will like to possess a reproduction of the manuscript (apart from its endorsement, which as will be shown presently is of small importance), together with a transcript of the forty lines of verse underneath the drawing, and a brief discussion of the principal problems the manuscript gives rise to. First then let us have the text before us in print:

> Enter Tamora pleadinge for her sonnes
> going to execution

Tam:	Stay Romane bretheren gratious Conquerors	
	Victorious Titus rue the teares I shed	
	A mothers teares in passion of her sonnes	
	And if thy sonnes were ever deare to thee	
	Oh thinke my sonnes to bee as deare to mee	5
	Suffizeth not that wee are brought to Roome	
	To beautify thy triumphes and returne	
	Captiue to thee and to thy Romane yoake	
	But must my sonnes be slaughtered in the streetes	
	for valiant doings in there Cuntryes cause	10

Oh if to fight for kinge and Common weale
Were piety in thine it is in these
Andronicus staine not thy tombe with blood
Wilt thou drawe neere the nature of the Godes
Draw neere them then in being mercifull   15
Sweete mercy is nobilityes true badge
Thrice noble Titus spare my first borne sonne

Titus: Patient your self madame for dy hee must
Aaron do you likewise prepare your self
And now at last repent your wicked life   20

Aron: Ah now I curse the day and yet I thinke
few comes within the compasse of [your *deleted*] my curse
Wherein I did not some notorious ill
As kill a man or els devise his death
Ravish a mayd or plott the way to do it   25
Acuse some innocent and forsweare my self
Set deadly enmity betweene too freendes
Make poore mens cattell breake theire neckes
Set fire on barnes and haystackes in the night
And bid the owners quench them with their teares   30
Oft have I digd vp dead men from their graves
And set them vpright at theire deere frendes dore
Even almost when theire sorrowes was forgott
And on their brestes as on the barke of trees
Have with my knife carvd in Romane letters   35
Lett not your sorrowe dy though I am dead
Tut I have done a thousand dreadfull thinges
As willingly as one would kill a fly
And nothing greives mee hartily indeede
for that I cannot doo ten thousand more & *cetera*   40

Alarbus.

The foregoing is a curious cento from *Titus*, composed of (i) ll. 1–17, the petition by Tamora,
Queen of the Goths, that Titus should spare her son Alarbus (*Titus*, I, i, 104–20), adapted, but
not consistently, so as to become a petition for more sons than one; (ii) ll. 21–40, a bloodthirsty
speech by Aaron from the scaffold (*Titus*, v, i, 125–144); (iii) ll. 18–20, a speech by Titus of
which the first line is made up of the beginning of I, i, 121 and the end of I, i, 125, and the
remainder is obviously invented by the scribe as a link between Tamora's speech and Aaron's;
and (iv) l. 41, the prefix to a speech, which is not given, by Alarbus who has no speech in the play.

The endorsement, not here reproduced, need not trouble us. Adams thinks the words are in
the hand of J. P. Collier, the early nineteenth-century scholar who went about forging Elizabethan
MSS. or adding to genuine documents in faked Elizabethan handwriting. The script, he says, is

like other pieces of his forged writing at the Folger Library; and even if he is wrong, the words are clearly nothing but an interpretation by a much later scribe of the "Henricus Peacham Anno m°q°g q^{to}" which appears in the margin near the foot of the recto. This dated signature or attribution implies, there can be little doubt, that the document was, to some extent at any rate, the work of one Henry Peacham, though it does not appear whether the name is intended to denote the well-known author of *The Compleat Gentleman*, who has left a number of other pen-drawings still extant and who took his B.A. degree at Cambridge in 1595, or his father, who was still living in 1605, or a different Peacham altogether. As for the date, whatever be the meaning of the third numerical symbol, which I follow Adams in reading 'g', though Chambers and the scribe of the endorsement take it for a '9', the first two symbols prove that some year in the sixteenth century is intended, and I feel pretty confident that '1594' or '1595' is the correct translation, the more so as I hope to show grounds in a forthcoming edition of *Titus* for believing that the play did not come into existence before 1593. All I wish to emphasize at the moment, however, is the century; and for this reason. Adams, the only student of the manuscript who has hitherto been in a position to collate the text with those of the First Quarto, subsequent Quartos, and Folio, argues that the forty lines under the picture were "transcribed from either the 1611 Quarto or the 1623 Folio, with a slight presumption in favour of the Folio". If that be so, it would follow, though oddly enough Adams does not himself draw the deduction, that the text with signature and date was added about a generation after the drawing was executed, assuming the scribe's date refers to the latter and is correct.

I do not wish to stress this point, though I think Adams is probably right in believing the Folio to be the source of the text. But I find it impossible to escape the conclusion that the text was at any rate added to the drawing by another man, even though the ink looks much alike in both, since that supposition goes far to clear up all the puzzles which have up to the present baffled students of the document. For assume with Chambers and Adams that drawing and text were produced by the same hand at the same time, and you are faced with the following unanswerable questions: (1) Why does the drawing seem to represent Tamora pleading for *two* sons, when in the play she has three sons and pleads for one only, her first-born Alarbus? (2) Why does the scribe alter the text to agree with the picture for the first half of Tamora's speech, and then revert to the original version in her last line? (3) Why does the name 'Alarbus', who is given nothing to say in the play, appear in the margin at the end of the transcript? (4) What is Aaron supposed to be doing in the picture, and why does the scribe go to the trouble of copying out his bragging speech from Act v, Scene i, and of inventing, or partly inventing, a short speech for Titus to link it on to Tamora's from Act I? (5) Lastly, why does he describe the Gothic princes as "going to execution" when what happens in the play is not an execution but a sacrifice to the manes of the Andronici?

Assume, on the other hand, that the drawing was executed by one man and the forty lines added some time after by another man who was attempting to provide an explanatory text for a picture he failed to understand, the foregoing questions will either not arise or find a ready answer. In the first place, the only thing wrong with the drawing is that it represents a different moment of the play from that which the later scribe imagined, and Chambers and Adams imagined after him. What the artist depicts is not the stage situation at the beginning of Tamora's supplication, but the tableau twenty-five lines later, immediately after Titus has refused her prayer and his sons have carried away the doomed Alarbus. At the outset of her speech Tamora has three sons with her: there are only two in the picture; what has happened to the third? At the outset of her speech again, Titus has *four* sons with him, to say nothing of attendant soldiers; in the picture there are only two figures at his side, soldiers in plus-fours and with partisans, whom I take to be men-at-arms (the one in helmet and armour being perhaps an officer), since the Andronici would presumably be dressed like Roman gentlemen as are their father, the Gothic princes, and Aaron; where have the sons gone to? Surely the stage-direction of the Quarto at I, i, 129, "Exit Titus sonnes with Alarbus", provides the answer to both questions. We may even tell from the picture that the 'exit' on Shakespeare's stage was by the stage door on the left, since Titus points his hand in that direction as the actor would naturally have done in speaking of the impending sacrifice. At the outset of Tamora's speech, yet once again, the members of the Gothic party ought to be showing signs of deference and humility, to accord with her words. The drawing, on the contrary, exhibits Aaron expostulating with one hand and flourishing his sword with the other; why is he thus acting, unless it be to give expression in violent dumb-show to the bitter indignation which Tamora, Chiron and Demetrius do not hesitate to utter in ll. 130–41 (Act I, Sc. i) of the play?

The scribe probably possessed vague memories of *Titus* on the stage, but little or no previous acquaintance with the play he copied from. Certainly, he seems to have entertained only a hazy notion of the scene depicted in the drawing and to have constructed his text from hand to mouth as he went along. It is conceivable, indeed, that he may have started with the idea, which Adams actually puts forward, that the negro flourishing a sword on the right was intended to represent an executioner. If so, that would account for his opening stage-direction; after setting down which, I imagine, he turned up the opening scene in a printed copy of the play and began transcribing Tamora's lines. He would find nothing there to disturb his preconceptions; for, though he alters 'sonne' in l. 106 to 'sonnes' to accord with his reading of the picture, he might have supposed this to be a misprint.[2] As for the reference to "my first borne sonne" in l. 120, it was open for him to interpret that as a special plea by Tamora for the elder of her two boys. At this point he probably realized, perhaps because somebody pointed it out to him, that the negro was not an executioner, but Aaron the Moorish paramour of the Gothic Queen. Only so can I explain his sudden turning to the fierce speech in Act v, Scene i. What he was proposing to do with the derelict 'Alarbus' speech-heading is beyond conjecture; but that he went so far as to contemplate a speech for him shows how little he knew of the play, and suggests that he threw up the sponge because he failed to find the speech he sought, while the "*& cetera*" and the blank verso also show, as Adams points out, "that the manuscript as we have it is complete". Enough said, however, on the subject of the transcription, which, made up in the patch-work fashion described above and almost certainly taken from one of the printed texts, is of small interest to an editor or to anyone else.

Very different must be our attitude towards the drawing, which, freed from the hesitations and bewilderments hitherto attached to it by the text, now takes on a new fascination and importance. Without a doubt it is the work of a cunning pen-and-ink artist, who depicts, equally without doubt, what he actually saw at a performance of the play. Nor is it difficult to understand why he selected this particular play and this special moment of it for his picture. The contrast between Aaron and Tamora (obviously played by a blond boy) cried out for black-and-white treatment, while the stage-tableau immediately after the exit at I, i, 129 furnished excellent material for a pretty piece of design. Note, for example, how the tall ceremonial hasta, the "staff of honour", which Titus holds in his left hand, divides the picture into two panels, how the lines on the one side, formed by the three scabbards, two partisans, and Titus's outstretched hand, all make the same angle with the central staff, and those on the other, formed by Aaron's sword, his expostulating arm, and Tamora's hands clasped in supplication, also run parallel, though at a different angle; lastly, how the intense blackness of Aaron's body[3] is carried on in the black hair and beard of the princeling kneeling next to him. "Incidentally", writes Chambers, the drawing "may inform students of *Othello* as well of *Titus* that to the Elizabethan mind a Moor was not tawny but dead black". It may tell them too something of the costumes adopted in the production of Roman plays; the lower classes being played apparently in "modern dress", whereas every effort was obviously made, contrary to the assumptions of our theatrical historians,[4] to attain accuracy in the attire worn by patricians. Moreover, since the actors shown in the drawing were probably members of Shakespeare's company—does that black profile belong to Burbage?—or at any rate of some London troupe like the Earl of Sussex's men, we may suspect that Julius Caesar, Brutus and Antony were so dressed on Shakespeare's stage, despite Casca's reference to the dictator's 'doublet'.[5] Then there is the use of the players' hands to be noted; gesture, it would seem, was a much more important part of acting then than it is now—"suit the action to the word, the word to the action" enjoins Hamlet. But, like Keats's Urn, the picture doth tease us out of thought. And if some feel that these reflections attempt to wring too much from the evidence, I would point to the elaborate hypothetical structures that have been erected from the material furnished by one Dutchman's copy of another Dutchman's sketch of what he remembered about the interior of the Swan Theatre after a single visit, and ask whether speculations based upon this much neglected, unique and finished drawing of Shakespeare's fellows in action on his stage and performing one of the plays of his canon, may not be more profitable.

Finally a word, necessarily inconclusive, on the identity of the draughtsman. If we assume that the scribe intended to attribute the drawing to Henry Peacham, that he did so with full knowledge, and further that we are correct in reading his date as 1594 or 1595, the possibility that he is referring to the author of *The Compleat Gentleman* seems to be slight. For though the latter was not too young, being 17 or 18 at this time and "ever naturally from a child...addicted to the practice" of "taking in white and black the countenance of someone or other",[6] he has left behind a number of drawings (viz. twenty pen drawings in the manuscript *Emblemata Varia* at the Folger Library, and a number of coloured illustrations in a manuscript of King James's *Basilicon Doron* at the British Museum), which Adams and Greg, who have examined these manuscripts respectively, agree are different in style from, and "very distinctly" inferior to, what Adams calls "the elaborate and detailed drawing at the top of the *Titus* document".[7] And when Adams adds in a footnote: "The faces in Peacham's work are entirely without character, the details often clumsy in execution, and the whole drawing lacking in vitality" he not only brings out by contrast the points in which the *Titus* artist is at his strongest but seems to me to rule out Henry Peacham junior altogether.

For a time I played with the idea that we have to do with a drawing by Peacham's father, also called Henry, and that the text may have been added by the son in an idle moment some twenty-five years later. Against this stands the fact that we do not know whether Peacham *père* could draw at all and that we do know that the handwriting of Peacham *fils* was as distinctly inferior to that of the beautiful text before us[8] as were his drawings to our illustration. My feeling, then, is that, until and unless some further evidence turns up, it is safest to regard that "Henricus Peacham" with suspicion. I have shown, I hope persuasively, that the scribe who wrote it knew very little about the drawing for which he provided his text; is it not at least possible that he attributed it to Henry Peacham in error? If, as Adams believes, he wrote his addition to the drawing in the second quarter of the seventeenth century, the author of *The Compleat Gentleman* was by then famous as a pen-and-ink artist. What more likely than that a calligraphist, such as the scribe undoubtedly was, coming into possession of this brilliant drawing, should attribute it without hesitation to Peacham's pen? Likely enough, but for one thing, the date which follows the name. For though he might guess at Henry Peacham, and feel confident about it, a confidence which extended to assigning the picture to a definite year seems to imply something more than guesswork. And so he still leaves *us* guessing.

[Since this document is so important for our knowledge of the Elizabethan stage and since it presents so many puzzling features difficult to interpret, I hope that this article of mine may induce others to join a symposium designed to elucidate its complex problems. J. D. W.]

NOTES

1. He has been good enough to inspect the manuscript afresh at Longleat, and the foregoing description is based upon his notes. For what follows, however, I take full responsibility.

2. It is noteworthy that the Folio reads 'sonnes' in ll. 107, 108 and 112.

3. The editor tells me that the black of Aaron is made by a brown-black wash, which conceivably might have been added later, and is now distinct from the ink which has become yellowed with time.

4. See Creizenach, *English Drama in the Age of Shakespeare*, pp. 157–8.

5. *Julius Caesar*, I, i, 267.

6. *The Compleat Gentleman* (Tudor and Stuart Library), p. 126.

7. Adams, *op. cit.* pp. 35–6.

8. *Ibid.* p. 35.

A NOTE ON THE SWAN THEATRE DRAWING

So familiar to all is the drawing of the Swan Theatre that it might seem as though no good purpose could be served by reproducing it once more in this volume. Full justification for its appearance here is, however, to be found in three rather surprising facts. First, most of the existing reproductions either have been taken from inadequate copies of the original or else have been rendered by line-block, thus partly destroying the quality of the drawing itself. Second, hardly ever is the reproduction of the sketch accompanied by the explanatory commentary to which it is attached. And, third, not one of the theatre histories which quote this commentary has given an impeccable transcription of the original. For these reasons it seems that those interested in the Elizabethan stage may find it convenient to have the Swan Theatre drawing and the relevant text reproduced directly from photographs made especially for this purpose.

The facts concerning the document in which the drawing appears are well enough known and need not be repeated here, but attention may be drawn to a recent article in which fresh biographical information is provided concerning Johannes de Wit or de Witt (who originally sketched the Swan Theatre during a visit to London) and Arend Van Buchel, his friend (who copied the drawing and recorded de Wit's comments upon it). The article presents the texts of numerous extant letters to diverse correspondents written by these two men. The reference is: A. Hulshof and P. S. Breuning, "Brieven van Johannes de Wit aan Arend Van Buchel en anderen" (*Bijdragen en mededeelingen*, Historisch Genootschap, Utrecht, lx, 1939, 87–208).

De Witt's comments regarding what he saw in London read as follows:

EX OBSERUATIONIBUS LONDINENSIBUS

JOHANNIS DE WITT

De phano D. Pauli. Huic Paulino Phano adheret
Locus ab asseruandis sacratioribus vestimentis sa
cristi dictus, omnino obseruatione dignus, quippe
quo DIANÆ delubrum fuisse ferunt. Sacellum
est rotundum, hemy[s]phericum concameratum, cuius   5
structŭra Romanam antiquitatem referre videtur.
Aiunt cum fundamenta templi iacerentur, effos-
sam ante huius ædiculæ fores innŭmeram ceruinorum
capitum copiam; inde colligi Dianæ sacrificia
(cui ceruis litabatur) ibi olim peracta esse eique   10
hanc ædem sacratam fuisse; in eodem phano sunt
epitaphia et sepulcra varia et præter ea quæ alio loc[o] a
me notata sunt. Gvillielmi Herberti Penbrochiæ
comitis Walliæ præsidis qui obijt Anno ætatis LXIII
Christi vero 1569.   15
Ibidem in æde Westmonasteriensi sunt monŭmenta cum
suis elogijs: Guill. Thynne armigeri ex antiqua Botte
villorum familiâ. Joannis Thynne fratris qui obijt 14.

Martij 1584. item Joannis Bourgh Duistburgi guber
natoris Anno 1596.   20
Amphiteatra Londinij sunt IV visendæ pulcritudinis quæ a
diuersis intersignijs diuersa nomina sortiuntur; in ijs varia
quotidie scæna populo exhibetur. Horum duo excellentio:
ra vltra Tamisim ad meridiem sita sunt, a suspensis sig:
nis ROSA et Cygnus nominata. Alia duo extra vrbem   25
ad septentrionem sunt, viâ quâ itur per Episcopalem
portam vulgariter Biscopgat nuncupatam. Est et
quintum sed dispari et structura, bestiarum concertati
oni destinatum, in quo multi vrsi, Tauri, et stupendæ
magnitudinis canes, discretis caueis et septis aluntur, qui   30
ad pugnam adseruantur, iucundissimŭm hominibus specta
culum præbentes. Theatrorum autem omnium prestan
tissimum est et amplissimum id cuius intersignium
est cygnus (vulgo te theater off te cijn) quippe
quod tres mille homines in sedilibus admittat, construc   35
tum ex coaceruato lapide pyrritide (quorum ingens
in Brittannia copia est) ligneis suffultum columnis
quæ ob illitum marmoreum colorem, nasutissimos quoque
fallere posse[n]t. Cuius quidem forma[m] quod Romani ope
ris vmbram videatur exprimere supra adpinxi.   40
Narrabat idem se vidisse in Brittannia apud Abrahamum de
Kynderen mercatorem Alberti Dureri omnia opera chartacea
elegantissima et absolutissima

NOTES

Line 12, *loco a*. Text reads 'loca a'.   Line 27, Catchword omitted.   Line 30, Catchword omitted.
Line 34, *cygnus*. The reading may be 'cygnus' or 'cignus'.
Line 34, *cijn*. The reading may be 'cÿn'. Dutch engravers frequently wrote the letter 'ÿ' as an umlaut to suggest an
    English pronunciation (for example 'Marÿ Overÿs' and 'baytÿng').
Line 42. There is a stroke of the pen, whether accidental or deliberate it is impossible to determine, through the word
    'mercatorem'.

THE BANKSIDE THEATRES:
EARLY ENGRAVINGS

BY

I. A. SHAPIRO

By the end of the sixteenth century there were four theatres in Southwark: (1) the Beargarden, rebuilt after its much publicized collapse in 1583, (2) the Rose, built by Henslowe in 1587 or 1588, (3) the Swan, built by Francis Langley probably in 1595, and (4) the first Globe, built by the two Burbages, Shakespeare, Heminges and others in the first half of 1599. About their sites and shapes there has been much controversy and attempts have been made to reconstruct the design of each. Unfortunately, these discussions are all vitiated by uncritical acceptance of certain Jacobean and Caroline engravings. The pictorial and documentary information about the Southwark playhouses must be considered as a whole before we can safely draw from part of it inferences about any one building; through lack of such general study erroneous assertions are current about every one of these theatres. This article is an attempt to survey the pictorial evidence, and to collate it with the relevant documentary data.

First, it is essential to determine the date and authenticity of various views and maps often put forward as evidence. A single example will serve to show the worthlessness of some of these. One view of Southwark and London that has frequently been reproduced is illustrated in Plate XII: although unsigned and undated, it has been commonly stated to belong to a period about 1604–5. Cursory examination of its portrayal of the Tower, London Bridge and St Paul's, not to mention other glaring errors, should have made it immediately suspect. It is in fact a rehash of the background of an engraved portrait (not Delaram's) of James I on horseback, unsigned but dated 1621, of which Plate XI reproduces the lower portion. Comparison will show that the engraver of the view has drawn on his imagination for those parts of the background masked by the horse's legs and tail in the portrait. Judging by its wild inaccuracy, the view was made far from London and Londoners, probably abroad. It must be later than 1621, and is worthless as topographical evidence.

The background of the portrait (Plate XI) gives a more credible view of London, but it also is open to criticism, especially in its portrayal of Southwark. It is probable that the engraver took his background from a picture made before 1621, but unless that picture was made centuries earlier one cannot account for the omission of Winchester House, and even that assumption will not explain the conspicuously inaccurate portrayal of St Mary Overie's Church in the centre foreground. Therefore we must dismiss as negligible its representation of a cylindrical building at the extreme left of the foreground. Until we learn when this background was first depicted, the most that can be claimed is that it confirms what we already know, namely that the Beargarden *or* the Rose *or* the Globe was cylindrical.

Some of the maps often produced as early evidence for the shapes or sites of the Bankside theatres are similarly misleading. Among these is the so-called 'Agas' map.[1] It is seldom realized that the two known copies of this map were printed in 1633. Although there is reason to suppose that the blocks from which it was printed were made in Elizabeth's reign, their original date is uncertain. Since the map shows the Royal Exchange and its bell-tower it must be later than 1569, and it may well be as late as 1590.[2]

The 'Agas' map seems to be taken in part from that published by Braun and Hohenberg in their *Civitates Orbis Terrarum* (Cologne, 1572), and sometimes referred to as the 'Hoefnagel' map of London, on the questionable assumption that its style shows it to be the work of Georg Hoefnagel. There are several reproductions of the whole map, none quite satisfactory.[3] It was clearly engraved by a foreigner very imperfectly acquainted, if at all, with the English language but it is possible that, like Braun and Hohenberg's map of Norwich, it is, except in spelling, a faithful reproduction of an English original. Since it labels as 'Suffolk Place' the building which its new occupants in 1557 renamed 'York House' it has been argued that its original source must date from before 1558. This, and other dates proposed on evidence of a change of name, must be rejected. Certainly if Braun and Hohenberg had used the name 'York House', that would date their original as drawn in or after 1557, but that they use the earlier name 'Suffolk Place' proves nothing. Old names commonly lingered on. For example, in 1540 the church of St Mary Overie (the present Southwark Cathedral) was renamed St Saviour's. Nevertheless, here and in maps and views as late as 1657, we find the earlier (but doubtless still current) name; and Hollar, on detailed views of this church dated 1647 and 1661, still uses the old name. This is not to be explained as due to ignorance. Stow, for example, records the change of name but continues nevertheless to use the older title, as do his seventeenth-century editors. One basic principle must be applied in any attempts to date these views by reference to topographical evidence: use of a particular name provides a *terminus a quo* but not a *terminus ad quem*. The same principle applies to depictions of buildings. That Braun and Hohenberg's map shows St Paul's with its spire, destroyed in 1561, does not by itself prove that its original was drawn before 1561. On the other hand, we may safely claim that, since the map seems to show the gallows erected at Charing Cross in 1554, its original must have been made between that date and 1572.

Braun and Hohenberg's map has been praised for its minute detail and its accuracy, and of the former there can be no doubt. Few maps of London reveal such fascinating detail when enlarged, but it is doubtful if this is always reliable. The representation of St Mary Overie's Church is certainly incorrect, and the layout of the Southwark roads is quite inconsistent with what we otherwise know about them. The turret conspicuous on the ridge of Winchester House roof is not shown in the large and detailed drawings of Wyngaerde[4] (c. 1540?) and Hollar (c. 1640), though, as we shall see, it appears in certain views whose authenticity is suspect; and exactly the same is true of the wall and road curving up to the north-west between Winchester House and its garden. Since Braun and Hohenberg's representation of Southwark invites such criticism we must regard with reserve its frequently reproduced picture of the Bull and Bear baitings.

It would lengthen this article unduly to set out here my reasons for ignoring altogether certain maps cited in previous discussions of the Bankside theatres, but it may be as well to mention that the so-called 'Ryther' maps, which are sometimes dated, without evidence adduced, as c. 1604, can be shown to have been published by Cornelis Danckerts at Amsterdam some time after 1633 and perhaps much later. I hope elsewhere to discuss in detail these and other pre-Restoration maps and views of London not germane to our present purpose.

The earliest extant map of any part of Southwark appears to be a manuscript preserved among the records of the Duchy of Lancaster in the Public Record Office[5] and made, judging by internal evidence, some time between 1541 and 1555. Although this map ends just west of Winchester House, and therefore does not include the site of any Elizabethan theatre, its north-eastern quarter is reproduced here in Plate V because it provides such a valuable check on the accuracy of later maps and also helps us to interpret certain documents relating to the Globe (cf. note 15).

The first map to show any of the theatres is Pieter van den Keere's engraving of John Norden's map of London for the latter's *Speculum Britanniae Pars...Middlesex* (London, 1593). It has often been reproduced, whole or in part,[6] but these reproductions are rarely documented. Since the original plate fell into the hands of Peter Stent, who used it with some alterations as late as 1653, and since Norden's map was frequently copied without acknowledgement,[7] the Bankside portion has been reproduced in Plate VI from a perfect and unusually fine copy of the original edition. Norden's reputation as an expert surveyor and cartographer would in any case encourage one to trust a map inscribed "Joannes Norden Anglus descripsit", and in fact its representation of Southwark is consistent with every other piece of reliable evidence we have. Moreover, the prominence of the Beargarden and the Playhouse (Henslowe's Rose) in the foreground invites scrutiny, and makes any obvious inaccuracy here unlikely. Norden represents both the Beargarden and the Rose Theatre as cylindrical buildings, and this agrees with diverse references to these buildings. The only 'evidence' for a polygonal Beargarden and Rose are the Visscher and Merian views and their hitherto unknown source.

It has always been supposed that J. C. Visscher's famous and often reproduced *View of London*[8] is an original work and that it provides an authentic representation of the exteriors of the Swan, the Beargarden and the Globe. Both these claims must, I believe, be rejected. The date of Visscher's etching is uncertain. The copy in the British Museum (Department of Prints and Drawings, K. 2134, 2 Tab.) has attached to its base a printed Latin description of London, with the colophon: "Amstelodami ex officina Judocii Hondii sub signo Canis Vigilis, anno 1616." This Latin description (taken mainly from Camden's *Britannia*) was clearly specially printed to be attached to the Visscher etching, and thus proves that the latter must have been made by 1616.[9] But we cannot be sure, although the assumption is frequently made, that the description was printed to accompany the *first* impression of Visscher's etching, which *may* have been made before that date. J. C. Adams in his *Globe Playhouse* (1943) claims, but without producing any evidence, that the original etching was made between 1606 and 1614 and survives only in the impression now in the Folger Library. He believes the B.M. copy to be a derivative of the Folger 'original', and mistakenly supposes it to have been etched by the Ludovicus Hondius whose signature is appended to the Latin verses inscribed in two tablets in its upper corners.[10] Adams's frontispiece showing the Folger Visscher's version of the Globe and the larger scale reproduction on the wrapper of his book by themselves suggest that in fact the Folger Visscher is later than 1616; study of a photograph of the whole of the Folger etching makes it clear that, so far from being an 'original', this is certainly a derivative, neither skilful nor accurate, of the British Museum Visscher.[11] However, this conclusion is now of little more than academic interest, since it may be asserted with confidence that the reliability of all versions of Visscher's view is suspect. There are so many inaccuracies in its representation of Southwark that it seems doubtful if Visscher was ever there,[12] and in fact there seems to be no evidence that he either worked in or visited London. Investigation of this problem has revealed his probable source and has disclosed a very important 1600 revision of Norden's map.

In the Royal Library at Stockholm is an engraved panorama of London from the south bank of the Thames in which are inset versions of Norden's maps of Westminster and London published in his *Speculum Britanniae*. The central portion, considerably reduced, is shown in Plate IV B, and other portions in Plates VII and VIII A; I hope shortly to reproduce the whole on a larger scale. The panorama has been printed from four copper plates and measures 35.7 × 125.1 cm. Across the top of the two centre sheets is spread the title CIVITAS LONDINI, and in the lower middle is a cartouche announcing that:

This description of the moste Famous City LONDON Was performed in theyeare of Christe 1600 and in the yeare of the Moste Wished and Happy Raigne of the Right Renowmed Quene ELIZABETH The Forty and Two. Sʳ. Nicholas Moseley Knight Being Lorde Maior And Roger Clarke And Humphrey Wylde Sherifes of the same.

Depending from this is a smaller cartouche inscribed: "By the industry of Jhon Norden. Cum privil. R. Ma." Below the panorama, on five smaller sheets measuring 11.1 × 121.5 cm. overall, is depicted a procession of twenty-one robed figures on horseback, preceded by a sword-bearer, two pages bearing tall decorated wands and two musicians, all on foot. Three of these sheets, each depicting three pairs of riders, have been printed from the same plate, and a fourth sheet showing only one pair of riders is a cut-down impression from the same plate. The fifth sheet shows a single rider and the sword-bearer, pages and musicians who precede him on foot at the head of the procession. The plates are not signed, and unfortunately there is no clue to the engraver's identity.[13]

The date of this panorama can be fixed within fairly narrow limits. The year '1600' probably indicates a date after 25 March: Humphrey Welde and Roger Clarke relinquished their shrievalties on 28 September. We can therefore date this panorama as probably after March and certainly before October 1600.

This is without doubt the view, hitherto supposed lost, which was described by John Bagford in his letter to Hearne of 1 February 1714–15:

The same Mr. Norden design'd a View of London in eight Sheets, which was also engrav'd. At the bottom of this was the Representation of the Cavalcade of the Lord Mayor's Show, all on Horseback, the Aldermen having round Caps on their Heads. The View it self is singular and different from all that I have seen, and was taken by Norden from the Pitch of the Hill towards Dulwich College going to Camberwell from London: in which College on the Stair-Case I had a Sight of it in Company of Mr. Christopher Brown. Mr. Secretary Pepys went afterwards to view it by my recommendation, and was very desirous to have purchased it. But since it is decayed and quite destroyed by means of the moistness of the Wall. This was made about the Year 1604, or 1606 to the best of my memory, and I have not met with any other of the like kind.[14]

For the student of Elizabethan drama the most interesting section of *Civitas Londini* is its inset map of London, of which the Bankside portion is reproduced in Plate VII. Norden has brought his map of 1593 (Plate VI) up to date by inserting the Swan Theatre, built *c*. 1595, and the Globe, built in 1599. His indication that the Globe was farthest south and east of all the Bankside theatres, and his location of it just south of Maid Lane, authoritatively settles the controversy over its site.[15] The Globe is shown as situated within the angle between the ditch on the south side of Maid Lane and another running south-east from it, while from the latter a third ditch runs due south from a point just west of the Globe. Ben Jonson's description of it in his *Execration upon Vulcan* as "Flank'd with a ditch and forc'd out of a marish" had more point than one supposed. Its thatched roof, to which there are several contemporary allusions, is clearly depicted. The little building to the east of the Globe may be the alehouse which was also burnt in the fire of 1613. The 'Playhouse' of 1593 (which must be Henslowe's Rose) is now named 'The stare'. Although it is exciting to come on a new theatre name, in default of any other reference to a Star theatre at this period one can only suppose that this is simply a mistake. Norden's siting of 'The swone' theatre is confirmed by the 1627 map of Paris Garden (Plate IX B) which will be discussed later.

We must now consider the accuracy of Norden's depicting all these four theatres as round buildings. Contemporary references to the Beargarden and the Rose as round buildings have already been noted and several prologues and epilogues mention the roundness of the Globe.[16] De Witt in 1596 described the Swan and the Rose as 'amphitheatra', and there are other allusions to circular theatres on the Bankside. In fact, apart from engravings whose authenticity is suspect, all the positive evidence confirms Norden's representation of these theatres as round.

It is sometimes asserted that in the 1627 map of Paris Garden Manor the ground-plan of the Swan Theatre is octagonal or decagonal. This is quite erroneous. The plan was first reproduced by William Rendle in his article on "The Bankside, Southwark and Globe Playhouse" in the New Shakespeare Society's edition of *Harrison's Description of England*, Part II (*Trans.*, Series VI, 5, 1878). In this reproduction the outer circle of the plan is irregular and might be taken to imply a polygonal building, and this probably accounts for references to a polygonal ground-plan by later scholars. In the text, however, Rendle describes the 'Old Playhouse' as a "round building, twenty-six poles due south from the landing-place at the Stairs", and in a later reproduction in his article on "The Playhouses at Bankside" in Walford's *Antiquarian Magazine* (VII, 1885, p. 209) the Swan plan is unquestionably circular. The map which Rendle reproduced is now in the Guildhall Library, unfortunately too stained to be suitable for photographic reproduction. It is a copy, which I should judge to have been made not earlier than the eighteenth century, of the original belonging to the Copyholders of the Manor of Paris Garden, which Rendle inspected "at the office of Mr Meymott, the Steward of the Manor". This original was reproduced in W. J. Meymott's privately printed *Parish of Christ Church, Surrey* (1881), which also gives a circular plan for the Swan Theatre. Efforts to trace its present location have been unsuccessful. About 1900 it was examined by the antiquary Philip Norman, who published a corrected version of Meymott's map in the *Surrey Archaeological Collections* (XVI, 1901, facing p. 55); the north-east corner of this is reproduced in Plate IX B. It will be seen that here also the theatre plan is circular.

When we turn from Norden's 1600 map of London to the panorama in which it is inset we come upon the first of the engravings which depict a Bankside theatre as polygonal (Plate VIII A). Since this panorama shows all four theatres as polygonal its accuracy of detail must be immediately suspect, for evidence of, at the very least, one 'round-house' among the Bankside theatres is overwhelming. The panorama is misleading about one theatre; is it misleading about all?

At this point we may observe that the representations of Southwark in the panorama and in the inset map are contradictory. The map shows St Mary Overie's Church where we know it to have been, the panorama puts it much too far west of London Bridge. The map shows Winchester House without a turret, the panorama puts one in the middle of the roof-ridge. The street lay-out of the panorama, its round turrets on the south transept and choir of St Mary Overie's, and indeed its presentation of the whole south aspect of that church, are demonstrably incorrect. How are we to explain this in view of the comparative accuracy of the inset map and Norden's high reputation?

It is important to remember that Norden was a surveyor and cartographer, not an engraver. It has been stated that as draughtsmen Norden and contemporary cartographers "regularly use the technical word *descripsit*:...the English equivalent is 'performed': and a map inscribed as performed by so-and-so means that it has been drawn but not engraved by him"[17] but Dr Lynam of the British Museum Map Room, an authority on Elizabethan cartography, informs me that as far as he knows the only use of the word 'performed' is by Speed, apparently with the meaning of 'compiled'. There can be little doubt that Norden 'performed' the maps in *Civitas Londini*, for they are revised versions of those found in his *Speculum Britanniae*. Are we justified in assuming that the inscription on *Civitas Londini* is intended to claim more for him than that? The contradictions between his map and the panorama, and the ambiguity of the inscription, compel the conclusion that the panorama, or at least that part which depicts Southwark, is by another hand. The prominence of Sir Nicholas Moseley's name and arms suggests that *Civitas Londini* was intended to commemorate him and his mayoralty. If so, he may have arranged for an already existing panorama to be brought up to date,[18] just as Norden's maps of 1593 have been brought up to date. Even if the whole had been supervised by Norden there would be nothing surprising in his passing this panorama, for much of it is so obviously purely conventional and 'artistic' that he would probably consider it unnecessary that its details should be correct. Another possibility is that Norden had drawn a view of London from the 'statio prospectiva' shown on the tower of St Mary Overie (see Plate IV B) and that for the Southwark foreground the engraver had had to supplement Norden's view from sources now unknown, or memory, or imagination, or a mixture of these.

But whatever its history, there is no question that this panorama is the source of the views by Visscher (1616?) and Merian (1638), and of several others also. Visscher follows closely *Civitas Londini* for his panorama of the north bank of the Thames, for London Bridge, and for "The eell schipes" and "The gally fuste" in the river. Perhaps the most obvious evidence of his dependence on *Civitas Londini* is his labelling of "St Dunston in the cast." The *e*'s in the lettering of *Civitas Londini* are frequently indistinguishable, except by their context, from *c*'s. This is particularly so in "St. Dunston in the *east*". Visscher's misreading here is another indication of his ignorance of London and of English. Nor is this the only one. He has inscribed the names of such famous landmarks as Somerset House, Arundel House and Essex Stairs about one inch west of the places to which they refer, and has misnamed Bridewell Dock as Bridewell 'Stairs'.

Visscher inserted in his View a number of names not given in *Civitas Londini*. One of these insertions is an erroneous labelling of a church-spire near the river as 'St Hellen', which, as Braines pointed out,[19] has been taken over in turn by Merian. It is interesting to find that Visscher has only partly reproduced the picture of Southwark in *Civitas Londini*, and for the most part follows here the Braun and Hohenberg plan. The incorrect layout of Maid Lane and other roads, the distorted and conventional representation of the Great Pike Garden and, more important still, the siting of two amphitheatres separated by the King's Pike Garden (almost masked in Visscher by its hedge of trees), all proclaim a derivation either from Braun and Hohenberg or from an early version of its derivative, the 'Agas' map. Visscher has inserted into this the conventional polygonal representations of theatres found in *Civitas Londini*, but instead of hexagons he shows a dodecahedron (the Swan) and two octagons (Beargarden and Globe). His carelessness and unreliability are shown in his siting the Swan on the edge of the river, though both *Civitas Londini* and Norden's inset map correctly place it much farther south. Finally, although Norden's map shows that the theatre just east of the Beargarden was the Rose, Visscher misnames it the Globe and omits the latter altogether, probably because his careless scrutiny failed to reveal its inconspicuous and easily overlooked representation in *Civitas Londini* (cf. Plate VIII A).

Probably enough has been said by now to demonstrate that Visscher's view has no independent authority. Nevertheless, for completeness it may be added that Visscher has taken over from *Civitas Londini* its demonstrably false representations of Winchester House and St Mary Overie's Church, but since he follows the Braun and Hohenberg plan his siting of these in relation to London Bridge is more correct.

Another derivative of *Civitas Londini* often cited in discussions of the Bankside theatres is the view of London engraved by Matthias Merian and published in J. L. Gottfried and Merian's *Neuwe Archontologia Cosmica* (Frankfort, 1638). There are many seventeenth-century versions of this as well as a modern facsimile by the London Topographical Society.[20] It has been generally recognized that Merian's view was based on Visscher's, but with additions from "some other view". This other view can now be identified as *Civitas Londini*. In his picture of Southwark Merian shows a balconied and turreted square building prominent in the foreground south-east of the Swan Theatre.[21] This building, which is sometimes identified as "Holland's Leaguer", is also shown in *Civitas Londini* (see Plate IV B). Further evidence is provided by Merian's insertion of a third theatre between the Beargarden and 'The Globe' as sited by Visscher. Merian must have noticed that *Civitas Londini* and Norden's inset map both show four theatres on the Bankside and decided to repair Visscher's omission; not realizing that Visscher had misplaced his 'Globe', Merian inserted the missing theatre in its correct relative position assuming Visscher's siting to be accurate. Unfortunately for Merian, the Rose Theatre had disappeared some thirty years before he made his engraving. It may seem strange to us that Merian, who must have consulted *Civitas Londini* before finishing his engraving, should have preferred to follow Visscher's view wherever these differ, thereby adopting the labelling of 'St Hellen' and "St Dunston in the cast", and Visscher's other errors. But we must remember that Merian would have known Visscher's view to be later than that of 1600, and would have supposed it therefore to be more up-to-date. He copies the earlier view only where its deeper foreground supplies information not included in Visscher's.

Returning to our chronological survey of extant views of Southwark, the next we have to record is that usually known as the Hondius View (Plate VIII B), an inset to the map of Great Britain in John Speed's *Theatre of the Empire of Great Britain* (1611). The map is inscribed "Graven by I. Hondius...1610", but it is probable that the inset view was merely engraved by Hondius from a drawing by another hand, possibly some years earlier in date. The representation of

London north of the Thames appears to be based on Kip's 1604 engraving of the Triumphal Arch erected in Fenchurch Street for James I's entry into the city.[22] Though there are some suggestions of indebtedness to *Civitas Londini* for the view of the south bank, this may be original. If the view is derived partly from Kip's engraving it must have been made later than 1604, when the theatre farthest south and east was the Globe; its emphatic representation of this as circular is contemporary evidence not to be brushed aside.[23] Since only one other theatre is shown, this must be the Beargarden, the Rose presumably having been pulled down (about 1605) before the original was drawn, and the Swan lying too far west to be included. The representation of the Beargarden is much closer to the conventional polygonal picture of *Civitas Londini* but it is noticeably indistinct and ambiguous in comparison with the delineation of the Globe. Had the artist distinct and lively memories of the shape of the Globe but not of the Beargarden?

Hondius's view is the last certainly made before the rebuilding of the Globe and the Beargarden in 1613–14. Summing up the evidence so far, we find that there is literary or documentary evidence of the circular shape of every one of these theatres. Of the maps and the views, Norden's portrays all four, Hondius's at least one, as circular. Independent evidence of polygonal structure is to be found only in *Civitas Londini*, for Hondius's polygonal Beargarden may be derived from *Civitas Londini*, and is therefore of uncertain value. But *Civitas Londini* is certainly wrong at least about the Swan and the Globe, and may therefore be wrong about all four theatres. Unless further independent evidence of polygonal theatres on the Bankside can be found, we shall be justified in discounting that of *Civitas Londini*.

Visscher's view, already discussed and shown to have no independent authority, was made not later than 1616, and probably little if any earlier. The next to be considered is Delaram's, which cannot be dated except within very wide limits. It is an engraved equestrian portrait of James I, signed "Francisco Delarame sculpsit...Compton Holland Excudit Londini". Its background, a view of London and Southwark from the south, is reproduced in Plate X from the only known impression of the original, that in the Royal Library at Windsor. A mezzotint copy of this was made in the nineteenth century by Charles Turner, and it is Turner's version which has always been reproduced in previous discussions.[24] Delaram's portrait of James I is sometimes described as a 'pendant' to Simon van de Passe's portrait of Queen Anne of Denmark, dated 1616, but since the two engravings differ in size and are not a pair there seems no necessary connection between their dates. As Delaram was born about 1590 and, according to Sidney Colvin,[25] worked about 1615–24, it is very improbable that he engraved this portrait before 1610.

Clearly there is some connection between the Hondius view of 1610 and the background of Delaram's engraving (cf. Plates VIII B and X). Both show a small round tower with spire just east of St Mary Overie; both give the same distinctive round gable to the central block of buildings on London Bridge; both give St Olave's, Southwark, a flat-topped tower without a turret, and there are other similarities. The Delaram background may have been derived from the Hondius view (the converse is clearly impossible) or both may be derived from the same original, now lost. If so, Delaram's background merely corroborates other evidence that the first Globe was circular, for its theatre farthest south must be the Globe; its point of view being farther south than Hondius's, it can show the Swan as well as the Beargarden. At first glance the viewpoint appears to have shifted also eastwards, since the Globe now appears left of the Beargarden, but the true explanation is probably careless copying of the original, as evidenced by the impossible representation of St Paul's as east of the observer. The crudity of the draughtsmanship makes one suspect that the background was left by Delaram to a journeyman; in any case it cannot be regarded as independent evidence.

Our next picture is a small view of London ($3 \times 1\frac{1}{4}$ in.) at the foot of the title-page of Henry Holland's *Herwologia Anglica* (Arnhem, 1620; see Plate IX A). The engraving is unsigned, but may have been done by Magdalen Passe or her brother William, who appear to have engraved the portraits in the book. The *Herwologia* view is often described as identical with or derived from the Hondius view, but perhaps that is because so few scholars have bothered to compare them It *may* be derived from the same original, but if so it gives more of it, for it shows the river from Whitehall to the Tower. It is a cruder engraving than Hondius's and it is difficult to be sure whether it is following the same source even for the north bank; there is no doubt about its difference for Southwark. Right in the centre of the foreground, on what we know to have been the sites of the Beargarden and the Globe, are two unmistakably circular theatres. There is nothing on the site of the Swan, which by 1620 was hardly ever used.

The background of the unsigned engraving of James I dated 1621 (Plate XI) and Matthias Merian's view of London (1638) have already been discussed and shown to have no independent authority. Our next piece of evidence was brought to my notice by Allardyce Nicoll, whose active interest and encouragement have greatly assisted this investigation. This is a pair of alternative designs by Inigo Jones for the first scene of Davenant's *Britannia Triumphans*,[26] the backgrounds of which give two different views of London from the south (see Plate XIV). Davenant's masque was performed on 7 January 1638, so these drawings can be dated not later than 1637. They were certainly not based on any view we have so far considered, and give every indication of having been drawn on the spot.

The viewpoint of Plate XIV A is slightly east of London Bridge, and being farther south than that of Plate XIV B it gives a smaller but more extensive view. For the first time we are able to record that St Mary Overie's Church is correctly shown with the roof of the choir higher than that of the nave. Winchester House is reduced to its proper proportions and the ridge of its roof is shown without a turret, as in the drawings of Wyngaerde and Hollar. In the foreground is a tower, presumably that of St George's, Southwark. A little to the left is a large circular building surmounted by a small superstructure, above which projects a flag-pole. This must be the Globe, correctly sited south of the houses on the Bankside and on the edge of the fields. Farther west, and apparently farther back towards the river, is a tall building whose lower outline is too faint to permit of certain identification. As it has no flag-pole, and as from this viewpoint the Beargarden should appear very close to, if not actually masked by the Globe, I doubt if this is meant to represent a theatre. Can it be the prominent, square, balconied building shown in *Civitas Londini*? Farther west, and south of the houses on the Bankside is a large building surmounted by a flag-pole, which must be the Swan. It is without any superstructure or 'huts', though the roof-line is slightly irregular. It is impossible to be certain whether the building is intended to be circular or not.

Plate XIV B was drawn from a point slightly west of St Paul's, and not so far south as that of Plate XIV A. It shows only one theatre, an unmistakably circular building with a roof-line unbroken except by a chimney-like projection on the extreme right, and with a flag-pole and flag rising from the centre. If the building is correctly sited this must be a nearer view of the

Swan, for that was the only theatre lying west of St Paul's. The Beargarden lay too far east to be included in this view, and the Globe of course was still farther east. These drawings show that the Swan existed as late as 1637, and provide independent evidence of its circular shape; they also corroborate part of Hollar's view, which we have to consider next.

Our only detailed pre-Restoration picture of the exterior of any theatre is found in Hollar's 'Long View' of London, published at Amsterdam in 1647.[27] Hollar's topographical drawings are too numerous, too detailed and too easily checked by reference to surviving buildings for doubt about their authenticity and faithfulness. It is difficult therefore to understand why his representation of the Globe and Beargarden (Plate XIII) has not received more attention.

Attempts have been made to discredit the 'Long View' on the grounds that it was made in Holland in 1647, some three years after Hollar's escape from England, and that the Globe had been pulled down a few months before Hollar left.[28] This ignores the facts that Hollar lived in the Strand from the end of 1636 until at least 1642, busily etching and drawing for his patron the Earl of Arundel, and that a considerable number of his London views date from these, his happiest and most successful years. There is every reason to suppose that when Hollar made the 'Long View' he had before him a large number of drawings and studies of the London scene, quite probably made with this project of a panorama in mind; many such are catalogued by Hind, who reproduces among others a detailed view of St Mary Overie also etched in 1647.[29] Hollar's picture of London Bridge shows the six northern arches denuded of houses by the fire of 1633, and the boards set up along the sides to prevent people falling into the Thames, until the houses were rebuilt in 1645. After Hollar's return to England in 1652 he made new panoramas which record this and other changes in the waterfront, always a favourite subject with him. There is no doubt that Hollar's 'Long View' faithfully records the southern aspect of London between 1637 and 1644. His ignorance of the destruction of the Globe in 1644 is not surprising, for in that year he was serving under the Marquis of Winchester in the defence of Basing House, where he was taken prisoner.

Braines's disregarded argument[30] that Hollar has labelled the two theatres wrongly, 'The Globe' being actually the Beargarden and vice versa, is strengthened by the discovery of Norden's map of 1600. An additional piece of evidence now to be considered is, I believe, conclusive. The contract for the new Beargarden of 1614[31] specifies a removable stage (to permit of bear-baiting) and requires the builder "to build the Heavens all over the said stage, to be borne or carried without any posts or supporters to be fixed or set upon the said stage". This could not possibly relate to the building Hollar has labelled "the Beere bayting", for its massive 'Heavens' must have required several stout "posts or supporters" of the kind the Hope contract expressly forbids. On the other hand the building labelled the 'Globe' has no such weighty 'Heavens' but only a roof-extension inwards which looks as if it could have been supported on arches springing from the sides of the auditorium, thus fulfilling the terms of the contract. Since Hollar's 'Globe' is sited exactly where we should expect the Beargarden to be, and vice-versa, there can be no doubt that the 'Long View' portrays these two theatres with Hollar's usual accuracy, but with names accidentally interchanged.

Another detail of Hollar's drawing corroborated by the contract is the exterior projection on the Beargarden ('Globe') wall; this obviously encloses one of the "two staircases without and adjoining to the said Playhouse...of such largeness and height as the staircases of the said playhouse called the Swan now are or be...", the second being out of sight on the other side of the Beargarden. Two similar projections are shown in Hollar's picture of the Globe (his 'Beere bayting'), and were probably a feature of other Elizabethan theatres as well as the Swan and the two Hollar portrays, for there were close similarities between all of them; the Beargarden of 1614 was to have not only two staircases like those of the Swan, but also to be built "of such large compass, form, wideness, and height as the playhouse called the Swan" and "the said Playhouse or game place to be made in all things, and in such form and fashion, as the said playhouse called the Swan".

No views made after 1647 add anything authentic to our knowledge of the pre-Restoration theatres. Summing up the pictorial evidence between 1614 and 1644, we find that it confirms that the Swan was circular, and is unanimous that the Beargarden and second Globe were so also. Indeed, throughout this and our earlier survey we found no unimpeachable evidence that any pre-Restoration playhouse was other than cylindrical in shape. Finally, we have been led to the conclusion that Hollar's 'Long View' provides reliable pictures of the Beargarden of 1614–56 and the Globe of 1614–44. Now that we know we stand on firm ground we can proceed to build upon it, for Hollar gives us not only a detailed picture of the outside of the Globe, but also a glimpse of its interior.

NOTES

1. The only entirely reliable facsimile is that published by the London Topographical Society. W. H. Overall's *Civitas Londinum* (1874) contains a valuable discussion of Agas and his map, but reproduces the Guildhall copy, in which the date has been altered in MS. by a previous owner; a reduced lithograph from Overall's facsimile was made for Besant's *Tudor London* (1904) and reprinted in G. E. Mitton's *Early Maps of London* (1908).

2. See W. H. Overall, *Civitas Londinum*, pp. 20–3.

3. That by the London Topographical Society is blurred in comparison with the original, and is made from a later state of the plate, after the insertion of the Royal Exchange. A useful but very reduced facsimile of the first state is given in Besant's *Tudor London*, p. 187, and reprinted in G. E. Mitton's *Early Maps of London*.

4. Reproduced in original size by the London Topographical Society, and reduced in W. Benham and C. Welsh, *Medieval London* (1901).

5. M.P. C. 64 (Records of Duchy of Lancaster, Maps and Plans, no. 74). A much reduced tracing forms the frontispiece of William Rendle's privately printed *Old Southwark and its People* (1878); the reproduction of the inscriptions is less accurate than that of the outline. A reduced photographic facsimile of Rendle's copy is given in the *Geographical Journal* (1908), XXXI, 625.

The map is on paper, since mounted on cloth, and measures 33 × 24 in. The southern edge suggests that originally it extended farther in that direction. In the Appendix to the *Thirtieth Report of the Deputy Keeper of Public Records* (1869), p. 39, it is listed as one of a box of maps and plans "chiefly descriptive of boundaries, extents and quantities of premises viewed under Commissions of Surveys, and for that purpose directed; and principally elucidating the claims of parties in disputes pending in the Duchy Court, or otherwise contested".

6. A full-size reproduction has been published by the London Topographical Society. Others are in Besant's *Tudor London*, G. E. Mitton's *Early Maps of London*, H. A. Harben's *Dictionary of London* (1918). Reduced facsimiles are given in T. F. Ordish's *Shakespeare's London* (1904), and in H. B. Wheatley's *The Story of London* (1904). Several others exist.

7. For example, a copy was engraved by Hondius as an inset to the map of Middlesex in Speed's *Theatre of the Empire of Great Britain* (1611). This exists in two states, neither giving an exact copy of the 1593 original, details of which are omitted as well as altered. Reproductions of Hondius's copy have sometimes been described as examples of the 1593 original.

8. The best is that published by the London Topographical Society. A reduced facsimile was published by the Folger Library in 1935, and another is given in "London Past and Present" (*The Studio*, 1916).

Reduced facsimiles of most of the View are given in T. F. Ordish's *Shakespeare's London*, and H. B. Wheatley's *Story of London*. Reproductions of smaller sections, and especially the Bankside section, are too numerous to catalogue.

9. Copies of the same impression, but without the printed description, are in the B.M. Dept of Prints (Crace Views, I, Sheet 13, no. 16), and in the Guildhall Library. Visscher's view of London is similar in format to a number of panoramas of famous European cities, published in Holland between 1616 and 1619.

10. Adams (p. 9) states that the B.M. copy is marked "Visscher delineavit: Hondius lusit", and that this means that Hondius engraved Visscher's drawing. This of course is an impossible meaning for 'lusit', but in any case Adams is quite wrong, as a glance at a facsimile will show. Visscher's etching is signed in the bottom left-hand corner "J. C. Visscher delineavit". In two tablets in the top corners of the map are sixteen Latin hexameters praising London, and it is these hexameters which are signed (in the top right-hand tablet) "Ludovicus Hondius lusit", meaning that Hondius composed these verses. This is a common use of *ludere* and no other interpretation is possible.

11. That the B.M. copy is signed "J. C. Visscher delineavit" while the Folger version is signed "J. C. Visscher excudit" in itself suggests the former is the earlier, since the younger J. C. Visscher was a printer, and was printing at Amsterdam as late as 1640. But the question is settled by collation of the two versions. If the B.M. copy were derived from the Folger it would reproduce its spelling mistakes; it does not. On the other hand the mistakes in the Folger version, e.g. 'Eismogers Hall' for 'Fishmongers Hall', are such as would result from careless re-engraving of the B.M. version. The right-hand plates of the Folger Visscher seem to have been done less carefully than the left-hand plates, and the last plate on the right has several topographical howlers of the first order because the engraver allowed his imagination to misinterpret the original.

12. Visscher's picture of St Mary Overie's Church conflicts with what is known about its structure and outbuildings at this period. The turret on the roof-ridge of Winchester House, and the east-to-west wall and road separating Winchester House from its garden, suggest misguided reliance on Braun and Hohenberg's map or on an early impression of 'Agas' for the view of Southwark.

13. Among the Crace Views in the British Museum Dept of Prints is a later impression of the two centre plates of the 1600 panorama, stretching from Paul's Wharf to a little beyond Billingsgate Dock, and thus unfortunately lacking the inset maps of London and Westminster. The sheets of the cavalcade are also lacking. The left or outer side of the left-hand plate has been reworked, and both plates have been retouched, presumably in consequence of wear. The impression in the Crace collection (Crace Views, I, Sheet 10, no. 12) is itself rubbed and worn.

14. *Leland's Collectanea*, ed. Hearne (1715, I, lxxxiii). Aubrey says this panorama was given to Dulwich College by William Cartwright, son of William Cartwright the actor who, with others, in 1618 leased the Fortune Theatre from Edward Alleyn, founder of Dulwich College (*Natural History and Antiquities of Surrey*, 1719, v, 356).

15. W. W. Braines, in his admirable *Site of the Globe Playhouse* (2nd ed. 1924), showed by an exhaustive survey of the documentary evidence that the Globe site could not have been north of Maid Lane, but his argument that it lay to the south necessitated an assumption which scholars were reluctant to grant, namely that a lease reciting a description of the Globe plot had misread the north for the south and the east for the west (*loc. cit.* pp. 17–18, 43–4).

Another problem which Braines encountered, the location of the Park and the Park Gate (*loc. cit.* pp. 21, 63–6, 70–3), is solved by the manuscript map in the P.R.O. (Plate V) which shows two 'Park Gates' to the south of the road later known as Deadman's Place.

16. Some examples are collected by E. K. Chambers, *Elizabethan Stage*, II, 524. The reference in *Tom Tel-Troth's Message* (1600) to "the Banke-sides round-house" might allude to the Swan *or* the Rose *or* the Globe.

17. Sidney Colvin, *Early Engraving and Engravers in England* (1905, p. 34).

18. In the panorama the Globe looks very much like an insertion after the plate had been engraved. Cf. n. 21 on 'Holland's Leaguer'.

19. *Site of the Globe Playhouse* (1924), p. 56.

20. A reduced photograph of a portion showing all the Bankside theatres is given in J. Q. Adams's *Shakespearean Playhouses* (n.d.), facing p. 256. Reproductions of smaller sections are numerous. Merian's engraving appears to have been the source of the "View of London from Southwark" attributed to Thomas Wyck (1616–77), of which a reproduction was published by the London Topographical Society (Publ. no. 78, 1945).

PLATE I

Titus Andronicus. Drawing and text attributed to HENRY PEACHAM, 1595

(The Most Hon. the Marquess of Bath, Longleat)

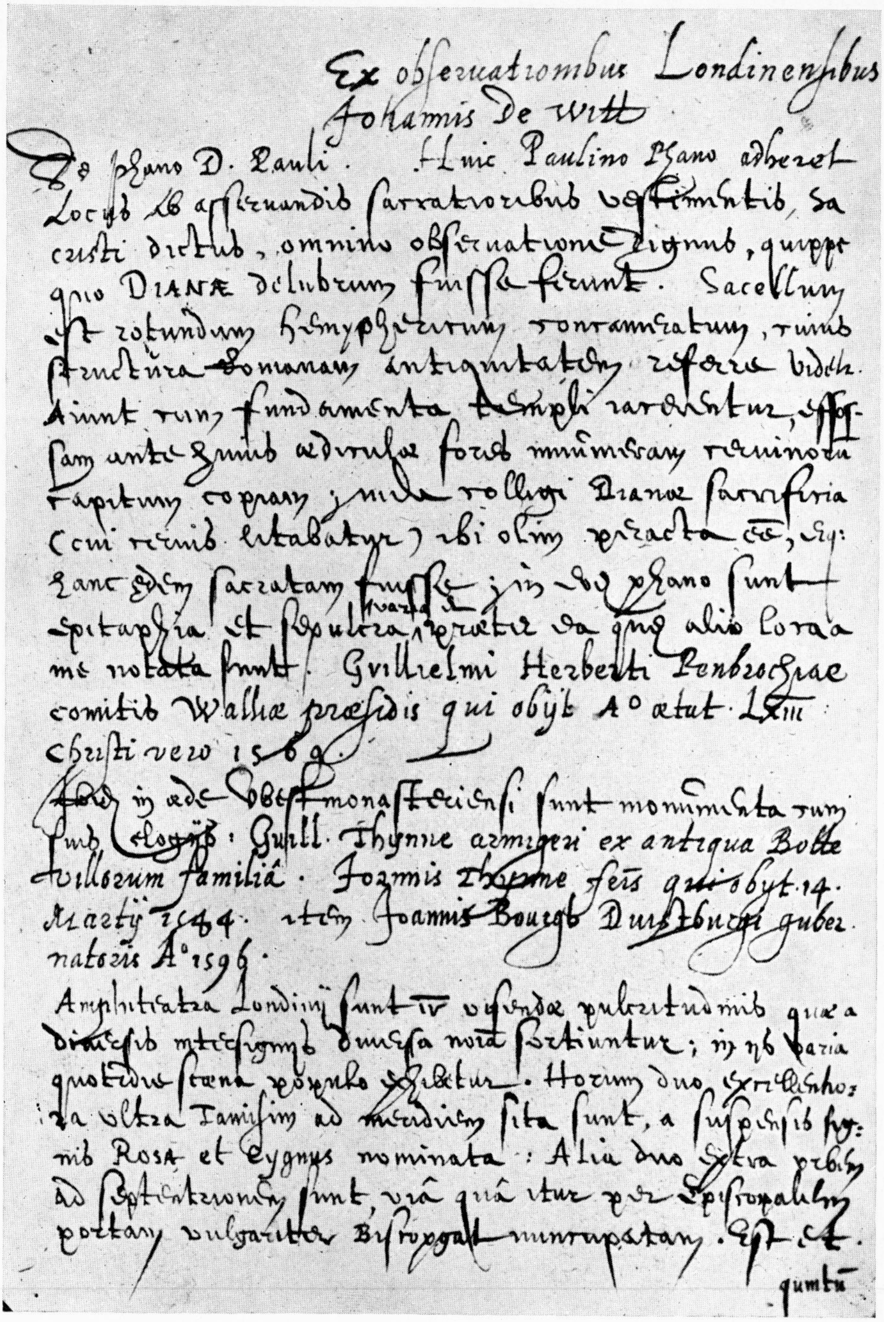

PLATE II

JOHANNES DE WITT: *Observations on London, c.* 1596

(*see Plate* IV A)

PLATE III

JOHANNES DE WITT: *Observations on London, c. 1596*

(*see Plate IV A*)

PLATE IV

A. Johannes de Witt: *Observations on London, c.* 1596. Copy by Arend Van Buchell of a drawing by Johannes de Witt together with the latter's observations on London
(Bibliotheek der Rijksuniversiteit, Utrecht, MS. 842)

B. View of London, 1600. Central portion, considerably reduced, of *Civitas Londini*
(Royal Library, Stockholm)

PLATE V

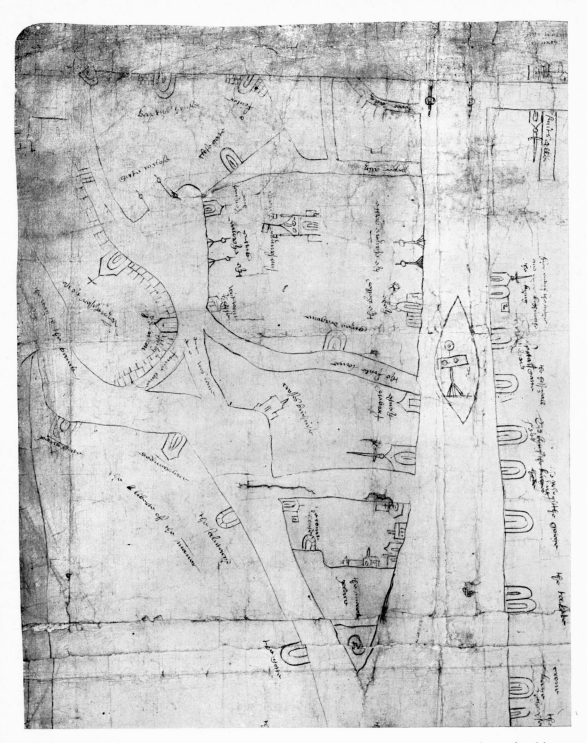

PART OF SOUTHWARK, *c.* 1550. North-east corner of manuscript map (considerably reduced) of Southwark, showing neighbourhood of St Mary Overie's Church

(Public Record Office, M.P. C. 64)

PLATE VI

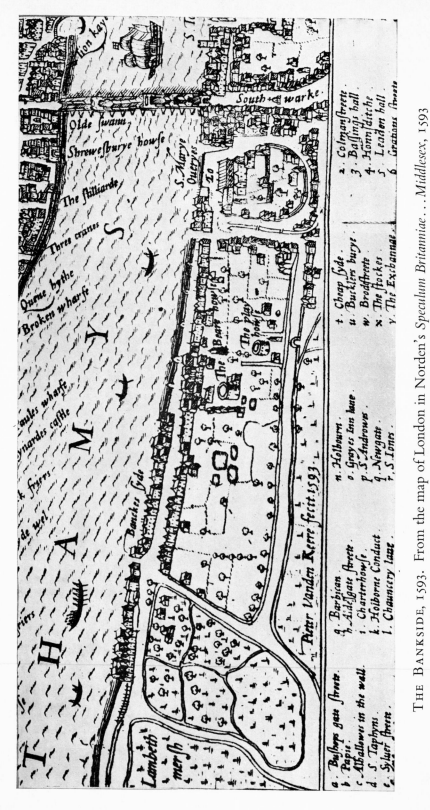

THE BANKSIDE, 1593. From the map of London in Norden's *Speculum Britanniae…Middlesex*, 1593

(Birmingham Reference Library)

PLATE VII

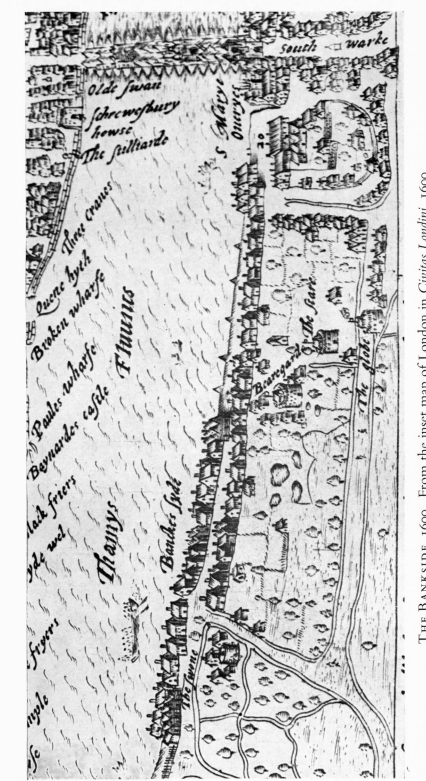

THE BANKSIDE, 1600. From the inset map of London in *Civitas Londini*, 1600

(Royal Library, Stockholm)

PLATE VIII

Swan   Beargarden   Rose   Globe

A. THE BANKSIDE, 1600. Detail from *Civitas Londini*, 1600
(Royal Library, Stockholm)

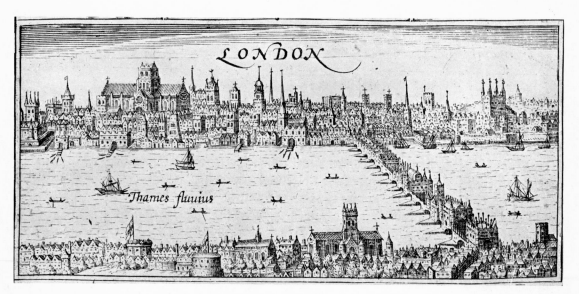

B. VIEW OF LONDON, engraved 1610. Inset from map of Great Britain engraved by
JODOCUS HONDIUS for JOHN SPEED'S *Theatre of the Empire of Great Britain*
(British Museum, G. 7884)

21. This is another building which looks like an insertion in *Civitas Londini* after the plate had been engraved. Cf. n. 18 on the Globe.

22. This is reproduced in Sidney Colvin's *Early Engraving and Engravers in England*, p. 67, and reduced in the illustrated library edition of Sidney Lee's *Life of Shakespeare* (1899), p. 190; a later impression is illustrated in Greg's *Bibliography of English Printed Drama* (1939), I, Pl. XLII.

23. The argument by which J. C. Adams seeks to discount this evidence is based on the quite unjustifiable and certainly·incorrect assumption that Delaram's background shows the Bankside as it was in 1603 (*Globe Playhouse*, p. 386; apparently a misunderstanding of Chambers's *Elizabethan Stage*, II, 354), and on the equally unjustifiable assumption that the Hondius view represents the Bankside as it appeared between 1587–99 (*ibid.* p. 389).

24. *Home Counties Magazine* (IX, 1907, 81); *Surrey Archaeological Collections* (XXIII, 1910, 186); J. Quincy Adams, *Shakespearean Playhouses*, p. 246; J. C. Adams, *Globe Playhouse*, p. 20.

25. *Early Engraving and Engravers in England* (p. 145). Colvin reproduces Passe's portrait of Anne of Denmark in his Pl. XXIV.

26. Both are described in *Designs by Inigo Jones*..., ed. P. Simpson and C. F. Bell (Oxford, for the Walpole and Malone Societies, 1924), p. 103; design no. 257 is reproduced in full in Pl. XXXIII.

27. A full-size reproduction of this beautiful etching was published by the London Topographical Society; a smaller one is to be found on Pl. XV–XX A of A. M. Hind's *Wenceslas Hollar and his Views of London* (1922). Numerous copies of Hollar's view, of varying degrees of inaccuracy, were published during the following three centuries, portions of some being occasionally cited in discussions of the Bankside theatres; all of course are worthless.

28. Cf. Adams, *Globe Playhouse*, p. 6. Adams's efforts to discredit Hollar's view, which contradicts his thesis, have led him to the strange argument that Hollar's selection of "an *actual* viewpoint atop the tower of St. Saviour's instead of the *imaginary* 'bird's eye' viewpoint used by Visscher and others" and his "perspective from a fixed point" proves his "lack of first-hand data, particularly with respect to certain land-marks in Southwark" (pp. 6–7, my italics). Adams's statements that "all other records deny his extensive rows of houses lying between St. Saviour's and the Thames" and that Hind's catalogue "reveals the artist's inattention to buildings in Southwark" are precisely contradicted by the facts.

29. Hind, *loc. cit.* Pl. XXX.

30. *Site of the Globe*, pp. 57–60.

31. E. K. Chambers, *Elizabethan Stage*, II, 466.

POSTSCRIPT

Strong support for the argument that Hollar interchanged the names of the Globe and Beargarden when etching his 'Long View' and proof that he made it from sketches prepared for the purpose before he escaped to Antwerp (see p. 34) have been brought to my notice by F. H. Simpson, Librarian of the Barber Institute of Fine Art. Two of Hollar's sketches, one showing the Globe and Beargarden and obviously the original of that part of the 'Long View' included in our Plate XIV, are reproduced in *The Connoisseur* (xcii, 1933, 320) by Iolo Williams, their owner. No building in either drawing is labelled. It is interesting to find Iolo Williams commenting independently that this "shows that the names were only put on while the plate was being etched— that is to say, not in England, but in Antwerp—and that, therefore, a mistake was very likely to occur". There is little difference between the representations of the theatres in the drawing and in the etching, the most considerable being the insertion of the Beargarden flag in the latter.

SHAKESPEARE AND THE BLACKFRIARS THEATRE

BY

GERALD EADES BENTLEY

It is necessary at the outset in a discussion of this sort to place Shakespeare in what seems to me his proper context—a context which none but the Baconians and Oxfordians deny, but which most scholars and critics tend to ignore. That context is the London commercial theatre and the organized professional acting troupe.

Shakespeare was more completely and continuously involved with theatres and acting companies than any other Elizabethan dramatist whose life we know. Most Elizabethan dramatists had only their writing connection with the theatres, but Shakespeare belonged to the small group which both wrote and acted. In this small group of actor-dramatists, the best-known names are those of Heywood, Rowley, Field and Shakespeare. Of this thoroughly professionalized band, Shakespeare is the one most closely bound to his company and his theatre, for he is the only one of the four who did not shift about from company to company but maintained his close association with a single acting troupe for more than twenty years. Besides this, he was bound to theatres and actors in still another fashion which makes him unique among all Elizabethan dramatists: he is the only dramatist we know who owned stock in theatre buildings over an extended period. His income was derived from acting, from writing plays, from shares in dramatic enterprises, and from theatre rents. From the beginning to the end of his writing career we must see him in a theatrical context if we are not to do violence to the recorded facts. At the beginning is our first reference to him in Greene's allusion to the "Tygers hart wrapt in a Players hyde"; at the end are his own last words, so far as we know them, in his will. This will is mostly concerned with Stratford affairs, but when he does turn to the years of his London life and his many London associates, he singles out only three for a last remembrance. These men are John Heminges, Henry Condell, and Richard Burbage—all three actors, all three fellow-sharers in the acting company of the King's men, all three fellow-stockholders in the Globe and the Blackfriars. If Shakespeare's proper context is not the London commercial theatres and the professional troupes, then evidence has no meaning, and one man's irresponsible fancies are as good as another's.

Now in spite of all the evidence that Shakespeare's dominant preoccupation throughout his creative life was the theatre, most scholars and critics of the last 150 years have written of him as the professional poet and not as the professional playwright. For the most part he has been studied as Spenser and Milton and Keats are studied. For a century and a half the great majority of studies of Shakespeare's genius and development have been concerned with literary influences and biographical influences and not with theatrical influences.[1] We have studied his sources and his text, his indebtedness to Ovid and Holinshed and Montaigne and Plutarch. Even in biographical studies the preference has always been for the non-theatrical aspects of Shakespeare's life—his boyhood in the woods and fields about Stratford, his marriage and his wife, the death of his son Hamnet, his relations with Southampton and Essex, his supposed breakdown, his retirement to Stratford. Now any or all of these facts, or alleged facts, no doubt had an influence on the great creations of Shakespeare. I do not suggest that our study of them should be discontinued. But given the verified documentary evidence which we have, is it not dubious practice to devote a large part of our investigations to the more or less problematical influences in Shakespeare's career and to devote a very small part of our efforts to that enormously significant influence which dominated the majority of his waking hours for the twenty-odd years of his creative maturity? A dozen or more unquestioned documents show that Shakespeare's daily concern was the enterprise of the Lord Chamberlain-King's company. Shakespeare had obviously read Ovid and Holinshed and Lord North's *Plutarch*; surely he must have mourned for the untimely death of his only son; but none of these can have occupied his mind for so long as his daily association with the enterprise of the Lord Chamberlain-King's men. Of the factors in his life and development which we can now identify, this was surely the most important.

Now what are the events in his long and absorbing association with this troupe which we can expect to have influenced his work? One of the first must have been the protracted plague closings of 1593 and 1594, for out of this disaster to all London players the Lord Chamberlain's company apparently rose.[2] Another must have been the assembling of the players and the drawing up of the agreement for the formal organization of the Lord Chamberlain's company. The record suggests that Shakespeare was one of the leaders in this organization, for when the new company performed before the court in the Christmas season of 1594-5, payment was made to Richard Burbage, the principal actor, Will Kemp, the principal comedian, and William Shakespeare.[3] How did the great possibilities offered by this new troupe, destined to become the most famous and most successful in the history of the English theatre, affect the writing of its chief dramatist?

In the winter of 1598-9 occurred another event which must have been of absorbing interest for all members of the company. This was of course the building of the Globe on the Bankside. Here was a theatre built for the occupancy of a particular company, and six of the seven owners were actors in the company. Assuredly it was built, so far as available funds would allow, to the specific requirements of the productions of the Lord Chamberlain's men. What facilities did Shakespeare get which he had not had before? How did he alter his composition to take advantage of the new possibilities? Can there be any doubt that as a successful man of the theatre he did so? Yet I know of no study which attempts to assess this vital new factor in relation to Shakespeare's development.

The next event which must have been of great importance for Shakespeare's company was its involvement in the Essex rebellion. This exceptional case has received the full attention of critics and scholars because of its supposed relation to a performance of Shakespeare's *Richard II*. Actually, however, the Essex rebellion, much though it must have excited the company for a few months, was the least influential of all these factors affecting the company's activities and Shakespeare's development. Apparently the company's innocence was established without much difficulty.[4] There is no indication that their later performances or Shakespeare's later writing were affected by the experience. Though the events were sensational, and though they must have caused great anxiety for a time, they cannot be thought of as events of long-term significance in

4-2

the history of this group of men who were so important and influential in Shakespeare's career and development.

Of much more importance in the affairs of the company was their attainment of the patronage of James I less than two months after the death of Elizabeth.[5] This patronage and the King's livery certainly became one of the important factors in creating the great prestige of the company. In the ten years before they became the King's company, their known performances at court average about three a year; in the ten years after they attained their new service their known performances at court average about thirteen a year, more than those of all other London companies combined.[6] They were officially the premier company in London; a good part of their time must have been devoted to the preparation of command performances. Surely this new status of the troupe must have been a steady and pervasive influence in the development of its principal dramatist, William Shakespeare.

The final event which I wish to mention in the affairs of the King's company was perhaps the most important of all. There is no doubt that it made a great change in the activities of the company, and I do not see how it can have failed to be a principal influence in Shakespeare's development as a dramatist. This event was the acquisition of the famous private theatre in Blackfriars. No adult company in London had ever before performed regularly in a private theatre. For thirty years the private theatres with their superior audiences, their concerts, their comfortable accommodations, their traffic in sophisticated drama and the latest literary fads, had been the exclusive homes of the boy companies, the pets of Society. Now for the first time a troupe of those rogues and vagabonds, the common players, had the temerity to present themselves to the sophisticates of London in a repertory at the town's most exclusive theatre. I suspect that this was one of the turning points in Tudor and Stuart dramatic history. Beaumont and Jonson and Fletcher had begun to make the craft of the playwright more socially respectable. The increasing patronage of the drama by the royal family, and the growing splendour and frequency of the court masques which were written by ordinary playwrights and performed in part by common players, were raising the prestige of the drama and the theatre from its Elizabethan to its Caroline state. The acquisition of the Blackfriars in 1608 by the King's company and the full exploitation of the new playhouse must have been the most conspicuous evidence to Londoners of the changing state of affairs. Surely it is impossible that the King's men and their principal dramatist, William Shakespeare, could have been unaware of this situation. Surely they must have bent all their efforts in the selection and performance of old plays and in the commissioning and writing of new ones to the full exploitation of this unprecedented opportunity. The new state of affairs must have been apparent in much that they did, and it must have influenced decidedly the dramatic compositions of Shakespeare.

So far, it has been my contention that all we know of William Shakespeare has shown him to be above all else a man of the theatre, that during the twenty years of his creative maturity most of his time was spent in closest association with members of the Lord Chamberlain-King's company and in thought about their needs and their interests, and that therefore in the affairs of this company we should seek one of the principal influences in his creative life. I have mentioned six events which (so far as we can tell through the mists of 350 years) seem to have been important in the affairs of that theatrical organization. These events are not all of equal importance, but each of them, except possibly the Essex rebellion, must have had a marked effect on the activities of Shakespeare's company and therefore on the dramatic creations of Shakespeare himself. Each one, it seems to me, deserves more study than it has received in its relation to the development of Shakespeare's work.

Let me invite your attention now to a fuller consideration of one of the most important of these events in the history of the Lord Chamberlain-King's company, namely the acquisition of the Blackfriars Theatre. What did this event mean in the history of the company, and how did it affect the writing of William Shakespeare?

Probably we should note first the time at which the Blackfriars would have begun to influence the company and the writing of Shakespeare. All the dramatic histories say that the King's men took over the Blackfriars Theatre in 1608, and this is true in a legal sense, for on 9 August 1608 leases were executed conveying the Blackfriars Playhouse to seven lessees: Cuthbert Burbage, Thomas Evans, and five members of the King's company—John Heminges, William Sly, Henry Condell, Richard Burbage, and William Shakespeare.[7] The few scholars who have examined in detail the history of the King's company have noted, however, that Shakespeare and his fellows probably did not begin to act at the Blackfriars in August of 1608. The plague was rife in London at that time; fifty plague deaths had been recorded for the week ending 28 July, and for a year and a half, or until December 1609, the bills of mortality show an abnormally high rate from the plague.[8] Though specific records about the closing of the theatres are not extant, we have definite statements that they were closed for part of this period, and comparison with other years suggests that there must have been very little if any public acting allowed in London between the first of August 1608 and the middle of December 1609. Therefore, it has occasionally been said, the Blackfriars was not used by the King's men much before 1610, and no influence on their plays and their productions can be sought before that year.

This conclusion of little or no influence before 1610 is, I think, a false one. It is based on the erroneous assumption that the actors and playwrights of the King's company would have known nothing about the peculiarities of the Blackfriars and that they would have had no plays prepared especially for that theatre until after they had begun performing in it. Actors are never so stupid or so insular as this in any time. The King's men, we may be sure, were well aware of the Blackfriars and the type of performance it required, or specialized in, long before they came to lease the theatre. There must be many evidences of this, but three in particular come readily to mind.

Seven years before, in 1601, the King's men had been involved in the War of the Theatres, which was in part a row between the public theatres and the private theatres. The chief attack on the public theatres and adult actors was made in Jonson's *Poetaster*, performed at the Blackfriars. Certain actors of the Lord Chamberlain's company, and possibly Shakespeare himself, were ridiculed in this Blackfriars play. The reply, *Satiromastix*, was written by Thomas Dekker and performed by Shakespeare's company at the Globe.[9] Certainly in 1601 at least, the company was well aware of the goings on at Blackfriars.

A second piece of evidence pointing to their knowledge of the peculiar requirements of the Blackfriars is the case of Marston's *Malcontent*. Marston wrote this play for the boys at the Blackfriars, who performed it in that theatre in 1604. The King's men stole the play, as they admitted, and performed it at the Globe; the third edition, also 1604, shows the alterations they commissioned John Webster to make in order to adapt a Blackfriars script to a Globe perform-ance, and in the induction to the play Richard Burbage, speaking in his own person, points out one or two of the differences between Blackfriars requirements and Globe requirements.[10]

Finally, and most familiar of all evidence that the King's men were quite alive to what went on at Blackfriars, is the "little eyases" passage in *Hamlet* and Shakespeare's rueful admission that, for a time at any rate, the competition of the Blackfriars was too much for the company at the Globe.

Clearly the King's men did not have to wait until their performances of 1610 at the Blackfriars to know how their plays needed to be changed to fit them to that theatre and its select audience. They had known for several years what the general characteristics of Blackfriars performances were. Indeed, the leading member of the company, Richard Burbage, had a double reason for being familiar with all the peculiarities of the Blackfriars, for since his father's death in 1597 he had been the owner of the theatre and the landlord of the boy company that made it famous.[11] We can be perfectly sure, then, that from the day of the first proposal that the King's men take over the Blackfriars they had talked among themselves about what they would do with it and had discussed what kinds of plays they would have to have written to exploit it. It is all too often forgotten that in all such discussions among the members of the King's company William Shakespeare would have had an important part. He had more kinds of connections with the company than any other man: he was actor, shareholder, patented member, principal playwright, and one of the housekeepers of the Globe; even Burbage did not serve so many functions in the company. Few men in theatrical history have been so completely and inextricably bound up with the affairs of an acting troupe.

When would the King's men have begun planning for their performances at the Blackfriars? We cannot, of course, set the exact date, but we can approximate it. There is one faint suggestion that consideration of the project may have started very early indeed. Richard Burbage said that Henry Evans, who had leased the theatre from him for the Children of the Queen's Revels, began talking to him about the surrender of his lease in 1603 or 1604.[12] These early discussions evidently came to nothing, for we know that the boys continued in the theatre for three or four years longer. Burbage's statement about Evans does suggest the interesting possibility that the King's men may have dallied with the project of leasing the Blackfriars Theatre as early as 1603 or 1604. This, however, is only the faintest of possibilities. The Blackfriars was tentatively in the market then, but all we know is that Burbage had to consider for a short time the possibility of getting other tenants for his theatre. Whether the King's men came to his mind and theirs as possible tenants, we do not know.

We can be sure that active planning for performances at the Blackfriars did get under way when Burbage, who was both the leading actor of the King's men and owner of the Blackfriars Theatre, knew for certain that the boy actors would give up their lease and that arrangements for a syndicate of King's men to take over the theatre could be made. Conferences among these men—the Burbages, Heminges, Condell, Shakespeare, and Sly—and probably preliminary financial arrangements would have been going on before a scrivener was called in to draw up a rough draft of the lease. Such preliminaries, which must come before a lease can be formally signed, often consume months. We know that the leases were formally executed on 9 August 1608;[13] therefore discussions in June and July or even in April and May are likely enough. We know that the Blackfriars Theatre was available as early as March 1608, for in a letter dated 11 March 1608 Sir Thomas Lake officially notified Lord Salisbury that the company of the Children of Blackfriars must be suppressed and that the King had vowed that they should never act again even if they had to beg their bread. General confirmation of this fact is found in a letter written two weeks later by the French ambassador.[14] Thus it is evident that in March of 1608 Richard Burbage knew his theatre was without a tenant. March to July 1608, then, are the months for discussions among the King's men of prospective performances at the Blackfriars.

What did this little group of Shakespeare and his intimate associates of the last fourteen years work out during their discussions in the months of March to July 1608? One of the things they must have considered was alterations of their style of acting. As Granville-Barker has pointed out,[15] the acting in the new Blackfriars before a sophisticated audience would have to be more quiet than in the large open-air Globe before the groundlings. It would be easier to emphasize points in the quiet candlelit surroundings, and "sentiment would become as telling as passion". There must also have been extended discussions of what to do about the repertory: which of the company's plays would be suitable for the elegant new theatre and which should be kept for the old audience at the Globe? Some of their decisions are fairly obvious. *Mucedorus*, which Rafe in *The Knight of the Burning Pestle* says he had played before the Wardens of his company and which went through fifteen editions before the Restoration, was clearly one of the Globe plays which might be laughed at by a Blackfriars audience. Similarly, *The Merry Devil of Edmonton* was not a good Blackfriars prospect. Certain other plays in the repertory might be expected to please at the Blackfriars; Marston's *Malcontent*, for instance, could easily be changed back to its original Blackfriars form, and Jonson's *Every Man in His Humour* and *Every Man out of His Humour*, though nine and ten years old, had been played by the company at court in the last three years and ought to be suitable for the Blackfriars.

These discussions of the old repertory, though no doubt important to the company then, are fruitless for us now. I know of no evidence as to their decisions. More important are the proposals for new plays for the Blackfriars, and I think we do have some evidence as to what these decisions were. The experienced members of the King's company were familiar with the fact so commonly recorded in the annals of the Jacobean theatre that new plays were in constant demand. With the acquisition of the new theatre they had an opportunity to claim for their own the most profitable audience in London. We know from the later Jacobean and Caroline records that this is just what they did.[16] It seems likely that one of the foundations of their later un-questioned dominance of the audiences of the gentry was their decision about plays and play-wrights made in their discussions of March to July 1608.

One of their decisions, I suggest, was to get Jonson to write Blackfriars plays for them. He was a likely choice for three reasons. First, because he was developing a following among the courtly audience (always prominent at the Blackfriars) by his great court masques. At this time he had already written his six early entertainments for King James—those at the Coronation, at the Opening of Parliament, at Althorp, at Highgate, and the two at Theobalds. He had written for performance at Whitehall *The Masque of Blackness*, *The Masque of Beauty*, *Hymenaei*, and the famous *Lord Haddington's Masque*. The sensational success of these courtly entertainments made Jonson a most promising choice to write plays for the courtly audience which the King's men did succeed in attracting to Blackfriars.

A second reason which would have led the King's men to Jonson as a writer for their new theatre was his great reputation among the literati and critics. In this decade from 1601 to 1610 the literary allusions to him are numerous, more numerous than to Shakespeare himself. The poems to Jonson and the long prose passages about him in this time are far more frequent than to Shakespeare; quotations from his work occur oftener, and I find three times as many literary and social references to performances of his plays and masques as to Shakespeare's. Poems about him or references to his work are written in these years by John Donne, Sir John Roe, Sir Dudley Carleton, the Venetian ambassador, John Chamberlain, Sir Thomas Lake, Sir George Buc, Sir Thomas Salusbury.[17] This is just the kind of audience which might be attracted to the Blackfriars, and which, eventually, the King's men did attract there.

There was a third reason which would have made Jonson seem to the King's men a very likely bet for their new theatre: he had already had experience in writing plays for this theatre when it was occupied by boys. Before the conferences of the King's men about their new project he had already had performed at Blackfriars *Cynthia's Revels*, *The Poetaster*, *The Case Is Altered*, and *Eastward Ho*. Possibly just before the time of the conferences of the King's men he had been writing for the Blackfriars another play, *Epicoene*, for he says in the Folio of 1616 that the play was performed by the Children of Blackfriars, but the date he gives for performance comes after their expulsion from the Blackfriars Theatre. Not only had Jonson had the valuable experience of writing four or five plays for the Blackfriars, but the Induction to *Cynthia's Revels* and his personal statements about boys of the company, like Nathan Field and Salathiel, or Solomon, Pavy,[18] strongly suggest that he had directed them in their rehearsals. What valuable experience for the King's men planning their first performance in this new theatre!

Now all these qualifications of Jonson as a prospect for the King's men are, in sober fact, only speculations. Perhaps they simply show that if *I* had been participating in the conferences about the Blackfriars I should have argued long and lustily for Ben Jonson. Alas, I was not there! What evidence is there that they really did agree to secure his services for the company? The evidence is that before these conferences he had written only four plays for the Lord Chamberlain's or King's company—three, nine, and ten years before—nothing for the company in the years 1605–08. After these conferences, he wrote all his remaining plays for the company, with the exception of *Bartholomew Fair* six years later, a play which he gave to his good friend and protégé Nathan Field for the Lady Elizabeth's company at the Hope, and *A Tale of a Tub*, twenty-five years later, which he gave to Queen Henrietta's men. Jonson's first play after the reopening of Blackfriars was *The Alchemist*; it was written for the King's men, and numerous allusions show clearly that it was written for Blackfriars. So were *Catiline*, *The Devil Is an Ass*, *The Staple of News*, *The New Inn*, and *The Magnetic Lady*. Of course we lack the final proof of recorded reference to a definite agreement, but the evidence is such as to suggest that one of the decisions reached by the King's men in the reorganization of their enterprise to exploit the great advantages of their new theatre was to secure the services of Ben Jonson to write plays for the literate and courtly audience at Blackfriars.

Another decision, which I suggest the King's men made at these conferences, was to secure for their new theatre the services of the rising young collaborators, Francis Beaumont and John Fletcher. These gentlemen were younger than Jonson by about ten years, and as yet their reputations were distinctly inferior to his, but they had already displayed those talents which were to make their plays the stage favourites at Blackfriars for the next thirty-four years,[19] and were to cause Dryden to say sixty years later that "their plays are now the most pleasant and frequent entertainments of the stage".

One of the great assets of Beaumont and Fletcher was social. In the years immediately before and after 1608, the London theatre audience was developing the social cleavage which is such a marked characteristic of the Jacobean and Caroline drama and stage. In Elizabeth's time the London theatre was a universal one, in which a single audience at the Globe could embrace Lord Monteagle, Sir Charles Percy, city merchants, lawyers, Inns of Court students, apprentices, servants, beggars, pickpockets, and prostitutes. The later Jacobean and Caroline audience was a dual one. The gentry, the court, the professional classes, and the Inns of Court men went to the Blackfriars, the Phoenix, and later to the Salisbury Court; the London masses went to the larger and noisier Red Bull and Fortune and Globe. This new state of affairs was just developing when the King's men had their conferences about the Blackfriars in 1608. They evidently saw what was coming, however, for in the next few years they understood and exploited the situation more effectively than any other troupe in London. Indeed, the very acquisition of the Blackfriars and its operation in conjunction with the Globe was a device which had never been tried before in London and which is the clearest evidence that the King's men knew just what was happening.

Under these circumstances, then, the social status of Beaumont and Fletcher was an asset for the company in their new house. Francis Beaumont came of an ancient and distinguished Leicestershire family, with many connections among the nobility. John Fletcher was the son of a Lord Bishop of London and one-time favourite of Elizabeth. To a Blackfriars audience the social standing of these two young men would have been more acceptable than that of any other dramatist writing in London in 1608.

Another asset which made Beaumont and Fletcher valuable for the new enterprise of the King's men was their private theatre experience. So far as we can make out now, all their plays before this time had been written for private theatres and most of them for the Blackfriars. *The Woman Hater* had been prepared for the private theatre in St Paul's, but *The Knight of the Burning Pestle*, *The Scornful Lady*, and *The Faithful Shepherdess* were Blackfriars plays. I think we can add to this list *Cupid's Revenge*. This play has been variously dated, but two forthcoming articles by James Savage[20] seem to me to offer convincing evidence that the play was prepared for Blackfriars about 1607 and that it displays a crude preliminary working out of much of the material which made *Philaster* one of the great hits of its time and one of the most influential plays of the seventeenth century. In any event, Beaumont and Fletcher were among the most experienced Blackfriars playwrights available in 1608. It is true that in 1608 none of their plays had been a great success; indeed the two best, *The Knight of the Burning Pestle* and *The Faithful Shepherdess*, are known to have been unsuccessful at first. The King's men, however, were experienced in the ways of the theatre; it does not seem rash to assume that at least one of them knew enough about audiences and about dramatic talents to see that these young men were writers of brilliant promise—especially since that one was William Shakespeare.

Beaumont and Fletcher, then, because of their experience and social standing were very desirable dramatists for the King's men to acquire in 1608 for their new private theatre. What is the evidence that they did acquire them? The evidence is that all the Beaumont and Fletcher plays of the next few years are King's men's plays, several of them famous hits—*Philaster, The*

Maid's Tragedy, A King and No King, The Captain, The Two Noble Kinsmen, Bonduca, Monsieur Thomas, Valentinian. The dating of many of the Beaumont and Fletcher plays is very uncertain because of their late publication, and it may be that two or three of the later plays were written for other companies, but at least forty-five plays by Beaumont and Fletcher were the property of the Jacobean and Caroline King's men.[21] None of their plays before 1608, when Blackfriars was acquired, was, so far as we can find, written for the King's men. It seems a reasonable assumption, therefore, that another of the policies agreed upon at the conferences of 1608 was to secure the services of Beaumont and Fletcher for the company in its new enterprise at the Blackfriars.

The third of these three important changes in policy which I think the King's men agreed upon at their conferences about the new Blackfriars enterprise in 1608, is the most interesting of all to us, but it was the easiest and most obvious for them. Indeed, it may well have been assumed almost without discussion. It was, of course, that William Shakespeare should write henceforth with the Blackfriars in mind and not the Globe.

Why was this decision an easy and obvious one? The company could assume, of course, that he would continue to write for them, since he was a shareholder and a patented member of the company and a housekeeper in both their theatres. Since the formation of the company, fourteen years before, all his plays had been written for performance by them, always, in the last ten years, for performance at the Globe. All his professional associations as well as his financial ones were with this company, and probably no one in the group even considered his defection. Burbage, Shakespeare, Heminges, and Condell were the real nucleus of the organization.

This new enterprise at the Blackfriars was a very risky business. As we have noted, no adult company had ever tried to run a private theatre before. The King's men not only proposed to make a heavy investment in this new departure, but they intended to continue running their old public theatre at the same time. Every possible precaution against failure needed to be taken. One such precaution would be the devotion of Shakespeare's full-time energies to the Blackfriars instead of the Globe. They could trust Shakespeare; he knew their potentialities and their shortcomings as no other dramatist did—indeed, few dramatists in the history of the English theatre have ever had such a long and intimate association with an acting company as William Shakespeare had had with these men. If anybody knew what Burbage and Heminges and Condell and Robert Armyn and Richard Cowley could do on the stage and what they should not be asked to do, that man was William Shakespeare. He could make them a success at the Blackfriars as they had been at the Globe if any one could.

Another reason for the transfer of Shakespeare's efforts was the fact that the Globe could be left to take care of itself with an old repertory as the Blackfriars could not. For one thing, there was no old repertory for the Blackfriars, since the departing boys appear to have held on to their old plays. For another thing, it was the Blackfriars audience which showed the greater avidity for new plays; the public theatre audiences were much more faithful to old favourites. They were still playing *Friar Bacon and Friar Bungay* at the Fortune in 1630 and Marlowe's *Edward II* at the Red Bull in 1620 and *Dr Faustus* at the Fortune in 1621 and *Richard II* and *Pericles* at the Globe in 1631.[22] In the archives of the Globe at this time there must have been a repertory of more than a hundred plays, including at least twenty-five of Shakespeare's. Moreover, certain plays written for the Globe in the last few years, like Wilkins's *Miseries of Enforced Marriage* and the anonymous *Yorkshire Tragedy* and *The Fair Maid of Bristol* and *The London Prodigal*, had provided playwrights who might be expected to entertain a Globe audience with more of the same fare, but who could scarcely come up to the requirements of sophistication at Blackfriars. Altogether, then, the Globe repertory had much less need of Shakespeare's efforts in 1608 than did the Blackfriars repertory.

Why should Shakespeare have wanted to write for the Blackfriars, or at least have agreed to do so? The most compelling of the apparent reasons is that he had money invested in the project and stood to lose by its failure and gain by its success. He was one of the seven lessees of the new theatre; he had paid down an unknown sum and had agreed to pay £5. 14s. 4d. per year in rent.[23] He had at least a financial reason for doing everything he could to establish the success of the Blackfriars venture, and what Shakespeare could do most effectively was to write plays which would insure the company's popularity with the audience in its new private theatre.

A third reason for this postulated decision of the King's men in 1608 to have Shakespeare devote his entire attention to the Blackfriars and abandon the Globe was that the King's men saw that the real future of the theatrical profession in London lay with the court and the court party in the private theatres. Their receipts for performances at court showed them this very clearly. In the last nine years of Elizabeth, 1594–1602, they had received from court performances an average of £35 a year; in the first five years of the reign of the new king, 1603–7, they had averaged £131 per year in addition to their new allowances for liveries as servants of the King.[24] The Blackfriars and not the Globe was the theatre where they could entertain this courtly audience with commercial performances. There is no doubt that in the next few years after 1608 the Blackfriars did become the principal theatre of the company. In 1612 Edward Kirkham said they took £1,000 a winter more at the Blackfriars than they had formerly taken at the Globe.[25] When Sir Henry Herbert listed receipts from the two theatres early in the reign of King Charles, the receipts for single performances at the Globe averaged £6. 13s. 8d.; those for single performances at the Blackfriars averaged £15. 15s., or about two and one-half times as much.[26] In 1634 an Oxford don who wrote up the company simply called them the company of the Blackfriars and did not mention the Globe at all;[27] when the plays of the company were published in the Jacobean and Caroline period, the Blackfriars was mentioned as their theatre more than four times as often as the Globe was.[28] Such evidence proves that the Blackfriars certainly did become the principal theatre of the King's men. I am suggesting that in the conferences of 1608 the King's men had some intimation that it would, and accordingly they persuaded William Shakespeare to devote his attention to that theatre in the future instead of to the Globe.

So much for the reasons that Shakespeare might be expected to change the planning of his plays in 1608. What is the evidence that he did? The evidence, it seems to me, is to be seen in *Cymbeline*, *The Winter's Tale*, *The Tempest*, and *The Two Noble Kinsmen*, and probably it was to be seen also in the lost play, *Cardenio*. The variations which these plays show from the Shakespearian norm have long been a subject for critical comment. The first three of them in particular, since they are the only ones which have been universally accepted as part of the Shakespeare canon, have commonly been discussed as a distinct genre. Widely as critics and scholars have disagreed over the reasons for their peculiar characteristics, those peculiarities have generally been recognized, whether the plays are called Shakespeare's Romances, or Shakespeare's Tragi-Comedies, or his Romantic Tragi-Comedies, or simply the plays of the fourth period. No competent critic who has read carefully through the Shakespeare canon has failed to notice that there is something different about *Cymbeline*, *The Winter's Tale*, *The Tempest*, and *The Two Noble Kinsmen*.

When critics and scholars have tried to explain this difference between the plays of the last period and Shakespeare's earlier work, they have set up a variety of hypotheses. Most of these hypotheses have in common only the trait which I noted at the beginning of this paper—namely, they agree in considering Shakespeare as the professional poet and not the professional play-wright. They turn to Shakespeare's sources, or to his inspiration, or to his personal affairs, or to the bucolic environment of his Stratford retirement, but not to the theatre which was his daily preoccupation for more than twenty years. Dowden called this late group in the Shakespeare canon "On the Heights", because he thought the plays reflected Shakespeare's new-found serenity. Such a fine optimism had, perhaps, something to recommend it to the imaginations of the Victorians, but to modern scholars it seems to throw more light on Dowden's mind than on Shakespeare's development. Dowden's explanation seemed utterly fatuous to Lytton Strachey, who thought that the plays of "Shakespeare's Final Period" were written by a Shakespeare far from serene, who was really "half enchanted by visions of beauty and loveliness and half bored to death". Violently as Dowden and Strachey differ, they agree in seeking subjective interpretations.

Best known of the old explanations of the peculiarities of the plays of this last period is probably Thorndike's:[29] the contention that the great success of *Philaster* caused Shakespeare to imitate it in *Cymbeline* and to a lesser extent in *The Winter's Tale* and *The Tempest*. In spite of the great horror of the Shakespeare idolaters at the thought of the master imitating superficial young whipper-snappers like Beaumont and Fletcher, no one can read the two plays together without noting the striking similarities between them. The difficulty is that although the approximate dates of the two plays are clear enough, their *precise* dates are so close together and so uncertain that neither Thorndike nor any subsequent scholar has been able to prove that *Philaster* came before *Cymbeline*, and the Shakespeare idolaters have been equally unable to prove that *Cymbeline* came before *Philaster*.

I suggest that the really important point is not the priority of either play. The significant and revealing facts are that both were written for the King's company; both were written, or at least completed, after the important decision made by the leaders of the troupe in the spring of 1608 to commission new plays for Blackfriars, and both were prepared to be acted in the private theatre in Blackfriars before the sophisticated audience attracted to that house. It is their common purpose and environment, not imitation of one by the other, which makes them similar. Both *Philaster* and *Cymbeline* are somewhat like Beaumont and Fletcher's earlier plays, especially *Cupid's Revenge*, because Beaumont and Fletcher's earlier plays had all been written for private theatres and all but one for Blackfriars. Both *Philaster* and *Cymbeline* are unlike Shakespeare's earlier plays because none of those plays had been written for private theatres. The subsequent plays of both Beaumont and Fletcher and Shakespeare resemble *Philaster* and *Cymbeline* because they too were written to be performed by the King's men before the sophisticated and courtly audience in the private theatre at Blackfriars.

So much I think we can say with some assurance. This explanation of the character of Shake-speare's last plays is in accord with the known facts of theatrical history; it accords with the biographical evidence of Shakespeare's long and close association with all the enterprises of the

Lord Chamberlain's-King's men for twenty years; it is in accord with his fabulously acute sense of the theatre and the problems of the actor; and it does no violence to his artistic integrity or to his poetic genius.

May I add one further point much more in the realm of speculation? Since John Fletcher became a playwright for the King's men at this time and continued so for the remaining seventeen years of his life, and since the activities of the King's men had been one of Shakespeare's chief preoccupations for many years, is it not likely that the association between Fletcher and Shakespeare from 1608 to 1614 was closer than has usually been thought? Shakespeare was nearing retirement; after 1608 he wrote plays less frequently than before; Fletcher became his successor as chief dramatist for the King's company. In these years they collaborated in *The Two Noble Kinsmen*, *Henry VIII*, and probably in *Cardenio*. Is it too fantastic to suppose that Shakespeare was at least an adviser in the preparation of *Philaster*, *A King and No King*, and *The Maid's Tragedy* for his fellows? Is it even more fantastic to think that Shakespeare, the old public theatre playwright, preparing his first and crucial play for a private theatre, might have asked advice—or even taken it—from the two young dramatists who had written plays for this theatre and audience four or five times before?

Perhaps this is going too far. I do not wish to close on a note of speculation. My basic contention is that Shakespeare was, before all else, a man of the theatre and a devoted member of the King's company. One of the most important events in the history of that company was its acquisition of the Blackfriars Playhouse in 1608 and its subsequent brilliantly successful exploitation of its stage and audience. The company was experienced and theatre-wise; the most elementary theatrical foresight demanded that in 1608 they prepare new and different plays for a new and different theatre and audience. Shakespeare was their loved and trusted fellow. How could they fail to ask him for new Blackfriars plays, and how could he fail them? All the facts at our command seem to me to demonstrate that he did not fail them. He turned from his old and tested methods and produced a new kind of play for the new theatre and audience. Somewhat unsurely at first he wrote *Cymbeline* for them, then, with greater dexterity in his new medium, *The Winter's Tale*, and finally, triumphant in his old mastery, *The Tempest*.

NOTES

Since this paper was prepared as a lecture for the Shakespeare Conference at Stratford-upon-Avon, it lacks the fuller documentation it might have had if it had been originally written for publication.

1. *The Cambridge Bibliography of English Literature* will serve as an example. The bibliography of Shakespeare fills 136 columns, of which one half-column is devoted to "The Influence of Theatrical Conditions". This is not to say, of course, that there have been no proper studies of the theatres and acting companies of Shakespeare's time. There are many. But there are comparatively few books and articles devoted to the examination of Shakespeare's work in the light of this knowledge or to a consideration of the specific influence such matters had on his methods and development.

2. E. K. Chambers, *The Elizabethan Stage*, II, 192–3 and IV, 348–9; *William Shakespeare*, I, 27–56.

3. *The Elizabethan Stage*, IV, 164.

4. *William Shakespeare*, I, 353–5; *The Elizabethan Stage*, II, 204–7.

5. *The Elizabethan Stage*, II, 208–9.

6. *Ibid.* IV, 108–30.

7. *The Elizavethan Stage*, II, 509–10. Technically Richard Burbage leased one-seventh of the theatre to each of the other six.

8. *Ibid.* IV, 351.

9. See J. H. Penniman, *The War of the Theatres*, and R. A. Small, *The Stage Quarrel*.

10. F. L. Lucas, *The Works of John Webster*, III, 294–309.

11. J. Q. Adams, *Shakespearean Playhouses*, pp. 199–223.

12. The Answers of Heminges and Burbage to Edward Kirkham, 1612, printed by F. G. Fleay, *A Chronicle History of the London Stage*, p. 235.

13. *William Shakespeare*, II, 62–3.

14. *The Elizabethan Stage*, II, 53–4.

15. *Prefaces to Shakespeare*, 2nd ser., pp. 249–50.

16. See Bentley, *The Jacobean and Caroline Stage*, vol. I, chap. I *passim*; II, 673–81.

17. See Bentley, *Shakespeare and Jonson*, I, 38–41, 65–7, 73–9, 87–90, and Bradley and Adams, *The Jonson Allusion-Book*, *passim*.

18. See "A Good Name Lost", *Times Literary Supplement* (30 May 1942), p. 276.

19. *The Jacobean and Caroline Stage*, I, 29 and 109–14.

20. "The Date of Beaumont and Fletcher's *Cupid's Revenge*" and "Beaumont and Fletcher's *Philaster* and Sidney's *Arcadia*".

21. *The Jacobean and Caroline Stage*, I, 109–15.

22. *Ibid.* I, 156, 174, 157, 24, 129.

23. *Shakespearean Playhouses*, pp. 224–5.

24. *The Elizabethan Stage*, IV, 164–75.

25. C. W. Wallace, *University of Nebraska Studies*, VIII (1908), 36–7, n. 6.

26. *The Jacobean and Caroline Stage*, I, 23–4.

27. *Ibid.* I, 26, n. 5.

28. *Ibid.* I, 30, n. 1.

29. Ashley H. Thorndike, *The Influence of Beaumont and Fletcher on Shakespeare*.

SHAKESPEARE'S BAD POETRY

BY

HARDIN CRAIG

*[A paper read at the Shakespeare Conference, Stratford-upon-Avon, August 1947.
Two portions delivered on that occasion have been omitted.]*

In my book, *The Enchanted Glass*, I endeavoured to emphasize the intense expressiveness of the English Renaissance, in accordance with the belief current at that time in the power of expressed truth. If these opinions should be called in question, it is only necessary to point out that rhetoric was the central core of Renaissance education and the very foundation of virtue. The power of speech distinguished men from the brutes, and rhetoric was the symbol of man's dignity. We know that the persuasive aim of ancient rhetoric had also been transferred to poetry. The object of humanistic education, as stated by my pupil Dr Madeleine Doran, was to prepare men to use rational discourse and persuasive eloquence in the service of truth and the public good. In this aim rhetoric and poetry came together. Poetry sought to teach with delight and to move men to great achievement, and, since the medieval conception of rhetoric as merely the ornamental aspect of discourse still prevailed, poetry in some sense superseded rhetoric, inherited the ancient estate of rhetoric, and itself became a primary agent for moving men to rational thought and virtuous action. The *word* itself was irresistible. Of course schools fell far short of their ideals, and rhetorical doctrine suffered mechanization. The whole paraphernalia of the divisions and patterns of oratory were ruthlessly applied to all discourse—to the composition of letters, to the writing of history, and even to the writing of poetry itself. Thus rhetoricians, or general teachers, saw the problem of drama, epic, and lyric in terms of oratory, its divisions and its style.

Renaissance poetry was typically preoccupied with style, and style regarded primarily as decorative at that. This being the case, the wonder is that in Elizabethan literature there is so little sign of flagging poetic power. Renaissance poets urged themselves on to energy and were exhorted to effort by their critics. The demands of rhetoric were thus carried over in full force to poetics. Renaissance poetic style, though based on the highest ideals, was so mandatory, so analytical, so burdensome that it is also surprising that so many poets mastered it. High degrees of mastery could be realized fully only by minds of the greatest genius. The doctrine of poetry, based on the practice of ancient poets shredded, as it were, out of Virgil, Horace, and Ovid— great poets all—was a way to great poetic utterance; but it was not a carefree, untutored way. It did not lend itself to "easy numbers" and "native woodnotes wild".

The primary quality of Renaissance poetry is certainly copiousness, or the results of amplification. Invention came to mean, not merely skill in the constructing of arguments, but verbal dexterity and "copious varying". Note, for example, the punning changes played on words, the multiplication of epithets, the figures of iteration, and the wide use of analysis; as also the insistent demand for analogy or illustration—all of these with omnipresent forms of comparison, such as simile, metaphor, metonymy, and personification, which are basal to all animated discourse. Obviously it was no easy thing to write acceptable Renaissance poetry. Shakespeare did write just such poetry, and it is not unreasonable to believe that it cost him effort and pains, indeed, that such poetry could not have been written without effort and pains. As Miss Doran says, in the hands of genius, copiousness, although dreary enough in Peacham and even Erasmus, becomes the fresh and varied opulence of Rabelais and Shakespeare. The copiousness of Renaissance rhetoric expressed itself in endless variety in Elizabethan drama—double plots, many episodes, multitudinous characters. Again, as Miss Doran says, exuberance, rather than economy, remains characteristic of Chapman, Marston, Webster, Shakespeare, and of Jonson himself. It brought with it variety, power, and subtlety of language, as well as largeness of imaginative vision and great expressive power.

From the rigorous requirements of Renaissance poetic art, obedience to which can be observed in thousands of places in Shakespeare's plays and poems, comes the homely suggestion that some of Shakespeare's bad poetry was never given the line by line finish that characterizes great poetic masterpieces like *A Midsummer Night's Dream*, *Richard III*, *Romeo and Juliet*, and *Antony and Cleopatra*. Unfortunately, it is difficult to support this natural-seeming hypothesis with the clearest arguments because passages and parts which might serve as illustrations have often been swept away as un-Shakespearian, are therefore in dispute, and to some degree disallowed as evidence. There are three plays, all of which have the trail of the asp of collaboration over them, which, nevertheless, I should like, as a matter of self-indulgence and with little hope of carrying conviction, to consider with you from the point of view of greater and less poetic elaboration in their parts; namely, *Timon of Athens*, *The Taming of the Shrew*, and *King Henry VIII*.

If one could be sure that *Timon of Athens* was never carried to completion by Shakespeare but left by him in an incomplete state, and this theory seems the most plausible one so far advanced, *Timon of Athens* would of itself furnish overwhelming evidence that much of Shakespeare's rejected poetry is unfinished poetry.[1] The play seemed to have been inserted into the First Folio irregularly in order to supply the place rendered vacant by the temporary withdrawal of *Troilus and Cressida*. This circumstance at least justifies a suspicion that *Timon of Athens* was not originally chosen for inclusion. More important is the fact that the play as printed in the First Folio has the very look and sound of a first draft. It shows overwhelming power in speeches and single lines scattered throughout the play and has along with them prosaic passages, odd bits of occasional rhyme, and many passages almost bare of poetic ornament. Examine, for example, I, ii, 137-50; III, iv, 1-79; IV, ii, 24-50; IV. iii, 147, 464-543; V, i, 1-119. Still more obviously, compare the two presentations of the Poet and the Painter. The first scenes are meticulously finished, if not *précieuse*; the second (v, i, 119) is partly in prose and partly in very rough verse.

The same situation of incompleteness may also appear in *The Taming of the Shrew*. Many of the parts of that play which have been assigned to a collaborator are not so much out of line with Shakespeare's language, thought, and methods as barer and more poorly developed poetically than are the parts assigned to Shakespeare. A correct theory of the origin of the play will give us ground for suspecting, if not haste in composition, at least a special situation in the composition of the minor plot, a situation which may have caused the minor plot to be written in a more restricted way than was the major plot. *The Taming of the Shrew*, as ten Brink contended long ago, is not based on *The Taming of a Shrew*, but is based on an original shrew play now lost. *The Taming of a Shrew* is not a bad quarto of *The Taming of the Shrew*, but is a bad quarto of the same lost original shrew play.[2] What Shakespeare, supposing him to be the author of the whole play as it appears in the Folio, may have done was to rewrite with much gusto the story of the wife-tamer, and to reject the rather formal, if not banal, love story of the two sisters of the heroine as given in the old shrew play. There is little to suggest that this rejected story had any connection with Ariosto's *I Suppositi*. Shakespeare, dissatisfied with the formal minor plot of his original, substituted for it Ariosto's brilliant intrigue and thus gave to the minor plot an element of dramatic suspense. Such a substitution would have been a special exercise, a sort of translation or adaptation, and might have been done more hastily and certainly less freely than was the more attractive major plot. In any case the minor plot has nothing in it unworthy of Shakespeare, but seems to be merely less highly finished as dramatic poetry. For example, consider the dialogue between Baptista and the Pedant in the fourth scene of the fourth act (ll. 19–71). It is in plain verse and has no sparkle, but it is clear and adequate in the presentation of necessary matter out of Ariosto. In some places the rejected portions do show spirit, but for the most part they are below the level, not of Shakespeare's good sense and dramatic skill, but of his highly wrought poetic style.[3] Consider also the puzzling case of the first seventy lines of v, ii, which are tied in with Petruchio's wager and necessary for its comprehension. They were rejected by Pope and are certainly very poorly written, and yet to reject them would throw out Petruchio's triumph and Katharina's carefully written speech (ll. 136–78), which offers a sort of justification for the whole comedy.

As to *Henry VIII*, the consideration that has perplexed me is, not that the play shows two styles, but that it shows many styles. We know from *The Winter's Tale* and *The Tempest* the sort of blank verse Shakespeare, when he was taking pains, was writing toward the end of his career. We call it Shakespeare's late style. It is a style which would demand exaltation of mood and great poetic effort both in language and thought. Nowhere is there greater mastery of poetic utterance than in the later style of Shakespeare. The degree to which condensed and elliptical syntax and flashing figures of speech in which metaphor is both ornament and substance appear in *Henry VIII* varies all the way and by regular gradation from the simple little picture scene (II, iii) between Anne Bullen and an Old Lady to the towering height of Wolsey's farewell to greatness (III, ii, 350–72). It is noteworthy that the higher style appears whenever the tension of dramatic suspense is greatest—in the speeches of Buckingham at his trial, in Queen Katharine's noble defence of herself, in Wolsey's agonies, and perhaps in Cranmer's prophecy. To account for this one may argue that Shakespeare wrote most of the bad parts of the play and a collaborator wrote most of the good parts, but it seems quite as reasonable to argue that in writing *Henry VIII* Shakespeare showed varying degrees of inspiration and industry, quite apart from the fact that some of the passages said to be in an early style may be defended as deliberate variations to suit characters and conditions. If *Henry VIII* broke into two clearly marked parts, as Spedding thought that it did, the one old-fashioned, the other very 'late', one would be willing to proceed to judgement; but, since the play shows every degree of freedom between the extremes, one hesitates to fix on a certain point and say: "I cannot permit Shakespeare at this late date to write more than such and such a percentage of double-endings, of extra syllables at caesural pauses, and of run-on lines", and to remonstrate with him on the ground that he had long passed that period in his career when he might use so many end-stopped lines and masculine endings; indeed, that he is behaving in an un-Shakespearian way.

We may well pass over without mention that extensive body of minor flaws in Shakespeare's verse which are probably due to cuts, patches, alterations, and other modifications which various plays underwent when these plays were staged in the Elizabethan theatre. They are well summarized by Sir Edmund Chambers in the seventh chapter, "The Problem of Authenticity", in the first volume of his *William Shakespeare*.

There is, however, another aspect of Shakespeare's less pleasing poetry which is well worthy of our consideration. I refer to Shakespeare's use of various conventional styles, particularly in his masque-like episodes and so-called masques. Such passages rarely give pleasure, and some of them have fallen under suspicion as to their authenticity. Did Shakespeare have a special style, or several different styles in which he composed pageants, apologues, little masques, and various extra- or epi-dramatic matters? Such episodes call for a heightening of the conventional level, and Shakespeare's genius reveals itself in his recognition of that artistic necessity. But such heightening of style does not always meet with the approval of critics and readers. It is doubtful if the play-within-the-play and the Hecuba passage in *Hamlet*, in spite of their greatness, give pleasure except to well-trained and catholic readers of Shakespeare. There can be no doubt that Shakespeare did adapt his style to his occasion in elaborately conventional set speeches like the Queen's obituary speech about Ophelia in *Hamlet* or Cleopatra's panegyric on Antony addressed to Dolabella in *Antony and Cleopatra*. But masque-like passages fall under suspicion. Even Sir Edmund Chambers thinks[4] that the speeches of the ghosts in *Richard III* (v, iii, 118–76) are "extremely ineffective" and may be "a spectacular theatrical addition".

If we follow the author through, we find (p. 404) that the verses of Hymen in *As You Like It* (v, i, 114–56) are regarded as markedly inferior in style to the rest of the play and may be "a spectacular interpolation not due to Shakespeare". The trochaic rhymes in *Measure for Measure* (III, ii, 275–96) are, he thinks (p. 455), "not much like Shakespeare". In *Macbeth*, he objects, along with most of us, to the iambic lines (III, v; IV, i, 39–43, 125–32) devoted to Hecate and says (p. 472) that the passages are characterized "by prettiness of lyrical fancy alien to the main conception of the witches". He agrees with other critics (p. 486) in regarding the masque in *Cymbeline* (v, iv, 30–150) also as "a spectacular theatrical interpolation". He is lukewarm about the masque in *The Tempest* (p. 493) and questions the authenticity of the song of Juno and Ceres (IV, i, 106–17).

There is a family resemblance among these rejected passages, since all are in some sense conventional or masque-like in nature. One is tempted to apply to them a clue given by the distinguished scholar himself in speaking of the Hecuba speech in *Hamlet* (II, ii, 474–519) and the play-within-the-play. He there suggests (p. 425) that these passages are written "in styles deliberately differentiated from that of the ordinary dialogue". He also drops an interesting hint in his discussion of *Measure for Measure* (p. 455). He there says that the Duke is 'choric' like "the old folk in *All's Well*". Is it not possible that Shakespeare adopted a different style when he was writing for musical spectacles (as distinguished from songs) and that he sometimes tried for quaint and archaic effects?

It is easy to find parallels in the masques of other writers to the seemingly commonplace style that often appears in the musical interludes in Shakespeare's plays. It may even be contended that there was a gentle, undramatic style employed widely in masques. Personally it seems to me that the effect is usually due to the use of iambic measures. Iambic pentameter in rhymed couplets occurs in Campion's *Lords Masque* and in Chapman's *The Masque of the Middle Temple* and *Lincoln's Inn*. Jonson usually employs the heroic couplet, but uses iambic tetrameter in *Pan's*

Anniversary, The Masque of Augurs, and elsewhere. There are other styles in masques, and masques are not conspicuous for great poetry. Is it not possible that, in some of the offending passages at least, Shakespeare consciously adopted a style in common use for masques and musical entertainments in his age? This would seem at least as probable as that he deliberately turned his pen over to somebody else or suffered some unknown person about the theatre to make spectacular additions.

Let us follow Sir Edmund Chambers's suggestion that the Duke in *Measure for Measure* is 'choric' like "the old folk in *All's Well*" and come to the masque in *Cymbeline,* usually rejected. There can be no doubt that in the Gower prologues in *Pericles* Shakespeare sought for the sake of quaintness to reproduce the effect of Gower's tale of Apollonius of Tyre as told in *Confessio Amantis.* The Gower that Shakespeare knew was not the Gower of standard modern texts, but of Caxton and Bethelet; and, even when the texts are the same, Shakespeare did not know, and nobody knew for two hundred years, the rules of scansion and accentuation to be followed in the reading of Gower's verse. The loss of the final *e* in pronunciation tended to throw heavy syllables together and to increase the number of trochaic feet in the line. These are the chief metrical eccentricities in the Gower prologues. Some lines in Gower when read without attention to the pronunciation of the original seem to lack a syllable or a foot, and they too are imitated. In other cases the pronunciation of syllables which would have been elided in Middle English verse causes the line to have a sprawling quality; and, since numerous extra syllables at the ends of Gower's lines tend to disappear, the verses end in accented syllables and seem less fluent. Gower, moreover, had his own metrical irregularities, and these too no doubt make their contribution to Shakespeare's gentle travesty of the old poet. Gower was popular in the age of Shakespeare, and a great deal of his wisdom and his poetic excellence must have come through in spite of his apparently disordered metre. The Gower prologues then are an example of what Shakespeare did when he sought to be quaint and old-fashioned. Let us see if there is anything similar in the situation of the masque in *Cymbeline.*

Let it be remarked, in the first place, that the masque in *Cymbeline* is carefully tied in with the text and situation of the play and that by no means all critics would cast it out.[5] One notes that these ghosts are old and very pitiful. Sicilius Leonatus is described as an old man attired like a warrior, leading in his hand "an ancient mother", his wife. They are very humble in their spirit; they refer to themselves as "we poor ghosts". *Cymbeline* itself is a romance of the long ago, and there seems a fair probability that Shakespeare thought of the scene as something out of an ancient world, something deserving commiseration. How would Shakespeare express that? I am sure I do not know. I see that there is a difference in conventional level. He must make the ancient still more archaic, and I think that he would deliberately differentiate the style from that of the ordinary dialogue. Intricately and awkwardly rhymed strophe-forms were certainly commoner in drama in preceding ages than they were at the time that Shakespeare wrote the play of *Cymbeline.* The verse itself would have seemed old-fashioned. All in all, it seems possible to defend the authenticity of this masque and other stylistic abnormalities on the ground that gods and those who speak to gods, especially if they themselves are spirits, must speak differently from creatures of this world.

My paper, which has not advanced much further than mere illustration of my meaning, has suggested that some of Shakespeare's bad poetry may have been adjudged to be un-Shakespearian because it is less painstakingly composed according to the poetics of the Renaissance than is his greater verse; also perhaps because what may have seemed good to Shakespeare and his contemporaries no longer seems good to us. To this I have added the idea that, when for some reason Shakespeare consciously varied his style to accord with special situations, we have not always approved of the results. Both of these ideas, I diffidently suggest, are worthy of further elaboration.

NOTES

1. See E. K. Chambers, *William Shakespeare: A Study of Facts and Problems* (Oxford, 1930), II, 480–4; with references.

2. See Hardin Craig, "The Shrew and A Shrew", in *Elizabethan Studies and Other Essays: In Honour of George F. Reynolds* (University of Colorado Press, 1945, pp. 150–4); Raymond A. Houk, "Evolution of *The Taming of the Shrew*", *Publications of the Modern Language Association of America*, LVII (1942), 1009–38; and "Strata in *The Taming of the Shrew*", *Studies in Philology*, XXXIX (1942), 291–302; Peter Alexander, *Shakespeare's Henry VI and Richard III* (Cambridge, 1929), pp. 6, 8 *et passim*; Chambers, *op. cit.* I, 322–8; with references.

3. See Florence Huber Ashton, "The Revision of the Folio Text of *The Taming of the Shrew*", *Philological Quarterly*, VI (1927), 151–60; with references.

4. Chambers, *loc. cit.* p. 303.

5. Sir Edmund Chambers, who would reject the masque, points out (*loc. cit.* p. 486) that, if the masque goes, so also must go the long passage referring to the vision (V, v, 425–59), a thing that would throw out matter which would never otherwise have fallen under suspicion.

THE FOLGER SHAKESPEARE LIBRARY

BY

JAMES G. McMANAWAY

"Whatever you do, Buy", urged Heminges and Condell in 1623 in their appeal "To the great Variety of Readers" of *Mr. William Shakespeare's Comedies, Histories, and Tragedies,* never dreaming that in the distant land of the American 'salvages' a lover of their friend Shakespeare's plays would one day own seventy-nine copies of the First Folio. Not elsewhere since Jaggard, Blount, Smethwicke and Aspley, at whose charges the book was printed, first offered it for sale three centuries ago, have four walls contained so many copies.

The man who gave such heed to Heminges and Condell and bought editions of Shakespeare more assiduously and successfully than any other was Henry Clay Folger. He was a lineal descendant of Peter Folger, who about 1635 emigrated from Norwich and settled ultimately on Nantucket Island in New England. Folger's parents lived in Brooklyn, where he was born on 18 June 1857. As a student in Adelphi Academy in Brooklyn, he manifested an interest in Shakespeare that increased during his undergraduate years at Amherst College under the stimulus of Emerson's Essays and his "Remarks at the Celebration of the Three Hundredth Anniversary of the Birth of Shakespeare". There was no thought at that time of a Shakespeare Library, but a Philadelphia edition of the *Works* which a brother gave him at Christmas in 1875 may be regarded as the first item in his collection.

After graduation in 1879, Folger was aided in securing a clerkship in the firm of Charles Pratt and Company in New York City by the same friends who had assisted him in surmounting the financial difficulties that had beset him in his last years in college. At once he began to devote his leisure hours to the study of law at Columbia, from which he received his LL.B. *cum laude* two years later. Though possessed of considerable ability as a writer and speaker, Folger was almost painfully shy, and his friends expected little of him.

His marriage with Emily Clara Jordan in 1885 brought to his side a well-educated young woman whose interest in Shakespeare was as intense as his own, and whose lifelong joy it was to assist and encourage him in his collecting. The young couple lived modestly in Brooklyn in those early days, devoting their leisure hours and most of their resources to Shakespeare. And even after Folger's industry and business acumen had brought him wealth in the old Standard Oil Company and elevated him in 1911 to the presidency of the Standard Oil Company of New York and the Chairmanship of its Board in 1923, their way of life continued to be simple and unassuming. Only in his later years did he permit himself the luxury of a summer house at Glen Cove, Long Island.

The purchase of a copy of Halliwell-Phillipps's reduced facsimile of the First Folio about 1879 brought to Folger an awareness of some of the textual problems in Shakespeare and inspired in him a passion for their solution that was to dominate his life. His initial venture into the book market is thus described:

In 1889 a copy of the Fourth Folio (1685) was advertised for sale at Bangs' auction-room in New York City, and Mr Folger, though still relatively a poor man, was tempted to make a try for it. "With fear and trepidation", as he expressed it—fear at his proposed extravagance, trepidation at a strange experience—he entered the auction-room, and, following up each competing bid with a small increment, finally saw the coveted volume knocked down to him for $107.50. Not finding it convenient to pay at once, he asked and received credit for thirty days. When, at the end of the month, he had settled in full for the volume, he proudly possessed his first Shakespearian rarity; and he had irrevocably launched himself upon the entrancing sea of collecting.[1]

Fifteen years later, with the skill that comes with experience and with greatly increased financial powers, he was able to carry off in the face of all competition the unique First Quarto of *Titus Andronicus* (1594) that turned up in Malmö, Sweden. This precious little book, no copy of which had been heard of since 1691, disappeared from view, as so many other Shakespeare items were then doing, the name of its purchaser unknown even to the newspaper reporters who made much of the selling price of £2,000.

It was Folger's practice to buy quietly, circumspectly, whether by private negotiation as books were brought to his attention, or through agents in the auction rooms; and though many rare items, especially Shakespeare Folios and Quartos, passed out of circulation, not even the great book-dealers could have guessed the extent and quality of his holdings in 1919 when he first came to public attention by paying $100,000 for the Edward Gwynn volume of the falsely dated Pavier-Jaggard Shakespeare Quartos of 1619.

The years between this purchase and his death were filled with activity. In the London and New York markets, Henry E. Huntington, W. A. White, and Sir Leicester Harmsworth were the most notable, but not by any means the only, competitors for Early English books. So when in 1928 Folger announced his plan of presenting his library to the American people and locating it in Washington, close to the Library of Congress, the public were amazed to read that he was the reputed owner of thirty, or possibly thirty-five, copies of the First Folio and of from 20,000 to 25,000 other books and manuscripts.

It is hardly accurate to write of Folger's library. Through forty-five years of active collecting, it was the custom of Folger and his wife to read booksellers' catalogues assiduously, order the items of their choice by letter or cable, devote their evenings to examining and listing each day's purchases, bundle up with the books the relevant catalogues and correspondence, and store them in bank vaults and warehouses. There they accumulated in some three thousand wood packing-cases until the library building was ready in 1931–2 to receive them. Single-minded in his determination to buy, he seems to have been unwilling to divert funds to the construction of a private library in his home. Though his lifelong ambition was to assemble the books which would enable students, himself among them, to determine the text of Shakespeare and produce a definitive account of his life, he deferred the joy of using his books until too late even to see the library building he had commissioned. His unparalleled collections were for nearly half a century equally inaccessible to the scholars who would gladly have consulted them and to their owner.

Paul Philippe Cret, the architect, and Alexander B. Trowbridge, the consulting architect, united in advising that the library building must harmonize architecturally with the nearby Capitol and Supreme Court buildings, both classic in style, and Folger was equally insistent that a stained glass window depicting the Seven Ages of Man in *As You Like It* and reproducing the stone-work of the apsidal window in Holy Trinity Church, Stratford, should dominate the

Reading Room. The conflict was resolved by designing a white marble exterior of modern-classic style and an interior of Tudor Gothic.

The Reading Room, a typical English Great Hall, with a high trussed roof, is lighted on the south by three bay windows and on the west, in deference to Folger's wishes, by the great Seven Ages window. The masterpiece of the D'Ascenzo Studios, this is one of the finest examples of modern stained glass in America. Opening off the Reading Room are four air-conditioned vaults for the rare books and manuscripts, and below it are two levels of book stacks. At the east end of the room a hall screen has for its central feature a reproduction of the Stratford bust of Shakespeare, and flanking it are portraits of Henry Clay Folger and Clara Jordan Folger by Frank Salisbury. For visitors there is an Exhibition Gallery, where paintings, sculpture, books, and manuscripts are displayed.

The auditorium suggests an Elizabethan public playhouse. It is in no sense a reproduction, though in size, shape and decoration it is strongly influenced by the specifications of the Fortune Playhouse of 1600, with three galleries, a platform stage provided with inner- and upper-stages and a 'shadow', and walls made of "frame, lime, lath, and hair". As a concession to modern comfort, the sloping flagstone 'yard' is covered with a roof, and both 'yard' and galleries have seats. The stage lighting is elaborate. Though not used for the performance of plays, the theatre is an instructive exhibit, giving thousands of visitors each year some idea of the physical conditions of an Elizabethan stage production.

Two weeks after the laying of the corner-stone, Folger died on 11 June 1930. Not quite two years later, on 23 April 1932, the building he had planned and the treasures he had collected were presented to the American people "for the promotion and diffusion of knowledge in regard to the history and writings of Shakespeare". By the provisions of the will, the land and buildings, valued at more than $2,500,000, the collections, and a generous endowment were to be administered by the Trustees of his Alma Mater, Amherst College. At the death of Mrs Folger in 1936, the endowment was substantially increased.

The extent and richness of the collections surpassed all expectations and are even now not generally realized. Instead of the estimated thirty-five First Folios, there were seventy-nine—no other library has more than five!—and enough fragments and single plays to make up two or three more. Probably the finest copy is that formerly owned by George Daniel and later by the Baroness Burdett-Coutts. One or, perhaps, two copies are in their original bindings. And many others have special interest for scholars or collectors because of their provenance or some bibliographical peculiarities. The Roden Folio, for example, contains one of the four known title-pages with the Droeshout portrait of Shakespeare in the proof state (a second copy of this title-page, discovered by Halliwell-Phillipps, is likewise at the Folger; the third and fourth examples of the proof state are at the British Museum and at the Bodleian). M. H. Spielmann, the authority on Shakespeare iconography, considers the proof state of the portrait the most nearly faithful likeness of the dramatist. The Roden Folio is likewise remarkable for containing the uncancelled first leaf [2] of *Troilus and Cressida*. In addition to the isolated leaf [3] of *Anthony and Cleopatra* containing the original proof-reader's marks and corrections, supposed by Halliwell-Phillipps to be unique, there is in the Jonas copy a page of proof which resolves the famous "And hell gnaw his bones" crux in the text of *Othello*.[4] But unquestionably the most famous copy and certainly the most prized by Folger, is that which William Jaggard presented to his friend Augustine

Vincent. It is the largest copy known and is partly in the original binding, stamped with Vincent's arms, and on the title-page is Vincent's dated autograph inscription.

Less rare and costly, and lacking the textual authority of the First Folio, the Second (1632), Third (1663/4) and Fourth (1685) Folios testify to the continuing popularity of Shakespeare in the seventeenth century; they also exerted considerable influence on the early editors. In one or more of the fifty-eight Folger copies of the Second Folio, the twenty-four examples of the Third, and the thirty-six copies of the Fourth, are practically all the 'points' and variants which collectors have noted. Many of them have passed through the libraries of personages of note and famous bibliophiles, including the Princess Elizabeth (daughter of James I), David Garrick, George Colman, and the Shakespearian editors Lewis Theobald and Samuel Johnson.

Much rarer even than the Folios are the sixteenth- and seventeenth-century Quartos of Shakespeare's plays. Published in inexpensive form and sold unbound, these perishable little books had a high mortality rate, and the more popular the play, the less likely the Quarto was to survive. No library has ever possessed a copy of every First Quarto. Folger, for example, could never get the First Quarto of *King Richard II*. With the purchase in recent years of a first edition of *King Lear* (the Pide Bull edition) and of several Restoration editions, the Folger collection now totals 205 Quartos, many more than are to be found in any other one place.[5]

As with plays, so with the first editions of Shakespeare's poems; no library can ever hope for completeness. These precious little volumes of amatory verse are yet scarcer than the plays, being so popular that even later editions are frequently known only by a fragment or a single leaf. Excluding the ten Folger copies of the *Poems* (1640), some of them remarkably fine, there are in the library twenty-two examples of various early editions of *Venus and Adonis*, *Lucrece*, the *Sonnets*, and *The Passionate Pilgrim*, six more than in the next largest collection.[6] These include the unique fragment of the first edition of *The Passionate Pilgrim*,[7] three copies of the first edition of *The Rape of Lucrece*, and two copies of the *Sonnets*.

The extent and richness of Folger's holdings will be most readily apprehended if at this point the kinds of materials in which he was interested are mentioned and his holdings in each are indicated in order. These are the Text of Shakespeare, his Biography, his Sources, his Influence and Reputation, and his Background, both English and Continental.

THE TEXT

The text of Shakespeare was Folger's primary concern, and to supplement the early editions already mentioned he collected the later reprints and translations on an unprecedented scale. The great eighteenth- and nineteenth-century editions are present in many copies—some with valuable marginalia by succeeding editors and critics and others even in the form of corrected proof sheets as well as in bound volumes—and minor editions by the thousands. The collection of theatrical editions, representing the acting versions, is unequalled. Not the least valuable of these are the hundreds of prompt-books (both Shakespearian and non-Shakespearian), frequently illustrated or accompanied by sketches or water-colour drawings of stage settings, scenery, and costumes. Those prepared by David Garrick are among the most important, for they record in the actor-manager's hand how he gradually eliminated the alien lines and scenes introduced by the 'improvers' of Shakespeare during the Restoration period and immediately thereafter, and restored the true texts of Shakespeare. Public taste and the individual predilections of actors and managers are further illustrated in the prompt-books of Kean, Kemble, Sarah Siddons, Booth, Irving, and Ellen Terry, to name only a few.

BIOGRAPHY AND ICONOGRAPHY

It is almost incredible that over 250 years after Shakespeare's death it should have been possible for a bibliophile, however zealous, to collect primary documents relating to his biography, but Folger had that good fortune. In describing this class of material, J. Q. Adams has written as follows:

Of early manuscripts relating to Shakespeare Mr. Folger gathered a collection that in extent and value admits no superior. Indeed Mr. Seymour de Ricci, after cataloguing the items before the year 1625, declares that, in the field of manuscript Shakespeariana, "the Folger Library stands out supreme...." As de Ricci observes, the Library "contains all the extant manuscripts of any portions of his works",[8] including the only play in a manuscript contemporary with the poet, a version of *Henry IV* prepared about the year 1611, for use, it seems, at Court or at some private house.[9] Of Shakespeare's signatures, all of unquestionable authenticity are attached to legal documents preserved in official archives where suspicion of forgery cannot be entertained; the Library, however, has a number of attributed signatures, one or two of which may be genuine.[10]

Those lines were printed in 1933. Just ten years later, it was Adams's good fortune to be able to publish an illustrated account[11] of his amazing purchase for £1 on 28 November 1938 at Sotheby's, as an undescribed item in a lot of four books, of a copy of William Lambard's *Archaionomia* (1568) which bears in the upper right-hand corner of the title-page the name, "W[m] Shaksp[ere]". "Obviously", he wrote, "there are three possible explanations of this signature: first, it may be a forgery made with intent to deceive; secondly, it may be a genuine signature of some unknown person with the name 'William Shakespeare'; and, thirdly, it may be the autograph signature of William Shakespeare the dramatist." Efforts to discover evidence that the signature was not contemporary with the poet have been unavailing. "Thus," Adams concluded, "although certainty cannot be claimed, so far as modern science can tell, there seems to be no reason to question its being the autograph of the poet."

Among the biographical documents are four successive titles to Shakespeare's house, the purchase deed of his Blackfriars property, and the two indentures of a fine levied on New Place, all from the Shakespeare muniment chest. Another group of manuscripts supplements and corroborates previously known records of the grant of arms to Shakespeare; these include a contemporary transcript of "Arms granted by William Dethick", annotated in the autograph of Ralph Brooke; William Smith's "A brieff discourse of the causes of discord among the officers of arms, and of the great abuses and absurdities comitted by painters to the great prejudice and hindrance of the same office" (holograph); and also his holograph "Abuses committed by painters ánd others to the praejudice of the officers of arms"; and several other treatises or note-books of contemporary or later date. The often-quoted account of the merry meeting with Ben Jonson and Michael Drayton that preceded Shakespeare's death is in another Folger manuscript, the voluminous diary of the Reverend John Ward, Vicar of Stratford.

The iconography of Shakespeare has already been alluded to in the account of the two copies of the proof state of the Droeshout engraving of 1623. The next two printed likenesses of the poet, Marshall's engraving for the *Poems* (1640) and Faithorne's print of 1655 are represented by several fine copies. Though there is no oil painting of Shakespeare that can be proved to have been painted in his lifetime and to have an unbroken line of ownership to modern times, several of the fine group of portraits in the Folger are entitled to serious consideration. The Felton portrait, for example, has frequently been attributed to the great Shakespearian actor Richard Burbage. The Sir Godfrey Kneller portrait has the merit of being painted by a renowned artist at the time when descendants of Shakespeare's fellow-actors should have been able to authenticate the portrait that was copied; it has also the honour to have been commissioned as a gift to John Dryden. Others of varying interest are the Janssens, the Ashbourne, the Lumley, the Zuccaro, the Cosway, the Dexter, the Zoust, the Gunther, and the Page. The busts and statues by Roubiliac, Ward, MacMonnies and others are even better known than some of the paintings.

Shortly before his death in 1946, J. Q. Adams secured for the Library the drawing which Edward Malone commissioned Ozias Humphrey to make of the Chandos portrait of Shakespeare, which was about to be cleaned and restored. The great Shakespearian scholar perceived the need to preserve for posterity a replica of this important canvas in its antique state. It will be the duty of experts to note and evaluate the differences between Humphrey's competent pencil drawing and the Chandos portrait in its present state, after a second process of restoration.

SOURCES

As a basis for the study of Shakespeare's creative genius, Folger assembled an almost complete collection of the familiar English source-books and many of the rarities. Worthy of special mention are the unique copy of Greene's *Pandosto* (1592), a copy of Lodge's *Rosalynde* (1590; one other copy known), and the only extant copy of the first edition of Marlowe's *Hero and Leander* (1598), from which Shakespeare quoted directly in *As You Like It*. The sources of *Titus Andronicus* are represented by several early broadsides of the 'Ballad' and the unique eighteenth-century chap-book of the 'Prose History'. Sometimes the acquisition of a Shakespeare source-book strengthens an already fine collection of the works of another poet. Thus Folger's excellent Daniel collection, though it contained the first edition of *Delia and Rosamund* (1592), lacked the second and third editions, one of which Shakespeare used. The recent purchase of *Delia and Rosamund, Augmented. Cleopatra* (1594; three other copies recorded) and of the 1595 reprint (one other copy recorded) fills these two gaps with books of excessive rarity.

Interest in source material extended to the books mentioned in the plays. One of Folger's great purchases, the mammoth scrap-books of Halliwell-Phillipps, contains fragments of the earliest English edition of *A C. Mery Tales*, named in *Much Ado about Nothing*, and the Library has added another item, Cartigny's *The Wandering Knight* (1581), referred to by Falstaff in *1 Henry IV*.

As might be expected, the Library has many editions of the Continental authors whose works were plundered by the Elizabethan dramatists and story-tellers. One of the rarest of the Shakespeare source-books, a fine copy of the 1535 edition of Luigi da Porto's prose version of *Romeo and Juliet*, has recently been acquired through the generosity of Lessing J. Rosenwald.

The collection of Continental books, though small, goes far beyond Ariosto, Bandello, Belleforest, Boccaccio, and Giraldi, and three groups of books deserve special attention. In Professor Bradner's "Check-list of Original Neo-Latin Dramas by Continental Writers Printed before 1650",[12] 110 items were located in the British Museum, 92 in the Staatsbibliothek, Berlin, and 56 in the Bibliothèque Nationale, while in America, the Folger led the field with 94 items. Plays not recorded by Bradner or acquired by the Folger Library since the publication of his list increase the number to about 150, apparently the largest collection in the world. Comparable statistics are lacking for Italian drama published by 1600, but scholars will find many rare and useful plays among the 430 Folger items.

The familiarity of Shakespeare and Spenser with emblem-books is indicative of the vogue of a type of literature of which there is no modern counterpart. Whitney, Quarles and Wither helped to popularize emblems in England, but the English market was supplied very largely by the Continental presses with sometimes beautifully illustrated editions of Alciati, Corrozet and Vaenius, to name only a few. Folger's collection of emblem-books up to the time of Shakespeare's death contains many items not readily found elsewhere.

INFLUENCE AND REPUTATION

The earliest allusion to Shakespeare supplies almost as much information for his biography as it does for a study of his reputation and influence, and it is a question where the Folger copy of Greene's *Groatsworth of Witte* (1592; one other copy known) should be mentioned, with its famous reference to the "upstart crow". The search for allusion-books was the most systematic part of Folger's collecting. He prepared a check-list of all known allusions through the year 1700 and attempted to acquire every title that came on the market. Furthermore, with the aid of assiduous dealers he possessed himself of many books that were unknown to the compilers of allusions. The search for early references to Shakespeare continues, but it is rarely possible to add to the 5,000 or more titles already in the Library.

Allusions in the eighteenth century are as yet uncollected. When the task of compilation is begun, hundreds of obscure pamphlets in verse and prose that would otherwise have perished will be found on the Folger shelves, preserved solely because a word or phrase has been quoted from Shakespeare.

Manuscript poetical commonplace-books are a mine of information about current tastes in poetry in the hundred years after Shakespeare's arrival in London. Many of those in the Folger were acquired for their interesting versions of bits of Shakespearian verse.[13]

SHAKESPEARE'S BACKGROUND, ENGLISH AND CONTINENTAL: ENGLISH DRAMA TO 1640

After fifteen years visitors frequently express surprise that the Library contains non-Shakespearian material. It was only natural that Folger should collect the plays of Shakespeare's predecessors and contemporaries. This he did with remarkable success, but even a careful reading of the first volume of W. W. Greg's *Bibliography* (the proofs of which were checked against the Folger copies) will fail to give an adequate idea of the richness of the collection, so many noteworthy items have been added in recent years. These include, among others, the unique *Commody of the Most Vertuous and Godlye Susanna* (1578) by Garter, which was known only by title until this copy was discovered, bound in a volume with twelve other rare plays, in the Beaumont Library in 1936. Another unique item in the volume is a complete copy of the third edition of *Jacke Jugeler* (c. 1565–70), known previously only in a fragment, and a third is a copy of the second edition of *Like Will to Like* (c. 1568).[14]

Among the additions to the Folger holdings of plays by the principal Elizabethan and Jacobean dramatists are Lyly's *Campaspe* (1584; two other copies known); Peele's *Edward I* (1593) and *The Love of King David and Fair Bethsabe* (1599, the only copy with the blank leaves); Greene's *Orlando Furioso* (1599); Marlowe's *Tamburlaine*, Part I (1605), his *Tamburlaine*, Part II (1606), *Dr Faustus* (1631), and *Edward II* (1611 and 1622, both issues); Kyd's *Spanish Tragedy* (1615); Lodge's *Looking Glasse for London* (1617); Heywood's *If You Know not Me*, Part I (1605, uncut), *If You Know not Me*, Part II (1606, the first issue, which joins the unique Folger copy of the second issue), his *Fayre Mayde of the Exchange* (1607, 1st ed. and 1625, 2nd ed.), his *Marriage Triumphe* (1613; two other copies known), and his *Foure Prentises* (1615, probably the finest of the four extant copies); Jonson's *Case is Alterd* (1609), *Catiline* (1611), *Love's Triumph through Callipolis* (1630) and *Chloridia* (c. 1630); Middleton's *The World Test at Tennis* (1620; six other copies), *Triumph of Honor* (1622, the only complete copy) and *Game at Chesse* (three different editions, all issued in 1625); Chapman's *The Gentleman Usher* (1606) and *Mask of the Middle Temple* (1613); and *Eastward Hoe* (1605, 1st ed., 2nd issue) by Chapman, Jonson and Marston.

Other plays of note that have been added are Seneca's *Troas* (c. 1560) and *Thyestes* (1560); *Damon and Pithias* (1571); *Freewyl* (c. 1572; only one other perfect copy known); and Gerard's *Entertainment in Norfolk and Suffolk* (c. 1578). The Folger copy of *The Tryall of Chevalry* (1605) is uncut and unopened. A unique copy of *The Insatiate Countess* (1613) has a cancel title, issued to change the attribution of authorship from John Marston to Lewis Machin and William Bacster. A copy of Alabaster's *Roxana* (1532) in the original vellum binding is important for its long presentation inscription by the author to John Selden. The collection of the printed works of Massinger, complete except for the first edition of *The Virgin Martyr*, was strengthened by the purchase of the eight Gosse quartos, all first editions, in which the author made hundreds of manuscript alterations. These copies are indispensable to the editor of Massinger. Among the additions to the plays by Beaumont and Fletcher the choicest is a first edition of *A King and No King* (1619), probably the finest copy in existence. No fewer than sixteen items by Shirley have been secured, so that now only one edition of one play is wanting.

Somewhat apart from the plays printed in England up to 1640 and yet intimately related to them are three volumes printed on the Continent in this period, each so rare that Folger was unable to secure a copy. The first of these is Ayrer's *Opus Theatricum* (1618). The second and third, entitled *Englische Comedien und Tragedien* (1620, 1630), contain versions of popular plays that were carried by travelling groups of Elizabethan actors to Germany and then crudely put into German for use by itinerant German actors. One of the plays is a curious alteration of *Titus Andronicus*, of absorbing interest for the study of Shakespeare. Several drolls and some of the early tunes sung on the English stage are known only in the texts supplied by these collections.

The manuscript plays of this period, though less numerous than the printed plays in the Folger, are not without interest and importance. Chief among them are the *Castle of Perseverance*, *Mankind*, and *Mind, Will and Understanding*, which J. Q. Adams acquired for the Library in 1936.

Next in importance is probably the Lambard volume of plays, bought by Folger; this contains, among others, Middleton's *Hengist King of Kent*, two plays by Beaumont and Fletcher, and Berkeley's *Lost Lady*. The Dering manuscript of Shakespeare's *Henry IV* has already been mentioned. A fragment of Marlowe's *Massacre at Paris* and one of *Gesta Grayorum* (1594) are two of the treasures collected by Folger, and the *Progress to Parnassus* and the so-called author's 'plot' of a lost or unwritten play about "Philander King of Thrace" are only a little less interesting. It has been the good fortune of the Library to add to Folger's collections such manuscript plays as Negri de Bassano's *Freewyl*; an adaptation from Sixt Birck of *Sapienta Salomonis* for the Westminster Boys about 1565; Greville's *Mustapha* (1596); Burton's *Philosophaster* (1606–18); an anonymous translation of Alabaster's *Roxana*; Lyly's *Harefield Entertainment* (1602); two manuscripts of Middleton's *Game at Chesse* (1624), one a preliminary version and the other, intended for presentation, with title-page in the author's hand; a copy of Montague's *Shepherd's Paradise* (1633) prepared for theatrical use, and another, with the unprinted prologue and songs, intended for presentation by the author; a version of Cartwright's *Royal Slave* (c. 1636) that differs markedly from the Quarto; and numerous academic exercises otherwise unrecorded.

For the historian of the early Tudor stage, 171 manuscripts from the muniment room of Loseley Park in Surrey await examination. They are the records of the Revels Office preserved by the Master of the Revels, Sir Thomas Cawardine, only a small part of which were printed in Feuillerat's *Documents Relating to the Revels*. These are now freely available to scholars for the first time, and many of them will be of even greater interest to the economic historian than to the student of drama for their detailed accounts of wages and the prices of materials in the reigns of Henry VIII, Edward VI, Mary, and the early years of Elizabeth.

Another group of 156 manuscripts from the same source gives the history of the Blackfriars Theatre property from the time of the disestablishment of the monasteries until the time of the Second Blackfriars, when Shakespeare and his fellows were acting there. One of these documents bears the signatures of Cuthbert and Richard Burbage.

ENGLISH DRAMA, 1641–1700

English drama from 1641 to 1700 was considered important by Folger because much of it was written in the traditions of Tudor and early Stuart drama and because the reprints, adaptations, and imitations of Shakespeare's plays give direct testimony to their influence and popularity. More than 1,400 editions or issues of plays and entertainments by various authors were published in this period, of which Folger collected a large number, devoting particular attention to the works of Dryden. In 1939 came the opportunity to secure the famous collection of Dryden and Drydeniana formed by Percy J. Dobell. After the duplicates of over 200 Dryden items already at the Folger had been put aside, more than 600 books remained to enrich the Folger collection, and Dobell's continuing interest has made it possible to secure a hundred or more other books.

The Dobell copies of Dryden's plays added so much strength to the collection of Commonwealth and Restoration drama that an intensive effort was made to fill the remaining gaps. By 1946 over 1,100 plays, exclusive of duplicates, had been brought together, the largest collection in America, particularly rich in prompt-books and in copies that exhibit bibliographical peculiarities.

The dramatic manuscripts of this period, though not numerous, include such important items as Killigrew's *Cecilia and Clorinda*, Parts I and II (*c.* 1650), prepared for stage use; two copies each of Boyle's *Mustapha* and *Henry the Fifth* (one copy of the latter is partly autograph); Katherine Philips's *Horace* and *Pompey the Great*; Dryden's *State of Innocence*; Wilson's *Belphegor* (1690); Wright's translation from Molière, entitled *La Mallad*; and Tate's *Constant Gallant*, possibly a version based on Echard's *Terence* (1694).

ENGLISH BOOKS, 1475–1640 (NON-DRAMATIC)

Important as was Folger's collection of some 9,000 English Renaissance books when the Library was opened in 1932, to-day the Library's holdings are vastly more important, for in the intervening fifteen years over 13,000 volumes have been added. It is likely that only the British Museum collection of pre-1641 English books exceeds in size that now housed in the Folger.

By the time of his death Folger had almost reached his limit in collecting early Shakespeariana and was intensifying his efforts to add to his drama collection. Some years earlier he had made the momentous decision to supplement these two collections with books and manuscripts representing all forms of literature and to make available to scholars all the recorded thought of the English Renaissance. At the outset he seems to have imposed certain limitations upon himself. To avoid competition with bibliophiles who specialized in those fields and frequently bid up prices to artificially high levels, he bought few books illustrative of the history of early English printing, few liturgies, only such editions of the Bible as would be of direct use to a student of Shakespeare or such copies as had association value, a limited number of almanacs, only a scattering of the proclamations of Elizabeth's predecessors and successors which did not relate to literature and the stage, and no items of Americana for their own sake. Even so, the Library opened with one of the five great collections of the volumes recorded in *A Short-title Catalogue of English Books, 1475–1640*.

One of the first tasks of J. Q. Adams, who resigned his professorship in English at Cornell University in 1931 to become Supervisor of Research at the Folger Library, and shortly became Director, a post he held until his death in November 1946, was to discover inductively the lines Folger had projected for his Library and to begin building along those lines.

From the beginning he enjoyed remarkable success. Few private collectors or public institutions were active in the book markets, as Huntington and Folger had been a few years earlier, and, though no great libraries like that from Britwell Court came up in the auction rooms, there was a steady flow of good books and manuscripts of this period, and by enterprise and skill Adams secured at least a fair share of them for the Folger.

In purchasing "*S.T.C.* books" [he wrote in 1942], the Director has sought to emphasize: (1) items that are, so far as can be discovered, unique (one thousand four hundred and seventy-four items—i.e. titles, editions, or issues—which, according to the *S.T.C.* are unique, have been acquired); (2) items that are not known to exist in America (in this category, so far as Bishop's recent but of course incomplete *Preliminary Checklist of American Copies of Short-title Catalogue Books* shows, the Folger now possesses upwards of four thousand items); (3) items that because of their superlative rarity or importance have a claim upon a library dedicated to Elizabethan research (one thousand two hundred and sixty-seven items recorded in the *S.T.C.* as existing in only one other copy have been acquired, and, of course, a far larger number of items recorded in only two or three other known copies); (4) items that complete—or nearly complete—Folger collections of specific authors or subjects; and (5) items that have for scholars some peculiar bibliographical interest.[15]

The most important single purchase in the history of the Library was the collection of early English books brought together in the Manor House, Bexhill-on-Sea, by the late Sir Leicester Harmsworth, consisting of some 9,000 volumes. These books were acquired in the spring of 1938; late in the summer of that year Dr Adams visited Bexhill and had the good fortune to come upon treasure trove in the form of 450 more books that Sir Leicester had received just prior to his death and had stored in a forgotten room. These, upon the gracious recommendation of Lady Harmsworth, were sold by the Trustees to the Folger Library for a modest sum. Fortunately, Sir Leicester had not an active interest in Shakespeare or the drama, though he had a copy of the Second Folio and also a number of excessively rare masques. Early English printing engaged his attention, and his eight Caxtons, including the first editions of Chaucer's *Canterbury Tales* and of Gower's *Confessio Amantis*, and seventy-one volumes printed by Caxton's successor Wynkyn de Worde, are a notable addition, for Folger had done little collecting in this field.

The history of the first English presses is further exemplified by Harmsworth books. Of the first fifteen or so earliest printers of Westminster and London, only two are not represented among the Harmsworth books. Among Wynkyn de Worde's books is *Scala Perfectionis* (1494), the first to bear his name. Other rarities are the first book printed by Pynson, *Dives and Pauper* (1493) and his edition of Brandt's *Shyp of Folys* (1509), the first English book to use Roman type.

Provincial presses are represented by Martyn Coffin's publication of Stanbridge's *Vulgaria* (1505), unique and the only book now traceable with an Exeter imprint, and books from Oxford (1482), York (1507), Hereford (1517), Tavistock (1525), Southwark (1522, 1530, 1535), St Albans (*not* printed by the Schoolmaster, alas, but by John Hertford, the second printer, 1534), Ipswich (1548) and Worcester.

Sir Leicester's primary interests appear to have been the history of Britain in all its aspects: political, religious, intellectual, and economic. All of the important annals, chronicles and histories are included, from Higden's *Polycronicon*, printed by Caxton in 1482, to the first issue of the first edition of Raleigh's *History of the World* (1614). These are supplemented, or rather glorified, by the poetical accounts in the *Mirrour for Magistrates*, Warner's *Albions England*, and the narratives of Spenser, Daniel, and Drayton. Volumes of statutes from the earliest years of Henry VIII, commentaries on the law, and manuals for civil servants illustrate the legal history of the country and throw light on Shakespeare's concept of such local worthies as Dogberry and Verges, and Justice Shallow.

During the Renaissance, the most lively topic of discussion both in Britain and on the Continent was theology, and more books were published in this field than in all others combined. It is only natural, therefore, that a high proportion of the Harmsworth books should be theological. Sir Leicester's interest may be gauged by the fact that he secured by private negotiation the theological section of the great Britwell Library before the announced date of public sale. Medieval Religion, Reformation, Anglicanism, Counter-Reformation and Non-conformity are all amply represented, and the number of unique items is remarkable: twelve of Augustine, four of Bernard, six of Thomas à Kempis, four of Luther, two of Calvin, thirteen of Knox, four of

Coverdale, three of Tyndale, six of Robert Parsons, and scores of others. Many of the books published by the Marian exiles are included, and there is an excellent collection of tracts relating to the Martin Marprelate controversy. The Puritan press at Leyden is represented by at least seven volumes, not to mention six books from the pen of John Robinson, pastor of the English Puritans there, and two others from his library. Another religious press is likewise well represented: that maintained by the Catholics at Birchley Hall in Lancashire. Eleven of the rare books from this press, the largest collection known, came to the Folger from Bexhill.

The sermons of the sixteenth and seventeenth centuries provide ample material for the study of prose style. They also supply first-hand information, not only about the current controversies over the divinity that "doth hedge a king", the right of free assemblage, of free speech and a free press, and of freedom of conscience—causes for which men bled and died—but also about current events of extraordinary interest that would be headlined in modern newspapers. It is in *A Sermon Preached at Pawles Crosse 3 Nov.* 1577 by Thomas White, for example, that is found the first printed reference to Burbage's Theatre. Two copies have survived, one in the British Museum and the other in the Harmsworth collection. Just a few years later, another clergyman, John Field, who in 1583 expounded the judgement of God as it had been manifested in the fatal collapse of the galleries at the Paris Beargarden, took his turn at denouncing lewd entertainments. Field's sermon, which contains an incidental fling at Burbage's Theatre and at the Curtain, survives in five copies, one of them among the Harmsworth books.

The intellectual history of Britain is amply recorded in the Harmsworth copies of reprints and translations of the Greek and Latin classics and of the literary monuments of Italy, France, Spain, and North-western Europe. Closely akin to these are the works of the great Humanists. Erasmus and Sir Thomas More appear to have had absorbing interest for Sir Leicester, but he also collected Brandt and Colet, Machiavelli, Castiglione, and Montaigne, as well as Petrarch, Boccaccio, Sir Thomas Elyot, and Cervantes. There are rhetorics in abundance, and rare, early school-books by John Stanbridge and Robert Whittinton, and selections from Terence, such as *Floures for Latine Spekynge* (1533), collected by the author of *Ralph Roister Doister*, Nicholas Udall, and known to and quoted by Shakespeare.

Scientific books received from Bexhill were not numerous, though there is a fine copy of William Gilbert's *De Magnete* (1600), and a number of medical books and herbals and numerous works dealing with astronomy, mathematics and navigation. These last are closely linked to the extensive group of books about voyages and travels, which it will be convenient to mention along with the collection of Americana.

The Harmsworth books in the field of economic history include many items that treat of the fishing trade and of foreign commerce. Many of these contain substantial or incidental information about the New Found World, such as Hood's *Regiment of the Sea* (1592), of which only one other copy is recorded in the *Short-title Catalogue*; Harcourt's *Relation of a Voyage to Guiana* (1626; two other copies traced); and Misselden's *Free Trade* (1622; four other copies).

Another category of Harmsworth books deserving attention is Music. Folger, who was himself a musician, had assembled a remarkable collection of Elizabethan and Jacobean song-books by Dowland, Watson, Weelkes, Wilbye, East, Ravenscroft, and others, including Morley's unique *First Book of Ayres* (1600), with the original setting of Shakespeare's "It was a lover and his lass", and a manuscript volume of instrumental music transcribed by Dowland. To these have

PLATE IX

A. View of London and Southwark. From title-page
of Henry Holland's *Herωologia Anglica*, 1620

(Birmingham Reference Library)

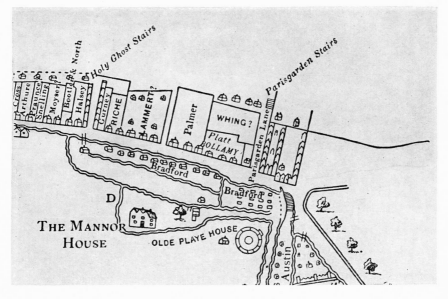

B. Paris Garden. North-east corner of Paris Garden Manor,
from map made in 1627

(Surrey Archaeological Collections, xvi, 1901, facing p. 55)

PLATE X

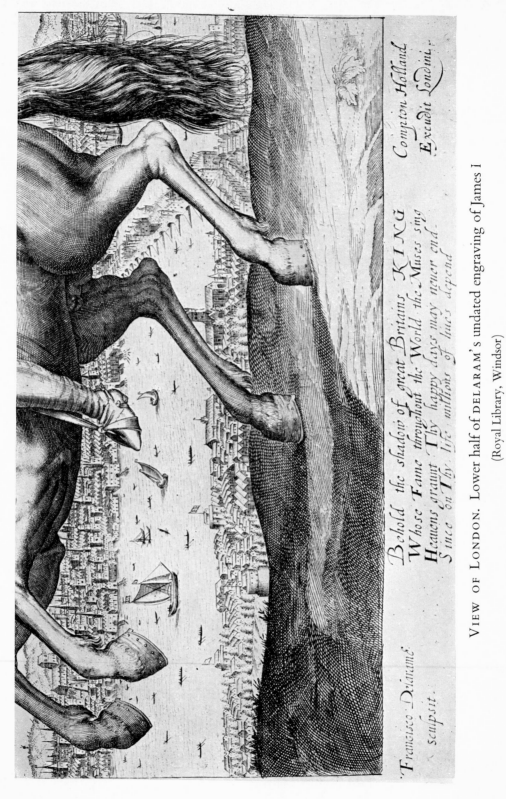

VIEW OF LONDON. Lower half of DELARAM's undated engraving of James I

(Royal Library, Windsor)

PLATE XI

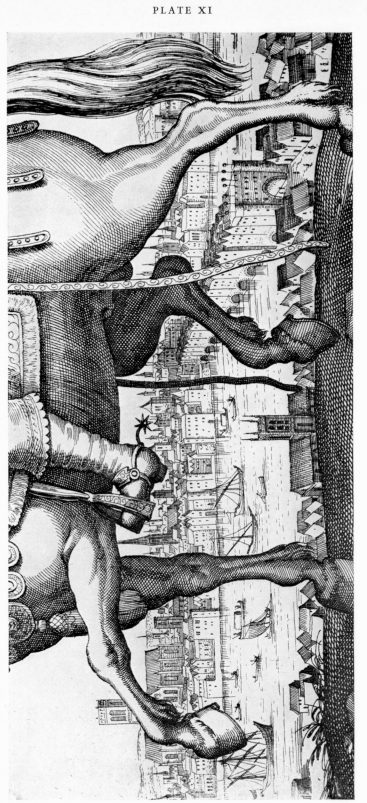

VIEW OF LONDON, engraved 1621. Lower third of unsigned portrait of James I

(British Museum, Crace Views I, Sheet 12, no. 14)

PLATE XII

VIEW OF LONDON. Unsigned and undated engraving of London and Southwark

(British Museum, Crace Views I, Sheet 31, no. 37)

PLATE XIII

THE SECOND GLOBE THEATRE AND THE BEARGARDEN. From HOLLAR's *Long View of London* (Amsterdam, 1647), on which the names of the Globe and the Beargarden are interchanged

(Guildhall Library)

PLATE XIV

A. VIEW OF LONDON, 1638. Background design by INIGO JONES
for D'AVENANT'S *Britannia Triumphans*

(His Grace the Duke of Devonshire, Chatsworth)

B. VIEW OF LONDON, 1638. Alternative Background by INIGO JONES
for D'AVENANT'S *Britannia Triumphans*

(His Grace the Duke of Devonshire, Chatsworth)

PLATE XV

A. THE FOLGER SHAKESPEARE LIBRARY, WASHINGTON

B. THE FOLGER SHAKESPEARE LIBRARY, WASHINGTON
The Reading Room

PLATE XVI

The Folger Shakespeare Library, Washington. The Elizabethan Stage

been added more than fifty volumes of early music collected by Sir Leicester, among them being Morley's *Madrigales* (1594); the *Triumphes of Oriana* (1601, a unique variant); Weelkes's *Ballets and Madrigals* (1608); Amner's *Sacred Hymnes* (1615); Byrd's *Mass for Three Voices* (c. 1588); and Attey's *First Book of Ayres* (1622), of each of which only one other copy is recorded.

It has been remarked that Folger did not collect Americana for their own sake, but many of the books that he purchased for other reasons have proved to contain interesting and important references to America. The Harmsworth Americana increase the holdings in this field to an almost unbelievable degree. In a recently published account of "The Distribution of Early British-Printed Americana in American Libraries",[16] W. W. Bishop notes 248 such works and tabulates the holdings of the larger libraries. In first, second, and fourth places, with 237, 208, and 150 items respectively, are the Huntington Library, the New York Public Library, and the John Carter Brown Library. Bishop continues as follows:

Third in the list is the Folger Shakespeare Library of Washington with 125 original editions and 35 variants and other editions, a total of 160. As this library is constantly adding to its collections, it is possible that these figures are already out of date, though they serve well enough to indicate the relative position of the library....All during the war this library has kept up its buying with the result that it has forged ahead into one of the leading libraries of the country in this as in other fields. In fact ownership of Americana is incidental with this library which specializes in the literary side of British printing.

From my own notes it is possible for me to revise Bishop's figures somewhat. Instead of 430 works that can be called Americana, my total is 493. And instead of 125 items at Folger, I note 276.[17]

Some of these books were purchased by Folger, as Gray's *A Good Speed to Virginia* (1609). Many of the more distinguished ones are Harmsworth books, among which should be mentioned Cartier's *Shorte and briefe Narration of the Two Navigations to Newe Fraunce* (1580); Drayton's *Poems* (c. 1606), with the "Ode to the Virginia Voyage"; both editions of John Donne's *Sermon...Preached to the Honourable Company of the Virginian Plantation* (1622, 1624); Mourt's *Relation or Journall of the Beginning of the English Plantation at Plimouth* (1622), Hariot's *Briefe and True Report of the New Found Land of Virginia* (1590); and six books by Captain John Smith. Yet others have been acquired recently by the Library, as Jourdan's *Plaine Description of the Barmudas now Called Sommer Ilands* (1613; the 1st ed. 1610, with the title, *Discovery of the Barmudas; or, the Isle of Devils*, was already on the Folger shelves).

Seventy notable volumes were purchased in 1940 from the famous Elizabethan library of William A. White, who in his lifetime had been one of Folger's dangerous rivals. At White's death, Folger had purchased many rarities, to the amount of $292,800. Eventually it was possible to secure such other items of importance as Lynche's *Diella* (1596; three others known); Craig's *Amorous Songs* (1606; one other copy recorded); Forde's *Parismus* (1599; the only other copy is in the British Museum); and Munday's *Palmerin d'Oliva* (1588; one other copy traced).

From miscellaneous sources, upwards of 5,000 books have been added to the general *S.T.C.* collection. Of those listed below several are unique and none is traceable in more than, at the most, three other copies. The classics may be represented by Sophocles, *Antigone* (1581); Demosthenes, Λόγοι ιε' (1597); and Cicero, *Foure Severall Treatises* (1577). Some of these books are by Continental authors, as Boccaccio's *Filocopo*, translated into English in 1567; Erasmus,

Bellum Erasmi, translated into Englyshe (1533); and Cervantes, *The History of Don Quixote*, Part I (1612; the gift of Leonard Kebler).

Of the books by English authors, early and late, that have been added to the Folger collections since 1932, it will be possible to name only a few, selected because of their rarity or intrinsic importance, or because they help to complete the collection of books by a major author, or on an important subject. Among these are Awdely, *The Fraternitie of Vacabondes* (1575); Ascham, *Toxophilus* (1545, gift of A. S. W. Rosenbach and Lessing J. Rosenwald. This copy contains the author's letter of presentation to William Parr, Earl of Essex and brother to the Queen); *The Delightful History of Celestina* (1596); Robert Crowley, *The Confutation of the Mishapen Aunswer to the Ballade called the Abuse of ye Blessed Sacrament* (c. 1548, much of the ballad is quoted); Daniel, nineteen items, including an apparently unique issue of *Delia* (1592), *Delia and Rosamond* (1595), and *Philotas* (1607); Davies, *Hymnes of Astraea* (1599); Angel Day, *The English Secretorie* (1586); Dekker, four items, including the first edition of *Lanthorne and Candle-light* (1608) with an allusion to *Hamlet*; Elyot, *A Preservative agaynste Deth* (1545); Forde, *Montelyon, Knight of the Oracle* (1640); Greene, seven items, including *A Maydens Dream; Upon the Death of Sir Christopher Hatton* (1591; this volume is of especial interest because of the gift to the Folger by Dr Rosenbach of a unique sepia drawing, 14 ft. long, of the Funeral Procession); Heywood, twelve items, including *A Curtaine Lecture* (1638); Kethe, *A Ballet...Intytuled, Tye thy Mare Tom Boye* (c. 1570); Nashe, *The Unfortunate Traveller* (1594); *A Pretye Complaynte of Peace that Was Banyshed out of Dyvers Countreys* (c. 1538; the gift of Arthur Amory Houghton); Christopher Saxton, *Atlas* (1574-9); *The Second Report of Doctor John Faustus* (1594; also given by A. A. Houghton); Stubbes, *The Anatomie of Abuses* (1583); and Swetnam, *The Araignment of Lewde, Idle, Froward and Unconstant Women* (1615).

Material additions have also been made to the collection of music books. Among those notable for their intrinsic merit or their rarity are Orlando di Lasso, *Receuil du Mellange* (1570, Superius part, unique; since the Folger has the Cantus part of his *Novae...cantiones*, it appears to be the only library with parts of both Lasso's English editions); Byrd, *Psalms, Sonnets, Songs* (1590, Bassus part only); Weelkes, *Ballets and Madrigals* (1598); Farmer, *English Madrigals* (1599); Pilkington, *First Book of Songs* (1605); Danyel, *Songs for the Lute, Viol and Voice* (1606); Cooper, *Funeral Teares* (1606); East, *Third Set of Books* (1610); Byrd, *Songs of Sundrie Natures* (1610); Gibbons, *Madrigals* (1612); Dowland, *Pilgrimes Solace* (1612); Campion, *Songs of Mourning bewailing the untimely Death of Prince Henry* (1613), Campion, *Ayres* (1614); Bateson, *Second Set of Madrigals* (1618); Hilton, *Ayres* (1627); Porter, *Madrigals and Ayres* (1632); and Butler, *Principles of Musik* (1636).

MANUSCRIPTS: NON-DRAMATIC

Scattered references have been made to the early manuscripts collected by Folger. A brief listing of those that were accessible in 1935 may be found in the late Seymour de Ricci's *Census of Medieval and Renaissance Manuscripts in the United States and Canada* (I, 267-450). The more important ones come from the Warwick Castle collection and the library of J. O. Halliwell-Phillipps, but Folger bought widely in his effort to collect autographs of royalty, the important nobility and the important literary men in Shakespeare's lifetime. There are autograph letters by

Elizabeth and James I, documents signed by members of the Privy Council, volumes of heraldry, commonplace-books, and such items of direct literary interest as Lodge's *The Poore Man's Talent* (autograph); Robert Jones's "The love of change hath chang'd the world through outt", with musical setting; Barnfield's *The Shepherde's Confession* and other poems; Harvey's marginalia in several volumes; Oxinden's commonplace-book; James VI's *Daemonologie*, in a scribal hand with numerous corrections in the autograph of the author; and a fragment of Henslowe's diary, bearing the signature of Dekker, Downton and Jubye. Among the manuscripts from the library of W. T. Smedley should be mentioned a fifteenth-century copy of Gower's *Confessio Amantis*, a number of classical manuscripts from the thirteenth to the sixteenth century, and also Peacham's beautiful *Emblemata Varia* (unpublished).

Additions to the collections of dramatic and theatrical manuscripts have been described elsewhere. From time to time it has been possible to enrich the non-dramatic collection. One of the most beautiful items is a fourteenth-century version of *Handlyng Sin*, on vellum, with the Clopton arms, that has not been examined by scholars. From the muniment room at Loseley Park was secured a collection of manuscripts of literary or historical importance, such as Henry VIII's proclamation at the disestablishment of the monasteries; a list of the ships and personnel of Drake's voyage to America in 1585; and the royal warrant for Raleigh's release from the Tower. From the same source came a collection of eighteen John Donne manuscripts, relating chiefly to his marriage with Anne More, but including the epitaph he wrote for her.

The Sidney collection is immensely strengthened by the acquisition of a transcript of about 1580 of his *Arcadia* in the original binding. This document, which did not come to light until 1907, bears the names of "Alex. Clifforde", "Will M. Clyforde" and "Mountgomery", a fact which reminded Feuillerat that Anne Clifford married as her second husband Philip Herbert, fourth Earl of Pembroke and Montgomery and nephew to Sir Philip Sidney. This Earl was one of the "incomparable brethren" to whom Shakespeare's First Folio was dedicated in 1623, and Shakespeare's indebtedness to the *Arcadia* for the Gloucester story in *King Lear* is well known.

Through the kindness of the Countess de Chambrun it was possible to secure a folio volume containing 105 manuscripts, including Spenser's *View of the Present State of Ireland*, which belonged, apparently, to the unfortunate Earl of Essex. Another Essex item, a contemporary copy of the portrait by Gheeraerts, has been placed in the Folger on indefinite loan by a friend who prefers to remain unidentified. It has frequently been suggested that Spenser wrote his *View* for Essex, whose patronage he was seeking, and it is remarkable that the Earl is the only contemporary noble referred to directly in any of Shakespeare's plays (*Henry V*).

Students of Chapman and Jonson, as well as of Dowland the composer, are indebted to Arthur Amory Houghton for presenting to the Folger a volume containing 137 manuscripts, chiefly personal letters, transcribed early in the seventeenth century. One of the letters is from Richard Martin, of the Virginia Company in London, to William Strachey, Secretary of the Colony, dated 10 December 1610, and sent to Jamestown on the ship *Hercules*.

Reference has been made to the manuscript of King James's *Daemonologie*, purchased by Folger. Alongside this may now be placed the original manuscript (1594) of his proclamation against witches, bearing his signature as James VI of Scotland. Both items are of surpassing interest to students of *Macbeth*.

One of the finest Folger collections of books by an individual author is that of Sir John Harington, kinsman to the Queen, poet, wit, and inventor. To this has been added the holograph manuscript of his *Epigrams*, dedicated to Prince Henry and illustrated by the author. This is still unpublished.

Only three other early manuscripts can now be mentioned. These came to the Folger at different times through the generosity of Lessing J. Rosenwald. The first is a lovely little book, written and illustrated by Esther Inglis, *Les C. L. Pseaumes de David, Escrites en Diverses Sortes de Letteres...à Lislebourg en Escosse* (1599); the second is from the pen of the same expert calligrapher, entitled, *Octonaries upon the Vanitie a. Inconstancie of the World* (1600). The third is a folio of absorbing interest, a pictorial and poetical commonplace-book, compiled in 1608 by Thomas Trevelyon, entitled, *Epitome of Ancient and Modern History*. Among the illustrations are the kings of Israel, the kings of England, the Nine Worthies, the Seven Deadly Sins, various alphabets, and a fine collection of textile patterns.

There are in all some 50,000 manuscripts, including letters, in the Folger collections.

MATERIALS RELATING TO THE THEATRE

The original Folger collections of materials relating to the theatre and the stage history of Shakespeare's plays are so extensive that little has been added to them. Two of the earliest items are playbills (*ante* 1700) of performances in London—one of them of Dryden's version of *Troilus and Cressida*. These are followed by day-books from Lincoln's Inn Fields and Covent Garden in the first decades of the eighteenth century and two sketches from the prompter's book of stage settings for *Richard II* (*c.* 1728). Invaluable details of eighteenth-century stage history are given in the Crosse-Hopkins diary and similar compilations. And primary records of nineteenth-century productions may be found in the scores of the official theatrical account-books of that period. To these have been added, as the gift of Ralph Brown, the financial records of Irving's first American tour.

The collection of some 250,000 English playbills of the English and American stages of the eighteenth and early nineteenth centuries has been partly arranged but is not yet catalogued. Already an important group of London bills for the 1730's has come to light.

Of great historical importance and immediate theatrical use are the 3,000 prompt-books in the Folger. These are frequently consulted by current producers of Shakespeare, as well as by scholars. The details of costume and stage-setting in the elaborate books of Charles Kean, for example, have more than once proved helpful. Hardly a great Shakespearian actor, actress, or producer but is represented in this section of the Library.

Supplementing these collections are the 50,000 theatrical and literary prints, engravings, photographs, drawings and small portraits brought together by Folger during his half-century of activity. Current additions include valuable material about Charlotte Cushman, the gift of Mrs Victor N. Cushman. Mr Arthur E. Muller presented a large collection of relics of Irving and Ellen Terry, including prompt-books, properties, costumes, and letters. Additional memorials of Ellen Terry have been secured with the assistance of David A. Randall, such as her annotated copy of *The Story of My Life*. Among the Sothern-Marlowe items presented by Mrs Julia Marlowe Sothern are books containing all the special music written for their productions. Other gifts of stage properties and theatrical materials are too numerous to mention; it must suffice to indicate the nature of the gifts and record the generosity of the Library's many friends.

An integral part of Folger's plan for establishing the text of Shakespeare was the collecting of all the reprints of the poet's work and all the significant translations and commentaries. Many of the choicest items came to him by way of the Warwick Castle Library and Marsden J. Perry Library from J. O. Halliwell-Phillipps, but his constant search for obscure editions enabled him to secure hundreds of volumes not to be found elsewhere. Shortly after the Library opened, Henry N. Paul of Philadelphia revealed the fact that he, too, had spent many years collecting editions of Shakespeare after 1700, and upon examination of his library it was discovered that he possessed over 2,000 volumes of the poems and plays that were not known to Folger. With a magnanimity exceeded only by his love of Shakespeare, Paul transferred these editions to Washington, giving to the Folger collections a richness beyond compare. Immediately the Library resumed the search for rare editions, and each year brings to light a hundred or more new items. Henry N. Paul and Giles E. Dawson, Curator of Folger Books and Manuscripts, have for a number of years been engaged in the compilation of a detailed bibliography of the editions of Shakespeare from 1709 to 1864.

Special reference must be made to the generosity of the Birmingham Reference Library, which at intervals sends lists of duplicates in its great Shakespeare Collection and presents to the Folger every item that is requested.

It is difficult to find gaps in the collection of Shakespeare commentaries with which the Library opened. A systematic check of the reprints of the contemporaries of Shakespeare has resulted in the purchase of hundreds of volumes, so that a complete record of Elizabethan scholarship will be at hand for the convenience of readers.

The private papers—letters, note-books, transcripts, and fair copies of manuscripts—of famous editors, critics, and actors of Shakespeare held a special appeal for Folger, who collected every scrap he could obtain relating to Garrick, Malone, Ireland, Collier, Halliwell-Phillipps, Swinburne —to name only a few. These documents, for the most part, await the study of scholars.

Wisely enough, Folger limited his purchases of Continental books very largely to those in circulation in Shakespeare's lifetime. It was with some surprise in 1938 that no fewer than 364 *incunabula* were discovered on the shelves. This number has since been increased to more than 370. According to Fremont Rider's revised tables of American holdings of *incunabula* (published in 1939), the Folger ranks fifteenth among American libraries—between Yale University and the Union Theological Seminary. The Folger is not interested in *incunabula* as such, but it is worth noting that in the Harmsworth purchase were twenty-three English-printed *incunabula*, and two Continental works have been received by gift (the first illustrated edition of Terence (1496), from A. S. W. Rosenbach and Lessing J. Rosenwald; and Roselli's *Tractatus* (1486), from Mrs Lydia Clothier Maxwell).

SERVICES TO SCHOLARS

It was the expressed intention of the Founder that the Folger should be a research library. Scholars and specialists—usually creative writers, actors, musicians and theatrical producers—are admitted to the Reading Room by card, usually after correspondence with the Director. To quote again the words of J. Q. Adams, the Folger

freely places [at the disposal of readers] its rare treasures, provides them with every facility to work under favorable conditions, and makes readily available to them the aid of its staff of experts in Elizabethan bibliography and paleography, and in other fields of technical research. But the Founder wished his library to extend to scholars more than a formal welcome. He stoutly insisted—so the architect, Mr Cret, relates—on adding to the Reading Room a practicable fireplace, saying in explanation that he desired to create in the building "the warm atmosphere of a private home", where readers would feel that they were his personal guests. Accordingly, every effort is made to render the Folger a place of friendliness and hospitality. Each afternoon the visiting scholars and the members of the staff—most of whom are themselves actively engaged in research—gather in the Founder's Room for tea. At these meetings, all formality and that reserve natural among strangers quickly vanish in a genial comradeship, while lively discussions of the investigations under way lead to stimulating suggestions, and often to actual co-operation in the solution of difficult problems. And throughout the entire Library this spirit—as of a friendly society of scholars working together for the advancement of knowledge—is cultivated.[18]

The same spirit of friendly co-operation pervades the correspondence of staff members with scholars throughout the world who call upon the Library for information or assistance. This service to scholarship is rendered freely and cheerfully, even though some projects require the attention of a staff member for a considerable time.

From the day it opened, the Library has been equipped to supply photostats of its books and manuscripts. In recent years, scholars have turned increasingly to the use of microfilm, because of the relatively small cost. Accordingly, the Folger is now installing a microfilm camera and a projector of a type perfected during the war for the armed forces, in order that scholars may quickly and inexpensively obtain the reproductions of the materials needed in their researches. Requests for photostatic or microfilm copies are invariably granted unless the physical condition of the original renders this inadvisable, or unless, in the case of excessively rare or unique items, the work is being reserved for publication by the Library or by a scholar who has already begun work on it.

FELLOWSHIPS

In 1936 the Trustees established two annual Fellowships to be awarded to young scholars of exceptional promise. These were awarded each year through 1941. Upon the resumption of the series, four Fellowships were awarded in 1946. Beginning with the academic year 1947, two Fellowships were awarded for the full year and two other Fellowships, with smaller stipend, were awarded for one semester. After 1947, this plan may be varied, according to the qualifications of the applicants, to include short-term Fellowships, as for one summer.

The purpose of the Fellowships is "to give a few well-trained and ambitious young scholars the opportunity early in their career to complete and bring to publication the contributions to knowledge they have begun, to lay foundations for further investigations, and so, perhaps, to become future leaders of productive scholarship in America. In this fashion the Library hopes to develop for our colleges and universities a small but steadily increasing supply of able teachers of Shakespeare and of Elizabethan literature."[19] The wisdom of this experiment is amply demonstrated in the publications and subsequent careers of the scholars who have held Folger Fellowships.

PUBLICATIONS

It was an inevitable result of Folger's method of building his library that the world of scholarship should desire immediate access to many of the treasures which had been out of circulation for many years. In response to this demand, the series of Folger Reprints was inaugurated in 1936 with the publication of the unique and hitherto unreproduced First Quarto of *Titus Andronicus* (1594), with full scholarly apparatus, under the editorship of the Director, J. Q. Adams.

This was followed by a collotype facsimile, with introduction and notes by Adams, of the Folger's unique *Ghost of Lucrece* (1600), written by Middleton under the influence of *The Rape of Lucrece*.

The third volume in the series was a reproduction, with introduction and notes by R. C. Bald, one-time Folger Fellow, of the Folger manuscript of Middleton's *Hengist King of Kent*.

The fourth volume reproduced the Folger copy of *The Passionate Pilgrim* (1599). Adams's bibliographical introduction presented evidence that the unique sheets in this fragmentary copy represent the first edition of this important book of amatory verses.

The fifth Reprint was a collotype facsimile of the Folger copy of the third edition (1612) of the *Passionate Pilgrim*, never before reprinted. The editor, Hyder E. Rollins, points out the fact that William Jaggard's little publication led to a bitter protest by Shakespeare and Heywood.

The sixth, and latest, volume in the series is a reproduction for the first time of the unique Folger copy of *Oenone and Paris* (1594), a close imitation by T. H. (probably Thomas Heywood) of *Venus and Adonis*. This volume was also edited by Adams.

To meet the needs of students, teachers, and the general public for inexpensive yet attractive and authentic pictures illustrating the age of Shakespeare, the Library has published four sets of collotype prints, each containing from eighteen to twenty separate items, of "Portraits of Shakespeare", "Stratford-on-Avon", "Shakespeare's London", and "The Shakespearian Theatre". There is also a collotype reproduction of Visscher's *View of London* (c. 1610), suitable for wall-display in schools. Views of the Folger Shakespeare Library and some of its more popular items are also made available to the public in post-card size, suitable for mailing. And in 1947 for the first time two series of Christmas cards, with collotype reproductions of scenes of the Nativity from Folger copies of early English liturgical books, were published.

A booklet containing a brief account of the Founder, a short history of the Library, and a summary account of its collections and principal activities is now in the press. This, like the prints and post-cards, will be on sale to visitors at approximately the cost of production.

CATALOGUES

As soon as the Folger books and manuscripts were unpacked, it was realized that the rarity of the items and the nature of the collections required unusual and elaborate cataloguing. Accordingly, Edwin E. Willoughby was invited to devise a special method of classification of books after 1700 to bring out their relation to Shakespearian studies and to set up a scheme for cataloguing the Early English books. This work began in 1935 and continued without interruption until December 1941, when it became necessary to select, pack, and store in a distant place upwards of 30,000 items. With the *S.T.C.* books removed, Willoughby and his staff turned to the cataloguing of Restoration books and those of the eighteenth century. This task they completed shortly after the return of the early books at the close of the war.

Books of the *S.T.C.* period are elaborately catalogued, and special card files are compiled of authors, editors, writers of prefaces and dedications, dedicatees, authors of commendatory verses, printers, publishers, booksellers, engravers and illustrators, binders, and former owners, in addition to the usual cross-references. For each book, the following information is also supplied: the title exactly transcribed (with the end of lines, the use of Roman, italic, and black-letter type, and of ligatures, indicated); a full collation by signatures; the title-borders, ornaments, and printer's device noted and identified; editions and issues carefully differentiated; all bibliographical peculiarities pointed out (with an attempt to explain their significance), important bibliographic studies cited; and, finally, any significant discoveries made by the cataloguer duly reported. So detailed are the mimeographed author cards that upwards of thirty American libraries have subscribed for copies (no file exists at present in Great Britain or on the Continent). These are issued to the subscribers at a nominal sum in lots of 1,000, as they are prepared.

It was originally intended that a catalogue of English books, 1475–1640, in book form, would be issued upon the completion of the cataloguing, in a format commensurate with the importance of the collection. But so rapid has been the growth of the Library that many years will pass before the cataloguing can be finished. In the meantime, scholars are deprived of the valuable information provided in the Folger catalogue cards. It will not be surprising if the original plan is altered to permit the publication of the catalogue one volume at a time as the work proceeds.

LECTURES

The Elizabethan theatre, which serves as an auditorium, is the scene of the annual celebration of Shakespeare's birthday. Some Shakespearian scholar is invited each year to deliver a formal address on 23 April. The lecturers in the past have been George A. Plimpton, Felix E. Schelling, George L. Kittredge, William A. Neilson, C. F. Tucker Brooke, Leslie Hotson, Allardyce Nicoll, Charles J. Osgood, and Samuel C. Chew.

In celebration of the publication of the First Folio of Shakespeare in November 1623, three addresses have been delivered: two by the distinguished bibliophile, A. S. W. Rosenbach, and one by the authority on the extant copies of the Folio, R. M. Smith.

EXTRA-MURAL RESOURCES

Capitol Hill, on which the Folger Shakespeare Library stands, is fast becoming one of the great library centres of the world. Nearby are the great reference collections of the Library of Congress and the law library of the Supreme Court. Plans are now being drawn for the superb Army Medical Library, to be located next door to the Folger. And not far distant are the growing art reference library of the National Gallery of Art and the splendid library of the Department of

Agriculture, with its fine collection of herbals. Compilation of a union catalogue of *S.T.C.* books in Washington libraries was begun several years ago by the Folger and the Division of Rare Books of the Library of Congress. This project was interrupted by the war but is to be resumed. The great Union Catalogue in the Library of Congress, listing the rare books in the principal American libraries, is of incalculable value to scholars working in Washington, who may by consulting it obtain needed books by inter-library loan, or by correspondence secure necessary information.

GIFTS

In this survey of the Library's possessions and activities, frequent references have been made to specific gifts of friends of the Folger Shakespeare Library by way of illustration, but many more benefactors have been left unmentioned than have been named, and not all the gifts of the most active benefactors have been listed. This account must not be concluded without a statement of the Library's gratitude to the Rockefeller Foundation, which in July 1940 offered to match, up to $50,000, any sum raised by the Trustees of the Library within the next twelve months. Within a year the offer was met, and the resultant $100,000 became available for accessions. The first purchase made from these funds was the John Donne Manuscripts (bound photographic copies of which were immediately deposited in the British Museum and the Bodleian Library). Many of the most important items secured by the Folger since 1941 could be purchased only by reason of this splendid gift.

NOTES

1. Joseph Quincy Adams, in *The Folger Shakespeare Library. Published for the Trustees of Amherst College* (1933), p. 15.
2. It is also present in three other Folger Folios. See Giles E. Dawson, "A Bibliographical Problem in the First Folio of Shakespeare", *Library*, 4th ser. (1941-2), XXII, 25-33.
3. Reproduced by Edwin E. Willoughby as the frontispiece of *The Printing of the First Folio of Shakespeare* (1932).
4. See Charlton Hinman, "A Proof-sheet in the First Folio of Shakespeare", *Library*, 4th ser. (1942-3), XXIII, 101-7.
5. For interesting details about the distribution of the early quartos in England and America, see the review by J. Q. Adams of Henrietta C. Bartlett and Alfred W. Pollard's "A Census of Shakespeare's Plays in Quarto 1594-1700", in the *Journal of English and Germanic Philology*, XXXIX (1940), 405-7.
6. Twenty-one items are recorded in the finding-lists compiled by H. E. Rollins in the Variorum editions of the *Poems* and *Sonnets*; the twenty-second, the sixth edition of *Lucrece* and the first to bear the author's name, was acquired at the Frank Hogan sale in 1946.
7. Described bibliographically and reproduced in facsimile by J. Q. Adams in 1939 in the series of Folger Reprints. The Folger copy of the third edition of 1612 (one other copy known) was edited by H. E. Rollins in 1940 in the same series.
8. In his enthusiasm, De Ricci seems to have forgotten the British Museum MS., *Sir Thomas More*.
9. The Dering MS., see Plate XVII. This and the manuscript commonplace-books which contain versions of his sonnets and other fragments of his verse might well have been mentioned in the discussion of the Text.
10. *The Folger Shakespeare Library*, pp. 20-1.
11. "A New Signature of Shakespeare?" *Bulletin of the John Rylands Library, Manchester*, XXVII (1943), 256-9.
12. *Publications of the Modern Language Association of America*, LXVIII (1943), 621-33.
13. See, for example, the poems and sonnets utilized by Rollins in his Variorum editions of the *Poems* and *Sonnets*.

14. Fortunately the Beaumont volume came to light in time for Dr Greg to describe the three unique plays in 'Additions' to his *Bibliography*, I, xxi–xxiii.

15. Adams, *A Report on Progress*, 1931–1941, pp. 15–16.

16. In *Miscellanea Giovanni Mercati*, VI (1946), 1–10.

17. Do not misunderstand me to assert that the Folger possesses the largest collection of *S.T.C.* Americana in the United States. I am confident that a free exchange of information would increase the totals of such items in the other libraries named, but not perhaps in the same proportion as at the Folger.

18. *A Report on Progress*, 1931–1941, pp. 50–1.

19. *A Report on Progress*, 1931–1941, p. 52.

THE HERITAGE OF SHAKESPEARE'S BIRTHPLACE

BY

LEVI FOX

"The truly heart-stirring relic of a most glorious period, and of England's immortal bard...the most honoured monument of the greatest genius that ever lived."

Such was the description of "Shakspeare's house", Stratford-upon-Avon, which appeared on a poster advertising its sale by public auction in London on 16 September 1847. The centenary of the sale and of the purchase of the property for preservation as a national memorial to the dramatist accordingly presents an appropriate occasion both for reviewing some aspects of the history of the fabric of the building and its associations and for relating the circumstances of the sale. It also affords an opportunity to record something of the work of the trustees who have been responsible for the preservation and administration of the property during the past hundred years.

The literature on the subject, though extensive, is of varying value, and no comprehensive study has yet appeared. The older descriptive guides, though generally reliable, are inadequate, and are too sentimental in their treatment.[1] A few items have been conceived in a spirit of partiality and are, therefore, misleading.[2] Much of the material relating to the sale in 1847 is scattered and needs to be pieced together, while most of the information regarding the latest chapter of the building's history is contained in minute-books belonging to the Birthplace Trustees.[3]

The visitor to the Birthplace is struck both by the size and the detachment of the building. Two explanations should accordingly be noted at the outset. Although the Birthplace now presents the appearance of a single, half-timbered building, it originally comprised two distinct properties: the house on the west, which came to be known as Shakespeare's house, with an adjoining property on the east (in later times used as an inn known as "The Swan and Maidenhead") also originally belonging to the family. The two properties are now joined together by interior doorways. Further, until less than a century ago both properties formed part of a continuous frontage of old buildings abutting on to Henley Street. The adjoining buildings were demolished in 1857 so as to isolate the Birthplace property with a view to diminishing fire risk, and further buildings which faced the Guild Pits (now Guild Street) at the rear were also removed to make possible the present lay-out of the garden at the rear of the Birthplace.

The history of the Birthplace fabric and its ownership is fascinating. No record of the erection of the building survives nor any specific reference to it before Shakespeare's time. Architectural features suggest that the greater part of it was built in the late fifteenth or early sixteenth century. Like most Stratford-upon-Avon houses of this period, the building consisted of a low foundation wall of local stone, supporting a substantial oak superstructure, the spaces between the timber framing being filled in with wattle and daub and the structure consolidated in the centre by a massive chimney stack and timber roof. Materials and workmanship were undoubtedly local.

The western end of the building still retains some of the original exterior timber work. The timbers on the ground floor frontage are of the early, close-studded type about nine inches wide and the same distance apart. The upper frontage has rectangular panels. The eastern half of the building follows the same style, but only a few beams on the front remain of the original timber work. A good deal of the interior timber of the whole building is original, and all the upper rooms except one are open to part of the roof. Only the 'birthroom' has a lower ceiling of later date, now covered by the signatures of generations of visitors. It is probable that the rear wing of the building projecting into the garden, also of rectangular timber framing but much restored, was added towards the end of the sixteenth century.

The question naturally arises as to the nature of the evidence supporting the Shakespeare connection with the property. This aspect of the subject received considerable attention some eighty years ago.[4] According to tradition John Shakespeare resided in the western part of the Birthplace either as tenant or owner during the whole period of his life in Stratford-upon-Avon, and it has been assumed that all his children, including William, were born there. The position as regards documentary evidence is conveniently summarized by Sir E. K. Chambers in his *William Shakespeare: a study of facts and problems.* There is documentary proof that John Shakespeare was living in Henley Street as early as April 1552, but whether as owner or tenant is not known. In 1556 property in Greenhill Street and a house in Henley Street which can be identified with the eastern part of the Birthplace property were transferred to him. A conveyance of 1597 shows that John Shakespeare was definitely occupying the western part of the Birthplace property and sold a strip of land adjoining it to his neighbour, George Badger.[5] How long he had been living there before that time is not known. The records do not indicate precisely at which house in Stratford-upon-Avon William was born. Local tradition alone assigns the western part of the Birthplace property as his birthplace.

The subsequent descent of the property has been satisfactorily established. It passed from John Shakespeare to the dramatist himself and then successively to his elder daughter and to his only grand-daughter, Lady Barnard. On her death in 1670 she bequeathed it to her cousin, Thomas Hart, the poet's grand-nephew and grandson of his sister, Mrs Joan Hart. Mrs Hart was occupying part of the property at the time of Shakespeare's death and continued there until she died in 1646. Some time before then, even possibly as early as 1603, the eastern part of the property was let to a tenant who used it as an inn, known at first as "The Maidenhead" and afterwards as "The Swan and Maidenhead".[6] This arrangement was continued for two centuries or more. Meanwhile the western part of the property remained in the occupation of the Hart family, and the whole was owned by Thomas Hart's descendants down to 1806. In that year the premises were sold to Thomas Court, on the death of whose widow they were again offered for sale in 1847, and then became public property.

Two developments occurred during the period between the seventeenth and early nineteenth centuries. On the one hand, the Birthplace became a popular showplace; on the other hand, the fabric of the building underwent certain changes. The story of neither aspect of the subject can be reconstructed in detail, but the general outline of each is clear.

When visitors first began to make their pilgrimage to Stratford-upon-Avon to see the house where Shakespeare was born is not known. The fact that Stratford was the place of his birth as well as his death was widely known in the seventeenth century, as evidenced by references in the works of a number of authors of the period; and it is reasonable to suppose that then, as now, readers were curious to see what they read about when opportunity occurred. The publication of popular local guides describing specific places of interest did not come till later, so that the most likely source of information for throwing light on the 'showplace' aspect of the property does not exist. It is also unfortunate that no detailed street plan or survey of seventeenth- or early eighteenth-century Stratford-upon-Avon exists.

Nevertheless, it is significant that the western part of the Henley Street property is specifically denoted as Shakespeare's Birthplace in the official map of the town by S. Winter published in 1759, and that in an engraving by B. Cole from a drawing of Richard Greene of Lichfield published in 1769[7] the two parts of the building are linked together as the house in which the dramatist was born (Plate XVIII A). Writing twenty years afterwards, Gough, in his additions to Camden's *Britannia*, expressly mentions "the house in which constant tradition has uniformly affirmed he first drew breath remains unaltered, being built of timber and plaister, like most of the town".

That the property should have figured prominently in the Garrick Jubilee of 1769[8] should accordingly cause no surprise. The town authorities erected a flag-pole opposite to its entrance, and a painting was placed by Garrick outside the window of the birthroom, bearing the motto: "Thus dying clouds contend with glowing light."

The continued recognition and increasing popularity of the Birthplace as a memorial to the poet were assured from this time. No reliable records of numbers of visitors during the eighteenth century survive. The auctioneer stated that in 1806 and for many years about a thousand persons visited the building each year, a number considerably increased in the years preceding its sale in 1847. Apart from numbers, other evidence indicates that the building enjoyed considerable pre-eminence as a place of interest visited by travellers. Walpole writes in his *British Traveller*: "We arrived in the month of July, 1777, at the White Lion. This is the inn represented in the entertainment of the Jubilee. In the yard is a sign of Shakespere. Three doors from this inn is the house in which Shakespere was born and here is shown his chair in which he sat in the chimney corner. It has been pretty much cut by different visitors...." Byng (1785) writes much in the same style. He "bought a slice of the chair equal to the size of a tobacco stopper" and bargained with Mrs Hart for the lower cross-bar, which he ultimately secured.[9]

Slightly later, from 1793 to 1820, the celebrated Mrs Hornby resided at the Birthplace and acted as cicerone.[10] She it was who assembled a collection of furniture and relics to which she attached fictitious Shakespearian associations for the benefit of visitors. When Washington Irving visited Stratford-on-Avon in 1815 Mrs Hornby conducted him over the house. He describes her in his *Sketch Book* as: "a garrulous old lady in a frosty red face, lighted up by a cold blue anxious eye, and garnished with artificial locks of flaxen hair, curling from under an exceeding dirty cap." He also gives an amusing list of the kind of relics exhibited in the house at the time: "There was the shattered stock of the very matchlock with which Shakespeare shot the deer, on his poaching exploits. There, too, was his tobacco-box; which proves that he was a rival smoker of Sir Walter Raleigh; the sword also with which he played Hamlet; and the identical lantern with which Friar Laurence discovered Romeo and Juliet...." Though profitable for its organizer, this kind of deception brought credit neither to Stratford nor to Shakespeare.

Meanwhile the property had been grossly neglected from the point of view of maintenance and its earlier appearance altered in certain respects. The drawing of 1769 shows the building with dormer windows and gable, a deep porch and projecting bay window. Ireland's sketch made in 1792[11] shows that the dormer windows and gable had been removed, the bay window altered into an ordinary lattice window, the porch taken away and the front fitted up as a butcher's shop. The use of part of the premises as a butcher's shop did not improve its appearance any more than did the use of the adjoining part of the building as an inn. Into what a poor condition the property had fallen, quite apart from any question of appearance, may be judged from the fact that when its owners offered it for sale by private contract in 1804[12] no purchaser was forthcoming. Three months later, on 7 March 1805, the property was offered for sale by auction, but still it remained unsold. Thomas Court bought it for £210 the following year and took possession in 1808.

It was at this date, or thereabouts, that the Swan and Maidenhead portion of the building was rebuilt at the front in red brick. Some of the old timber framing was removed, but the main cross-beams remained and were hidden behind the new brick frontage. Views of the Birthplace property showing this 'improvement' indicate how drastically it altered the earlier appearance of the building. Shakespeare's house itself remained alongside, "a small mean-looking edifice of wood and plaster", in the words of Washington Irving. Stratford's local historian, R. B. Wheler, describing its appearance in 1824, says: "The external appearance of these celebrated buildings is not very attractive, nor does the internal arrangement encourage the idea of their having afforded that domestic comfort to a respectable family of which they were nevertheless capable in the reign of Elizabeth." He attributed the decay of the building to "the lapse of more than two hundred years" and the want of sufficient repairs whilst in the possession of the Harts in the eighteenth century, who were burdened with a heavy mortgage and in humble circumstances.[13]

The condition of the property, however, did not deter visitors from coming specially to inspect it. Wheler wrote his historical account of the building primarily for their benefit. The owners encouraged patronage. One of Mrs Court's cards, dated May 1822, runs as follows: "Mrs Court respectfully invites the nobility and gentry visiting Stratford-upon-Avon to gratify their own laudable curiosity and honour her by inspecting the house in which the immortal Poet of Nature was born." The visitors were said to have numbered 2,240 in 1844, 2,400 in 1845 and 2,430 in 1846. Many of the signatures cut in the glass of the window of the birthroom date back to these years.

Court's widow died in 1846 and arrangements were made immediately to sell the property. The representatives of the owners were sufficiently astute to place the sale in the hands of the well-known London auctioneer, Mr George Robins. The sale poster, with its emphatic bold type, speaks for itself. The sale catalogue, comprising sixteen quarto pages, was equally a masterpiece of advertisement.[14] To supplement the actual particulars of the sale lengthy extracts from the works of Wheler, Knight, Drake and Irving were quoted and views of the Birthplace, the church, Anne Hathaway's Cottage, the Globe Theatre and portraits of Shakespeare, Queen Elizabeth, King James and Ben Jonson were included. The sale was announced to take place at the Mart, London, on Thursday, 16 September 1847 at 12 o'clock.

The publicity accorded to the announcement by the Press aroused widespread interest in the future of the building and many Shakespeare lovers welcomed the opportunity to help to secure the property for preservation as a national memorial. A rumour to the effect that a plan was on foot to remove the fabric to the United States of America seems to have produced immediate action. At a meeting held on 22 July 1847, the Shakespearian Monumental Committee at Stratford-on-Avon, which had existed since 1835 for the purpose of preserving Shakespeare's tomb and of restoring the chancel of Holy Trinity Church, extended its objects to include the preservation of Shakespeare's house.[15] Under the new name of the Shakespeare Birthplace Committee, the Committee proceeded to purchase for £820 four cottages adjoining the Birthplace offered for sale by Mrs Izod and to appeal for funds "to purchase and save from further desecration the walls which sheltered the cradle of William Shakespeare". An appeal notice, dated 2 August 1847, signed by Dr Thomas Thomson, Chairman of the Committee, announced that His Royal Highness the Prince Albert had donated £250 towards the object.[16] A similar Committee was set up in London under the chairmanship of Thomas Amyot and an appeal issued on similar lines. Subsequently the efforts of both Committees were co-ordinated. A rival appeal was sponsored by George Jones, an American tragedian who organized the People's Central Committee of the Shakespeare Memorial Fund; but Jones's efforts met with considerable criticism and his project failed.

The response to their appeals was sufficient to justify the Stratford and London Committees to go forward with their plan for purchasing the property. Special performances and entertainments were given in aid of the funds: for instance, *Henry IV* was staged at the Royal Olympic Theatre on 26 August and *Twelfth Night* at the Theatre Royal, Liverpool, on 9 September. How widespread was popular interest may be illustrated by J. S. Coyne's musical extravaganza *This House To Be Sold (the Property of the Late William Shakespeare); Inquire Within*, which was staged at the Theatre Royal Adelphi on 9 September 1847. Another effort to raise money was the publication by Francis Crew of *The Shakspere Newspaper*. The first number was "planned and brought out within a week".

The sale-room scene must have been a memorable occasion. A drawing of it, made by J. W. Archer for the *Illustrated London News*, and in the possession of the Birthplace Trustees, vividly illustrates its quality. A special Shakespeare number of that periodical was published on 18 September 1847, price 6d, containing an account of the proceedings of the sale together with a series of engravings of Stratford, Shottery and Charlecote by W. J. Linton from drawings specially made for the occasion by E. Duncan. Among those present in the sale room were Mr Amyot[17] and Dr Thomson, chairmen of the London and Stratford Committees respectively, Peter Cunningham (treasurer), F. G. Tomlins (honorary secretary), J. P. Collier, F. W. Fairholt, J. O. Halliwell(-Phillipps), Charles Knight and T. Purland. Edmund Robins conducted the sale, George Robins having died earlier in the year.

At one o'clock [says the *Illustrated London News* report], Mr Robins ascended the rostrum, amidst loud cheers. He then addressed the company, explaining that the vendor had no interest in the property, he simply acted as the trustee of several minors to whose interest he was bound to look; and in bringing the property before the public for sale, he was merely following a course which the Court of Chancery would have directed if it had been appealed to in the matter. He next stated there to be a property attached to the house which yielded a yearly rental of £30. He then read the conditions, and explained that the title to the property would descend to the purchaser or purchasers, from the will of the Great Poet. A person here interposed, and called upon Mr Robins to prove that the house he was about to sell was the identical one in which the poet was born. Mr Robins replied that tradition pointed out this house as that of Shakespeare's birth. His father lived in it, and there could be no doubt that the great Poet was born in the house and spent the greater part of his life in it. (Cheers.) They must take it as a matter of course. He wished that those who were sceptical on the point would stay away, instead of starting doubts which had no foundation to rest upon. The house was transferred from the hands of Shakespeare's descendants, in 1806, to the present owners....

The bidding started at 1,500 guineas and continued with bids of £2,000 and £2,100; at that juncture an offer of £3,000 was handed to the auctioneer on behalf of the two Committees.[18] This offer was accepted and so the property was secured for preservation as a national memorial.

The original idea was to place the property, once purchased, under the protection of the Government. Negotiations were at once started by the London Committee with the Chief Commissioner of Woods and Forests with a view to achieving that object. Meanwhile, further efforts were made to raise funds. In December 1847 a sum of £500 was still required to relieve the two Committees from liabilities incurred in connection with the purchase. A Shakespeare night in aid of the fund was held at the Royal Italian Opera House, Covent Garden, on 7 December 1847, when scenes from Shakespeare's plays were performed. On 20 December 1847, an amateur performance of *Henry IV*, *Part I*, was given at the Theatre Royal, Manchester, for the same object and similar amateur performances were given in different parts of the country. Slightly later, Charles Dickens sponsored an appeal for the endowment of a perpetual curatorship of Shakespeare's house. His plan was to make Sheridan Knowles, then in great financial need, the first curator. Dickens organized amateur performances to this end in London, Manchester, Birmingham and elsewhere, in which he and other literary figures of the day took part—among the most notable amateur productions of their time, indeed of the whole century. Although he raised a considerable sum of money, the project failed, presumably because it did not eventually prove acceptable to the Stratford Committee.

It is clear from the minutes of their proceedings that the Stratford Birthplace Committee took the initiative and assumed from the beginning that they were to be responsible for the property until such time as it might be taken over by the Government. Thus they arranged for the property to be conveyed by Mr Wheler, a Stratford solicitor, and for it to be inspected by Mr Gibbs, a local architect, and a sub-committee. Having secured possession of the property they engaged a lady custodian to be in attendance to collect subscriptions. In 1850 the Committee arranged a loan to complete the purchase and made plans to raise funds to liquidate their debt. To this end they decided to admit the public to the Birthplace by ticket only, price one shilling, to be obtained from the principal inns and booksellers of the town. An official visitors' book was also instituted.

Negotiations with the Government for taking over the property were still taking place in 1853, but by that time with little hope of success. The following year the Committee began to make other plans for the repair and future conservation of the property. As a temporary measure, various urgent repairs were carried out and the Swan and Maidenhead portion was re-let, but not as licensed premises. Income from visitors gradually increased. In 1853-4 as many as 2,878 persons visited the Birthplace, and these included visitors from Holland, Turkey, U.S.A. (461), Jamaica, Australia, Ceylon, Austria, Hong Kong, Denmark, Canada, Belgium, France, Norway,

Newfoundland and Hungary. By 1856 the Committee had succeeded in liquidating the debt incurred in connection with the purchase.

At this juncture, a fortuitous circumstance arose which produced far-reaching results. A John Shakespear of Worthington, Leicestershire, who claimed to be a descendant of the poet, made known his intention to donate by deed of gift a sum of £2,500 to preserve and restore the Birthplace fabric. Encouraged by this unexpected windfall the Committee immediately made plans to carry out the necessary work. As a first step, the Birthplace property was isolated on either side and at the rear by the demolition of adjacent properties. The tenant occupying the Swan and Maidenhead portion was removed and Mr E. M. Barry, architect, was called in to report in detail upon the state of the property. Barry's report, dated 6 July 1857, recommending the general lines of the restoration, was accepted by the Committee. In general terms the object was "to remove at once those portions of the building which are modern and formed no part of the original edifice; to avoid as far as possible touching the existing portion of the old building shown as the Birthplace and to confine the works to restoring that part of the building known as the Swan and Maidenhead in accordance with the old drawing". In particular, the restoration was to be so designed as "to remove with a careful hand all those excrescences which are decidedly the result of modern innovation, to uphold with jealous care all that now exists of undoubted antiquity, not to destroy any portion about whose character the slightest doubt does now exist, but to restore any parts needing it in such manner that the restoration can never be mistaken for the old work though harmonizing with it, and lastly to adopt such measures as modern science enables us to bring to our aid for the perfect preservation of the building". In view of misleading statements which are made concerning the restoration of the Birthplace from time to time, the principles governing the restoration, as quoted, cannot be too strongly emphasized.

Mr Edward Gibbs, architect, was commissioned to prepare an estimate of the cost, with proper working plans. The estimate amounted to £692 exclusive of heating and ventilation. Tenders for the "Works to Shakespeare's House" were then invited and in August 1857 the Committee entered into a contract with William Holtom. Holtom seems to have proceeded at once, for by April 1858 the major part of the work was completed. On removing the brickwork in front of the Swan and Maidenhead portion it was found that, although the subsidiary timbers had been removed, the main beams remained showing the mortice holes. This enabled replacement to be carried out exactly on the lines of the original structure. A photograph (Plate XIX A; cf. Plate XVIII B) taken at the time of the restoration also confirms this interesting point with regard to the survival of some of the original exterior fabric on the western frontage.

In August 1858 the Committee prescribed definite hours when the Birthplace property might be seen: from 8 A.M. to 8 P.M. daily, but not after that hour; nor on Sundays during the time of divine service.

At this juncture John Shakespear died, bequeathing £2,500 for the general funds of the Committee and a sum of £60 for the maintenance of a custodian. The Committee accordingly proceeded with plans for further improvements: the restoration of the penthouse and dormer windows at the front of the building; the fitting up of the Swan and Maidenhead portion as a museum; the installation of a heating system; the planting of a yew hedge on either side of the property and the laying-out of the garden at the rear. When in the following year the solicitors refused to pay John Shakespear's legacy the Committee were faced with the expensive course of appealing to the High Court. A most serious financial position arose when the Lord Chancellor ruled that the bequest was not valid. Undaunted, the Committee proceeded. A further appeal to the public for funds to liquidate the debt was made in 1860 and all kinds of devices to raise money were used. For instance, small pieces of oak from Shakespeare's Birthplace, authenticated by a small steel die, were sold to visitors and Halliwell(-Phillipps) presented 500 copies of a reprint of Wheler's history of the building to be sold to aid the fund. The offer of a loan of £300 free of interest eventually enabled the restoration to be completed[19] and the garden to be laid out with Shakespearian trees, plants and herbs (Plate XIX).

The museum was ready by 1863 and numerous accessions of considerable interest and value had already been given or deposited. Most important were the collections of books and topographical material belonging to R. B. Wheler and Captain Saunders. The Town Council showed its interest by placing the town records and other items in the Birthplace, and the Governors of the Grammar School by depositing a sixteenth-century desk from the school. Slightly later, J. O. Halliwell(-Phillipps) and W. O. Hunt made considerable gifts of books and in 1864 the Ely Palace portrait of Shakespeare and the old oak chair from the Falcon at Bidford, known as Shakespeare's chair, were presented. These were the beginnings of the present considerable collections of books, original documents, pictures and other items illustrative of the life, works and times of Shakespeare, and of the history of Stratford-upon-Avon and locality, now in the possession of the Birthplace Trustees.[20]

In consequence of the death of two members of the Committee in 1866, it was decided to convey the Birthplace property to the Corporation of Stratford-upon-Avon and to entrust its management to a Committee consisting of certain life trustees together with *ex-officio* personages of the town and county. A deed of trust dated 4 July 1866 detailed the new arrangements which lasted until 1891, when the Shakespeare Birthplace, etc. Trust Act[21] formally incorporated the Trustees and Guardians of Shakespeare's Birthplace. The Act vested in the Trustees the Birthplace property as well as Shakespeare's New Place estate which had been purchased independently by public subscription as a national memorial in 1862. The Act contained express provisions for the maintenance of a library and museum in connection with Shakespeare's Birthplace and authorized the acquisition of any other properties "which are of national interest as being associated with the life of William Shakespeare, or his wife or parents". In accordance with these provisions the Birthplace Trustees purchased Anne Hathaway's Cottage at Shottery in 1892 and Mary Arden's House at Wilmcote in 1930 for preservation as national memorials.

The story of the administration of the Birthplace property during the last seventy years is recorded in detail in the minute-books and annual reports of the Trust. The number of visitors making their pilgrimage to the Birthplace has increased almost year by year. In 1868–9 visitors numbered just over 6,000, of whom 1,000 were Americans; during the years preceding the War of 1939–45 the number averaged nearly 100,000 a year, of whom some 40,000 came from overseas, representing over seventy different nationalities. Gifts and purchases of books, records, pictures and other exhibits have been made in increasing numbers. The Trust appointed its first part-time secretary in 1866 and its first librarian in 1873.[22] Its first full-time secretary and librarian, Richard Savage, held office from 1884 to 1910 and was succeeded by F. C. Wellstood (1910–42). In 1903 two cottages adjoining the Birthplace garden on its eastern boundary, which were occupied by the Horneby family during Shakespeare's lifetime, were presented to the Trustees by Andrew Carnegie and have since been used as offices of the Trust. In 1913 an adjoining building at the rear was partly reconstructed for use as a library, and in 1936 commodious fire-proof record rooms were erected on an adjoining site. The exhibits in the Birthplace now form only a small part of the collections owned by the Trust. An amendment to the Trust Act in 1930[23] widened the constitution of the governing body so as to include representative trustees appointed by the Universities of Oxford, Cambridge, London and Birmingham in addition to local *ex-officio* trustees and life trustees. At the same time further powers and responsibilities of an educational character were accorded to the Trust. Besides maintaining Shakespeare's house and the other Shakespearian properties, the Trust now seeks to promote knowledge of Shakespeare and his works and everything of Shakespearian interest. The services afforded to students by its library and record rooms during recent years have been steadily increasing and plans for future developments, in co-operation with the Governors of the Memorial Theatre, the British Council and the University of Birmingham, should greatly increase their usefulness.

All this had its origin in the purchase of the Birthplace property one hundred years ago.

NOTES

1. The best is R. B. Wheler's *Historical Account of the Birthplace of Shakespeare* (1824), revised and republished by J. O. Halliwell(-Phillipps) in 1863. F. W. Fairholt's *The Home of Shakespeare* (1845), republished in 1847 and 1862 and subsequently rewritten by Samuel Neil, enjoyed considerable popularity. A short modern essay is contained in Brown and Fearon's *The Shakespeares and the Birthplace* (1939).

2. For example, *The Stratford Birthplace* published by the Bacon Society.

3. A continuous series of minutes exists from 1847.

4. Especially by J. O. Halliwell(-Phillipps) in his *The Abstract of title to the house in Henley Street* (1865); *Collectanea respecting the Birth-place of Shakespeare* (1865); *Abstracts and copies of Indentures respecting estates...in Henley Street* (1866); *A letter to Professor Karl Elze* (1888); and *New Evidences in confirmation of the traditional recognition of Shakespeare's Birthroom* (1888).

5. The original deed is preserved among the Birthplace collection.

6. Two painted signboards which hung in front and at the back of the inn from 1806 to 1847 are preserved in the Birthplace. The smaller board has at the bottom the name of the proprietress, "Eliz[th]. Court", who died in 1846.

7. Published in the *Gentleman's Magazine*, vol. VIII (1769), facing p. 345, with the caption: "A House in Stratford-upon-Avon, in which the famous Poet Shakespear was Born". The writer of the letter which accompanied this engraving says: "I do not know whether the apartment where the incomparable Shakespeare first drew his breath can, at this day, be ascertained, or not; but the house of his nativity (according to undoubted tradition) is now remaining. My worthy friend Mr Greene, of this place [Litchfield] hath favoured me with an exact drawing of it (here inclosed) which may not possibly be an unacceptable present to such of your readers as intend to honour Stratford with their company at the approaching jubilee...." A slightly later but almost identical representation is an etching by Colonel Philip de la Motte, 1788, preserved among the Birthplace collection. There is a drawing of about the same date in the King's Library, British Museum.

8. The Birthplace Trustees possess a large collection of material relating to the Garrick Jubilee.

9. Torrington diaries, Stratford section, preserved among the Birthplace collection.

10. A silhouette portrait of Mrs Hornby (20 May 1841) is exhibited in the Birthplace.

11. S. Ireland, *Picturesque Views on the Upper or Warwickshire Avon* (1795).

12. *Birmingham Gazette*, 26 November 1804.

13. Byng refers to the poverty of the Hart family in 1785.

14. The auctioneer's copy, containing his notes and record of the bids, as well as the certificate of purchase, is preserved among the Birthplace collection.

15. This and subsequent statements of the Committee's activities are based on the evidence of the Committee's minutes.

16. Copies of the appeal notices, playbills, etc. mentioned are preserved among the Birthplace collection.

17. An engraved portrait by Wageman of Thomas Amyot (1775–1850) is exhibited in the Birthplace.

18. The original autograph of the offer is exhibited in the Birthplace.

19. A photograph taken in 1864, reproduced as an illustration, shows the penthouse reconstructed in accordance with the earliest representations by Greene and de la Motte.

20. The Birthplace exhibits are described in F. C. Wellstood's *Catalogue of the Books, Manuscripts, Works of Art, Antiquities and Relics exhibited in Shakespeare's Birthplace*.

21. 54 Vict. cap. III, 1891.

22. Charles Jackman, librarian (1873–9); succeeded by Bruce Tyndall (1880–2).

23. Shakespeare Birthplace, etc. Trust (Amendment) Act, 20 Geo. V, cap. LIX, 1930.

THREE SHAKESPEARIAN PRODUCTIONS:
A CONVERSATION

BY

MICHEÁL MacLIAMMÓIR

SCENE *A stone terrace in Sicily*

PERSONAGES

HILTON EDWARDS, *a producer*   MICHEÁL MACLIAMMÓIR, *an actor and designer*

MACLIAMMÓIR (*emerging into the evening sunshine as he continues a sentence presumably launched upon indoors*) ...and anyway, who wants to talk of the stage in such a setting? Are you anxious, now you have escaped to Paradise for a season, to recall the agonies endured in a dusty theatre in Dublin, to consider seriously the drawbacks and advantages of the Elizabethan manner, to rack your brains in an endeavour to remember exactly why you were a little bored by any modern effort to revive that manner, or why the Shakespearian producer is at sea the moment that manner is abandoned?

EDWARDS I would not have been bored in Shakespeare's day. Not because my own mentality as a spectator would have been different, but because the actors themselves, with their fresher understanding, their surety of purpose, their reliance on their own craft instead of the electricians' and the dressmakers', their direct contact with their audience which is a forgotten secret of Shakespeare's magic, would have revealed the plays as no mouthing nineteenth-century Hamlet or muttering, impotent Othello of our own day can do, with all the ingenuity of our lighting, our swiftly-changing scenery, our amusing, fashionable disguises. Still I admit—

MACLIAMMÓIR Whatever you admit, you have not told me why we must discuss the theatre. I might as well have come to Sicily with William Poel or Gordon Craig. Everything you look at is bounded by the borders of the proscenium.

EDWARDS (*unconscious of any interruption*) I admit that the stage of Shakespeare's day had its limitations. An absolute visual monotony can be as distracting to the pleasure of the ear as the dazzling vulgarity and variety of a non-stop revue....Did I hear you mention a proscenium just now?

MACLIAMMÓIR You did. I was about to say it had ruined your life.

EDWARDS It has ruined the lives of better Shakespearian producers than I. It is one of the first things that, if I were able to build the theatre I should like, I would abolish.

MACLIAMMÓIR And yet how delightful it is! One arrives in front of that great hidden altar of the stage, the red velvet or the golden damask blooms with light, the orchestra is tuning up—

EDWARDS Clicking, scraping, whispering and coughing; a lot of tired trade-unionists in a dazzle of reflected light that illuminates everything but their own scores. The visible presence of these gentlemen, whether waiting for some cue for their incidental infernalia, or creeping noisily in and out of a creaking door under the stage, is an outrage on the actors and the play. They should be seldom heard and never seen.

89

MACLIAMMÓIR   A breath of wind causes the curtains to tremble. The lights are lowered in the auditorium. Who knows what is in store for us?

EDWARDS   If you are thinking of a Shakespeare production I can tell you precisely what's in store for us. A choice of three types of spectacle: The Benson School: rostrum at the back, chairs, tables and thrones in isolated places, pillars supporting nothing in particular, tasteful curtains, a bowdlerized version of operatic Renaissance cum pseudo-Elizabethan costume and setting, generally borrowed from other plays—Orlando wearing Romeo's tights and the battlements of Elsinore passing themselves off as Portia's garden at Belmont. West End: an inconceivably super-mechanized simplicity with sliding doors, revolving staircases and hydraulic lifts, revealing an occasional magnificent full set in one style followed by a succession of frontcloths in another; two or perhaps three performances that are really first-rate, and a support cast of beautifully-bred young things who have never learned to breathe. Experimental: a bare stage with possibly a square or triangular block or so of unknown origin, a few pools of light that appear and disappear like fireworks at a *festa*, Malvolio in a bowler hat and Rosalind in jodhpurs, and Lear or Richard II entrusted to a young man who has just published his third volume of verse (very slim) at his own expense and is now turning his attention for the first time to acting.

MACLIAMMÓIR   And how often at the Gate in Dublin we have emerged with a production that had the best and the worst of all these elements. How easy it is, when viewing one's own work or that of other theatres from a distance, to see what is wrong. It is their distance from the human struggle that leads one to suspect the integrity of the critics or the justice of the Almighty. How easy for us, now that we look back on our own work, to see what was wrong with our *Antony and Cleopatra*, in spite of its popularity, or with our six different productions of *Hamlet*, or with our *Merchant* last year, though this I think was our best endeavour in Shakespearian comedy, as certainly Shylock was the best performance you have given. *Antony and Cleopatra* suffered from a multiplicity of styles; the problem posed by Shakespeare of a story that moves rapidly from Egypt to Rome, to Sicily, and to a series of battlefields in varying places, is, architecturally alone, once one has abandoned the Elizabethan system of allowing the script to perform the function of the scenic artist as well as that of the actor, impossibly difficult.

EDWARDS   So what did we do? Saddled from the outset with the presence of a proscenium...

MACLIAMMÓIR   Ah, we're back at the proscenium.

EDWARDS   Would that we could ever leave it. Hampered by its inevitable presence as my compatriots are hampered from birth by a sense of law and order and yours by the terror of the life to come, we decided on a pictorial method that the shifting from Egypt to Rome and back again made impracticable the old trick of having arches and pillars as a permanent framework for movable pieces, and we started off, if you remember, by having as our only solid structure the one architectural form that could conceivably be the same in both countries: the floor.

MACLIAMMÓIR   Yes, the international groundwork. Bakst would have designed a series of wonderful arabesques, and Picasso have ignored it altogether, but we were dealing not with dancers but with actors, so we built a rostrum with a series of shallow steps which remained steps as long as one trod on them, but which, when spread with carpets, mantles and cushions by the handmaidens of the Queen, when surrounded by negroes bearing fans and tridents and

THREE SHAKESPEARIAN PRODUCTIONS: A CONVERSATION

the images of the gods borne upon gilded staffs, and when sat upon by Cleopatra, became the throne of Egypt; when reclined upon by Meriel Moore as the Queen and by myself as Antony they appeared to be a couch for the cooling of a gypsy's lust; when sprawled over by drunken officers and canopied by painted sails drawn down from the flies by a group of seemingly sea-faring supers they became the deck of a barge; when four Roman soldiers stood there with banners and lictors they became the royal seat of Caesar, and so on.

EDWARDS   So far, so good. At both sides of these rostra, incongruous as it may sound, there rose, if you remember, great black towers, square towers that had no nation; in many of the scenes the entire stage was sealed in blackness, and the scarlet and gold of the Roman troops or the white and turquoise and lapis-lazuli, the litters and the lotus flowers and the serpents of the Egyptians were the only indications of locality: a *décor* composed solely of players and pro-perties. And very satisfying it was; but you with your claustrophobic desire for fresh air, your restless demand for change and your terror of the audience's wondering exactly where they were at any given moment, insisted on opening the blacks at the back to reveal the sky or alternatively a series of cloths painted in the manner of Egyptian frescoes. I never really liked the mixture, for although the sky gave luminous depth and the frescoes a mysterious archaic quality, they represented two directly opposite methods of handling and the full blacks represented a third, and that was where we went astray. Our first idea of a completely neutral and unchanging background—or rather my idea, for it was you who opposed it—was more akin to the method of the stage for which Shakespeare wrote although its appearance was new, for in it the actors told the story and the lines they spoke or the properties they carried in their hands or drew down from the borders gave the essential keynote of the setting; and although I admit that your innovations lent us an amusing variety and were in themselves very pleasing—your tent scene at Philippi and the interior of the pyramid in the last act, emerging gradually from the surrounding blacks into a blaze of colour and seeming as if painted upon the darkness, were very lovely—no, don't bow and fool about, I'm quite serious —they were essentially wrong.

MACLIAMMÓIR   Theoretically, yes. But I have an instinctive distrust of any theory in the theatre that is not borne out by the reaction, not only of myself, but of the audience. In fact, the audience's visual and aural faculties were stimulated simultaneously by our *Antony*: that surely is what is important.

EDWARDS   Visually they were stimulated in jerks. That is offensive. And while I agree with you that no theory is worth while in the theatre that does not prove itself by instantaneous result, I would point out that if Shakespeare himself had written higgeldy-piggeldy in order to produce a series of disconnected sensations, if he had followed no long line, if in short he had had no theory at all, the plays would not be what they are.

MACLIAMMÓIR   He wrote alternatively in blank verse, rhyming couplets and prose.

EDWARDS   But always with a purpose, never disconnectedly. Our *Antony* sets represented a clever but not completely honest avoidance of incidental difficulties; and while you achieved a series of pleasing spectacles as well as continuity of action, the necessity of which has never apparently occurred to continental producers of Shakespeare, you did not achieve a continuity of emotion or of style, and this seems to me, more and more, the chief problem concerned in the presentation of the plays.

91

MacLiammóir Ah, continuity! That is your greatest obsession, and I must admit that after experiencing the long programme-rustling, torch-searching intervals that succeeded each short scene in Berlin or in Venice or in Athens, I have come, in spite of the elaborately built-up *décor* that followed them, to agree with you.

Edwards One thing, of course, must be said. In Europe, I mean in real Europe, not our island fringe, the stress is laid on the player, not on the producer, and that surely is nearer to Shakespeare's aim than the most harmoniously ingenious continuity of production ever devised. If Cleopatra is perfectly played, who cares how long one waits before her throne is ready to receive her?

MacLiammóir Cleopatra is never perfectly played. I did not see Constance Collier's performance and perhaps that is why I have yet to find the actress who could combine the gypsy's lust with the immobile majesty of Egypt, the petulant child with the immemorial wisdom of the serpent. Still less have I found the actress to agree with me that Shakespeare's heroine was one who at her most ecstatic moments saw, from almost disembodied eyes of an inconceivably diabolic sophistication, the occasional deliberate absurdity of her own rhapsodies. Cleopatra's tantrums, her treatment of messengers and servants, her monotonous insistence on the inferior charms of her rivals, her deadly playfulness, her fatuous incompetence, her poisonous interference, are tedious beyond endurance if they are taken with solemn literality by the actress: the four-square portrait of the barbaric *femme fatale* is not enough to satisfy us any more and we can be certain it never satisfied the poet; no, surely something more subtle, more ingenious, more fifth-dimensional is at work, and that something is the ability to step out of the conscious self and to watch its antics as from a remote distance with the silent ferocious pleasure of the spectator of disaster. Mrs Patrick Campbell, who possessed in her own life this curious detachment from herself—it was indeed her chief quality—might have expressed it: I think she never played the part, and certainly, perhaps because of this very faculty, that suggests, as in Cleopatra herself, a demon unwilling or unable to be mastered by a greater mind than her own, she was no Shakespearian. But apart from this you will say that if a poor production lacking continuity or an indifferent *décor* wanting in cohesion and harmony cannot seriously impair the value of an actor's performance, how much less can the presence of these, discreetly utilized and kept deliberately in a position of subservience to the actor's art, do so.

Edwards It is an irritating trick of yours, this habit of forecasting what one will say. I have a good deal more to say on the subject of the relations of the Shakespearian actor with the production than the observation that a perfectly prepared field of action is less likely to hamper a performance than one that is ill-prepared. That is too obvious for comment, although there are still in the world of the theatre actors who believe that the old indiscriminate jumble of full-sets, front curtains, and back-cloths that look like monstrous enlargements of third-rate water-colour landscapes of the spinster school, are less distracting as a background to their art than the most unobtrusive of innovations.

MacLiammóir One sees what they mean, of course. The late Victorian public, of which so many survivals fill the dress-circle to the present day, accepted what we might call the Tunbridge Wells manner as a matter of course, so it and all its modest horrors are forgotten when the actor begins to speak.

EDWARDS Exactly. Even a poor convention can grow in the mind of the well-trained spectator into the correct position of an accepted and fully comprehended background of secondary importance, like the table from which a meal is served. Then why, the Elizabethans having achieved the obvious table for the Shakespearian meal, and the poet himself having clearly prepared his dishes for that particular style of table, why must we serve him up on packing-cases, the tops of wardrobes, mantle-pieces, swinging shelves, Axminster carpets, the grass of public parks—anything and everything but the table originally designed for the purpose which, in spite of inadequacies, is still by far the nearest to the ideal that anyone has yet discovered? That it was not wholly adequate to satisfy the changing taste and more elaborate demands of a dwindling public imagination I do not deny—it is strange, by the way, that the greater the decline of the imaginative faculty the more ravenous becomes its appetite for synthetic food in the shape of realistic trappings—and in fact our answer is probably this. The principle of the Elizabethan manner of presenting Shakespeare remains by far the most satis-factory yet discovered, but there seems to be no reason why this should not be augmented and embellished by certain modern advantages.

MacLiammóir We want in fact a form that combines the excellencies of modern ingenuity with the evocative potency of the Elizabethan stage: the plays are here, and our generation has—in spite of its Edwardian training— its wits about it still. But if, apart from the questions of acting and of popular success, you feel we failed in *Antony and Cleopatra* because of a mingling of styles, how do you regard our last *Hamlet* which we played in modern dress in a setting of Gothic arches and pillars and tapestries that had a faintly Byzantine appearance due, no doubt, to my having been with you in Greece the previous summer?

EDWARDS Describe it: I can't remember it: it was the sixth attempt at a play that has always filled me with despair, and of which, on looking back, I have forgotten everything except how tired I am of playing Claudius. Didn't we have a curving rostrum that surrounded the stage, with three flights of steps—cutting out all thought of that infernal invention called a front cloth with the use of light?

MacLiammóir That was the second production or possibly the fourth. No, in our last we used an enormous central pillar with flying buttresses; the pillar was bedecked with banners—

EDWARDS Dear me!

MacLiammóir They were very dim banners. And very high up. Also there were two sets of tapestries drawn up, simultaneously or alternately, to meet the pillar, forming—when they were closed—a big triangular interior. A glorified front cloth in fact.

EDWARDS Yes, but a front cloth that supplied not merely an acting space but a shapely one, furnished with two permanent arches, a pillar with a stone seat at its base, and other seats and steps that gave the actor something more to do than merely to stand about and declaim in a corridor. These tapestries when opened revealed either exterior sets or inner rooms, whose furnishings had been set during the period in which the tapestries were closed. A sound if somewhat hackneyed device.

MacLiammóir Theoretically smacking of the charade, but in practice inevitable, and not— if carried out *pianissimo* by the staff—unpleasing. The light, too, gradually changed in view of the audience, and the curtain was only lowered to notify an interval. There was no need, except that of social convention and an immoral desire for applause, to lower it at all.

EDWARDS That's better.

MACLIAMMÓIR I felt much happier as Hamlet in a double-breasted black suit than I had ever felt in the doubtful authenticity of a doublet that was neither Danish, Italian, nor English. Modernity of the detailed kind that brings plus-fours, cigarettes and whiskys-and-sodas to the majesty of Shakespeare's speech is loathsome, but we did, I think, preserve the sense of the play's timelessness more successfully by the use of a dignified and non-committal contemporary costume—the men in uniforms or evening clothes with orders, the women in court dress with tiaras, long gloves and bouquets of orchids and gardenias—than by the most picturesque abstractions of 'period' origin. Your admiration and use of Dover Wilson's analysis—notably that of Hamlet's overhearing of the plot between the King and Polonius—I found invaluable, though I remember quarrelling bitterly with some of the points before we had put them into action; and on the whole, though it was far from perfect, our sixth and seventh productions of *Hamlet* (they were almost identical) were the best we have done. The only thing I disliked was the frequent loss of the use of the full stage—an inevitable result of dividing the acting-space into three or more parts by pillars, arches and curtains. The Queen's closet, I felt, was cramped, although by your diagonal use of moonlight on the down-stage portion of the set you included this as part of a rambling and oddly shaped room which allowed to Coralie Carmichael and myself the full use of the forestage when the action demanded it, and the battlement scenes were not improved by the overshadowing presence of the central pillar against the sky, that made one feel one was being watched from a gigantic loggia. However, on the Elizabethan stage of which you are so fond one wouldn't have a sky at all; still less, I suppose, that marvellous dawn you caused to creep at the heels of the cloaked and helmeted figures at the end of the first act, or the shafts of evening light that heralded the approach of Fortinbras at the end of the play, and seemed to break from the interminable gloom of sulphurous clouds as if in relief at the death of that poisonous royal family. How poisonous they really are, and what a legacy they must have bequeathed to Hamlet's blood: the sluggish undercurrent in the river of fire! And how right I was to insist upon the colours of the court, not in scarlet and gold as is so often imagined, but in thick silvers and greens and purples and cyclamens, the orchids and gardenias, the orders and the jewels, the corruption of a sort of martialized hothouse, with the one black note of mourning in the figure of the prince.

EDWARDS The double-breasted suit. Yes. But all this is visual, and even visually our *Hamlet* has never completely satisfied me, though somewhere the secret lies of the perfect mould for its expression, and a simpler mould, too, than is demanded by many of the plays because the action is less scattered: except for the Polish captain scene the story unfolds itself in and about Elsinore and some great structure with the slightest and most silent of changes should suffice. But what *Hamlet* really needs, what all the plays need, is the full apron-stage, or if you like, the circus ring; an acting space not merely confronted by the audience, but surrounded by them. Think of the solidity, the reality of it all—the reality, not the mere realism. Think of the contact with the audience, that living stream that flows between performer and spectator, that miracle of the theatre which Shakespeare more than any dramatist since the Greeks understood so fully, and which remains the only quality of the theatre unconquerable by the cinema, however perfected it may become.

MACLIAMMÓIR I like that. The art of the painter retiring before that of the sculptor, so that the players, instead of appearing as remote two-dimensional figures on a framed tapestry, become live statues in our midst, and we see Othello's rage or Lear's madness from every angle, the back of the neck, the sinews of the thighs, doing their work as well as the painted mask. But would one not lose the setting, not merely the picture, but the visible indication of whereabouts, the valuable background, the whole keynote of the scene? And how would your actors make their entrances and exits?

EDWARDS What is to stop an apron-stage from the possession of a permanent ordinary stage from which it springs? With a curtain and even a proscenium and any sort of setting you like? The only difference would be that it would no longer be the only or even the principal field of action, any more than the alcoves of our Gothic-Byzantine twentieth-century production were for *Hamlet*. As for the furniture—never an overwhelmingly important factor in Shakespeare: a divan, a throne, a couple of stools, he seldom insists on more—this could be placed on the apron at will by property men in the Chinese manner, or better still by servants who are also characters in the play. Do you remember the eight pierrots in our *Merchant of Venice*?

MACLIAMMÓIR I was about to remind you of them. The *Merchant of Venice*, although we used no apron-stage, seems to me by far the nearest approach to what we are both seeking than anything else that we have done.

EDWARDS I always felt you resented the eighteenth-century innovation.

MACLIAMMÓIR Only at first. The idea on paper or in words smacks of pointlessness and affectation, and there is still to my ears something a little odd about handing over Shakespeare's characters to Goldoni, especially in settings that were like a series of Veronese pictures; yet how well it all worked out. And what a reality the snuff-boxes and the three-cornered hats lent to those awful Salarios and Salanios and Salerinos; what conviction there was in the scene where Shylock returns to find an empty house, fighting his way through the crowds of masked and garlanded revellers under showers of streamers and petals; what solidity the more precise and easily understood period lent to the relations of Bassanio and Antonio, and to the Charles Perrault fairy-tale atmosphere of the casket-scenes. When the first curtain rose on Molly MacEwen's setting of Renaissance arches with their looped and festooned curtains and wreaths and gilded cupids, and one saw the figures of the *Commedia dell' Arte* dance forward with the great banner bearing the words "The Tragical-Comical History of the Merchant of Venice by William Shakespeare", and all to the accompaniment of Frascobaldi's languorous gaiety so divertingly pointed to by the background of masked and lace-shrouded dancers, one felt the authentic Venetian thrill and knew that one was in for something that, however incongruous, was going to be good. Then the pierrots pulled a little café with chairs and tables on to the pavement, and one of them, throwing a napkin over his arm, became a waiter; Harlequin beat with his wand upon an enormous *portière* swung between the marble pillars and lo! we were in a public place in Venice, and the dandies and idlers came sauntering over a ridiculous little bridge (also set by the pierrots to one of Scarlatti's brisker moods), tapping with their canes upon the table, ordering their wine, and discussing the anatomy of melancholy. Yes, I was easily won over to the swinging forward of the story to the grand century: it gave at the same time lightness and brilliance and conviction to a play of which we are all secretly a little tired, and did not obscure the action or the characterization as a still more beautiful and far more mechanically elaborate production at Stratford some years ago tended to do; and the Dublin audience, as weary as any in the world of the pseudo-Renaissance literal treatment of Shake-speare and of this play in particular, rewarded us by thronging to the doors. Of course this was mainly to see your Shylock and Ginette Waddell's Portia; but the gaiety and the freedom of the handling, the Scaramouche-like Gobbo, the pierrots who turned into Spanish courtiers or Moorish guards, the Harlequinesque changes of scene, had something to do with it too. It was completely your production, more even than most, and the settings were Molly MacEwen at her very best, so I can praise for once with no fear of the clutching hand of modesty or self-mistrust at my heart.

EDWARDS The critics didn't agree with you. At least not all of them. Wait though; the daily papers as far as I remember approved, but some of the monthly magazines ignored it altogether and at least one weekly objected to the idea of dressing up the Bard in order to intrigue the public, the writer adding bluntly that he preferred his Shakespeare straight. What, I should like to know, is straight Shakespeare? Only one: the Elizabethan, open-air stage and all; and it is unlikely that this was what any Dublin weekly would have in view. Possibly what was meant was a rehash of the Benson school with new curtains if essential. But the Benson school was in itelf an innovation, and was no straighter than any other innovation thought out by generations of distracted producers since the day when the wooden O, the three doorways, and the central balcony were deserted. We cannot wholeheartedly return to this austerity, partly because the weather in our islands must have changed or the public hardiness deteriorated since Elizabeth's day, and partly because we have nowadays, among other less excellent things, certain mechanical advantages of the stage that it would seem foolish to resist using; and also because the plays are not in their essence confined to their period, and there seems no good reason beyond those of scholarship on the one hand or on the other of mere artiness to present them simply as museum-pieces. Their endless complications, however, once the producer leaves their original form of presentation behind him, have become not only a delight, but a torment to him, and though I share with you a small satisfaction in remembering our *Merchant*, especially the idea of having a band of actors who are in and yet not of the play to do the work usually allotted, in a childish hide-behind-the-curtain secrecy that deceives nobody, to the scene-shifter, I do not believe for a second that this is a final answer to the question of how to do the plays. At present there is a perpetual quarrel between representational scenery and the demand for continuity, between the theatre of the spoken word, which is slowly but surely finding its expression in the radio, and that of visual appeal which has already given satisfaction in the cinema. In fact the theatre, that should give voice to what is happening now, as opposed to the art of the screen, which is, as you yourself have often complained, a mere record of what has already happened in the past, the modern theatre is faced with how to discover continuity, beauty, and consistency when dealing with the works of Shakespeare; and this problem we have so far not solved ourselves, nor indeed have we seen it solved by others. A revolving stage occurs to one's mind, but I have an instinctive mistrust of a question that is fundamentally artistic being handed over lock, stock and barrel to the inventiveness of the engineer. This is what has happened in the world of the cinema, with the result that the film is becoming more and more the product of the laboratory and less and less the medium for the art of acting. No, we must rediscover the secret of Shakespeare for ourselves; and though I know you do not altogether agree with me in this, I still believe that somewhere lies the formula, close to the one for which Shakespeare wrote, yet more beautiful, more evocative, and more varying, that would be a key to them all. It would be a manner further removed from that of the cinema than any used by the stage since the end of the seventeenth century, for its first principle would be that contact of the player with his audience that is the most precious quality of the living theatre, and that survives to-day, ironically enough, only in the music-hall; and whenever an actor has objected to the direct address, the direct appeal, the calling of the public into his confidence and the sharing with them of his secret, which is a vital part of the soliloquy, I feel it in my bones that what prompts his objection is the framed-in isolation of the proscenium and footlighted stage that sets a barrier between itself and the auditorium, and that renders any attempt on the actor's part to break that barrier down a self-conscious and artificial process. Therefore the big oval-shaped apron would be one of the first things which in the theatre I really want I would insist upon; and I am not at all certain that Shakespeare and the other Elizabethans are the only authors for whom it could be used. By that curious reaction of what at the moment we call modernity towards archaicism of form, Rouault and Picasso in painting, and Joyce and Gertrude Stein in the novel, we see already writers in the theatre whose tendencies are all towards the old direct appeal, and whose plays cry out for a breaking up of this infernal frame-work that the cinema has not only copied but improved. I am thinking, of course, of Cocteau, Sartre, O'Casey, Thornton Wilder, and our own early Denis Johnston. But this is no place to talk of contemporaries.

MacLiammóir No: in Sicily nothing is new except of course the roulette at the Hôtel Flora and the value of the lira. That is what is so superbly uneuropean about it, and what makes it so restful for the worker in the theatre, even if that worker does come to its shores from Ireland. For whatever in Ireland we think about the theatre to-day, we may be sure that northern Europe, at any rate, has thought of and probably discarded yesterday, and that at least is something that Ireland possesses in common with England. Look, it is almost dark. In an hour's time we shall dine, and a Sicilian dinner annihilates all desire for discussion. Why don't we walk down to the Greek theatre...there is no proscenium there, or any painted cloth except that of the evening sky over Etna to enrage you; and if it is not too late in the year, let us see if we cannot hear the solution of Shakespeare in the conversation of the Birds and the Frogs.

FOUR LEARS

BY

CHARLES LANDSTONE

The middle-aged and the old admit that the English Theatre is, to-day, at the richest point within their memory. Wealth is offered on every side and certainly no generation before has been given the opportunity of seeing four different interpretations of *Lear* in as many months, all offered by companies of reputation. I myself, with my grey hairs, have only twice before seen the play.

So much has been written about the London Old Vic production that I will be brief about it. At the risk of being deemed a blasphemer, let me say that I did not think this a great *King Lear* nor did I think it one of Sir Laurence Olivier's great performances. I did not feel that it could compare with either his Richard Third or his Oedipus, in both of which parts he had sought and found the soul of the character. In *Lear*, it seemed to me, he was not concerned to identify himself with the raging torrent that stormed through the mind of the poor madman; his chief aim, I felt, was to make the public accept his own objective interpretation of an old dotard. One should not be hide-bound by tradition, but it is difficult to believe in a Lear whose "Every inch a king" is not a boastful assertion of his unquestionable majesty, but a casual aside which, to those who do not know the play, might pass unnoticed. Surely the words demand declamation and no other intention can have been in the author's mind. It is only the incomparable magnetism and vigour of Olivier's personality that made one understand the carefully thought-out reason behind this interpretation. His Lear is a king who has always been a king, who has never questioned his own majesty, and when Gloucester asks him "Is it the King?" the matter to him is so obvious that it hardly seems worth a reply. It was on this conception that the whole performance was built. The deliberate caprice and pranking of the first act gave us a testy old man for whom it was difficult to obtain sympathy in the later scenes; but it would be wrong to suggest that it was possible to sit unmoved whilst Olivier's overwhelming sense of poetry wafted us through the grandeurs of the last act. Olivier is master of the unexpected.

I always long to see a dogma refuted, so it made me sad to find here the proof of the old axiom that a leading actor should not be his own producer. The scenes in which Lear himself did not appear were masterpieces of brilliant construction. Watch and note how Regan turns as she spits out at Gloucester "Why to Dover?". The effect of that move is to increase a thousandfold the malice of her words.

The success of the evening was achieved by Margaret Leighton. Here is an actress whose work so far has not been above the commonplace. At one stride, as the treacherous, vengeful Regan, she reached the front rank. The eye-gouging scene, which she commanded, had real greatness. Pamela Brown gave evil to Goneril—but it was an actress, acting evil. And as for Cordelia—oh, naughty Joyce Redman! Where is the Solveig that once tore at our hearts?

This is not the place to dilate upon Alec Guiness. His Fool was exquisite, tender, tragi-comic and pathetically human. Coming as it did shortly after his brutal and egoistic violence in Sartre's *Vicious Circle*, it showed that his way to stardom is surely mapped out.

There was an almost unhealthy hysteria both inside and outside the theatre on the first night. Elbowing my way through the crowd in the street (cheering they did not know what), I noticed in front of me a young man wildly clapping his hands. As I could see ahead of me the burly figure of Mr John Wilmot, the Minister of Supply and a Governor of the Old Vic, I presumed that this was just some keen young Socialist applauding his party. But as I drew level, the young man applauded just as heartily, and as I have no delusions about my own importance, I realized this was nothing but mass hysteria. However, I think that when all the tumult and the shouting has died down, this production will be given its true perspective, both in the history of the Old Vic and in the history of Olivier's career.

Some weeks later I went to Huddersfield to see the West Riding production. I did not particularly want to go. I felt that I had had my ration of *Lear* for the year. But I had not long been sitting in this sprawling Victorian theatre, before I realized that it had been the Old Vic production which had failed to whet my appetite. I found that the chief asset of Gabriel Toyne's production was that it presented a tale which actively sustained one's interest in its development. The set, a blasted rocky heath reminiscent of Stonehenge, was unchanged throughout, and the dim-out at the end of each scene, followed by the varying uses of exits and entrances, really gave the illusion of changing locale. Simple in details, the production was carried out as one continuous unstressed movement and made the whole play a straightforward story, which could be easily understood and appreciated even by the most juvenile mind. Only the lighting was here and there at fault, the storm scene having no sense of brooding doom.

I hope I shall not be thought patronizing if I say that this offering by an ambitious Repertory organization reflected the greatest credit on the actors, the producer, the designer and the English theatre as a whole. Philip Morant, a young actor in his thirties, gave a performance as Lear which was something more than a fine effort. Except for small patches it reached definite achievement. It was a consistent attempt to build up the character from that of the doting old man to the madman, followed by the return to the quiet placidity of the recovered mind. Sometimes it did not reach the heights (principally in the storm scene), but the gentle pathos of the line "Let me not be mad" was something to be remembered. His conception and his interpretation were magnificent. Occasionally his imagination was at fault. Yet it was a *Lear* well worth the doing and well worth the seeing, and Morant is an actor well worth the watching.

The supporting cast was repertory of a high standard with two outstanding performances. Willoughby Gray was a fine villainous Edmund, with a sound command of voice and technique; Ninka Dolega brought integrity and loveliness to Cordelia. Her voice could not, at times, conquer the range, though otherwise she has all the gifts of an accomplished actress.

It may be that I was unfortunate in seeing the production of the Bristol Old Vic Company on the second night, when not only was there the usual inevitable reaction, but also it happened that there had been a matinée in the afternoon. *Lear* is a long work and it cannot be easy at any time to play for what amounts to eight hours at a stretch with only a short pause half-way—to do so on top of all excitement of a first night is to ask for superhuman effort. I am prepared to believe that, seen under more favourable circumstances, the performance would have given a greater elation.

William Devlin's Lear has too settled a framework. Within that framework it is massive, impressive, at times anguishing in its overpowering immensity, but its mould is too firm. From the first line the actor has announced himself, and one knows that never will he step out into the unexpected. The result is that the doting father turns into the madman, the madman outbids the storm, there is the thunder of the elements in his majesty as he asserts every inch of his kingliness, we have spent nearly four hours in the presence of barbaric and primeval passions, expressed with a violent and beautiful sense of poetry, and yet the emotional experience has never reached the sublime.

But perhaps 'never' is too violent a word. When this Lear is outraged by his two daughters, when he feels the storm breaking both on his head and within his mind, then Devlin reaches greatness. The brain is still in full command, but there dawns upon it, for the first time, the possibility that it may loose its grip, and all the knowledge of a losing battle being fought is thronged into the one line, "Let me not be mad". It is not a cry built upon pathos. It is the reasoned plea of a majestic mind. Save in the final scene Devlin does not reach that majesty again.

There are other factors which, one feels, contribute to the lack of elation. The picture is over-crowded with scenery too circumstantial for so small a stage. Hugh Hunt is a master of production. He brings deft touches in which one recognizes his original genius. I liked especially the moment when Lear, storming at Kent, seizes the royal emblem from his standard bearer to emphasize the line, "Hear me, recreant! On thine allegiance, hear me!" and I liked very much the groupings in his first and final scenes. Very clever also was the way Goneril was made to play with Oswald's love. But Hunt will not work within his medium. He demands a setting which will match not the playhouse, but the majesty of the play. For this purpose, Guy Shephard, the designer, is his man. His work is superb, and it is not his fault that at times it preponderates over the action.

The other performances—a finely spoken Kent, a glamorous, devilish Edmund, a likeable Fool who just failed to extract all the possibilities from the part, and the greatest Goneril of our time.

It is difficult to take one's eyes from Rosalie Crutchley when she is upon the stage. There is a malevolent evil in her every movement; here indeed is the beauteous devil incarnate. To her all men are fools, and she has nothing but scorn for the old dotard who is her father, but she knows how to dissemble in order to gain her ends. There is decision in her simulated languor; and her lank fingers have the beauty of swaying tendrils and the urgency of a beast of prey. The rasp of her voice can chill her husband or make the Fool tremble, but she can coo like a dove so that Oswald or Edmund melt in her arms. As she sits brooding in her chair, the mind of the onlooker trembles at the terrible thoughts which are so evidently racing through her brain. A beautifully designed dress by Kathleen Ankers added a finish to an overpowering performance.

Robert Eddison is certainly the most handsome Edmund that ever trod the stage, and with it he is an accomplished villain. He gauges the part rightly in that he plays upon the charm which it is inevitable the man must have if all the world are to become his dupes. There is strength throughout this performance and nothing craven in his death.

The fuel restriction and cancelled trains made me miss the opening scenes at Liverpool Play-house. I arrived at Regan's court, to find Kent and Oswald in tussle. At this point one character only has really shot his bolt—Edmund's chief scenes have passed and it would be unfair to judge him by his performance in the rest of the play. Though it is a pity not to have seen the partitioning, or the violence of Goneril in the second scene, there was enough of the real meat of *Lear* left to make the passing of a judgement permissible.

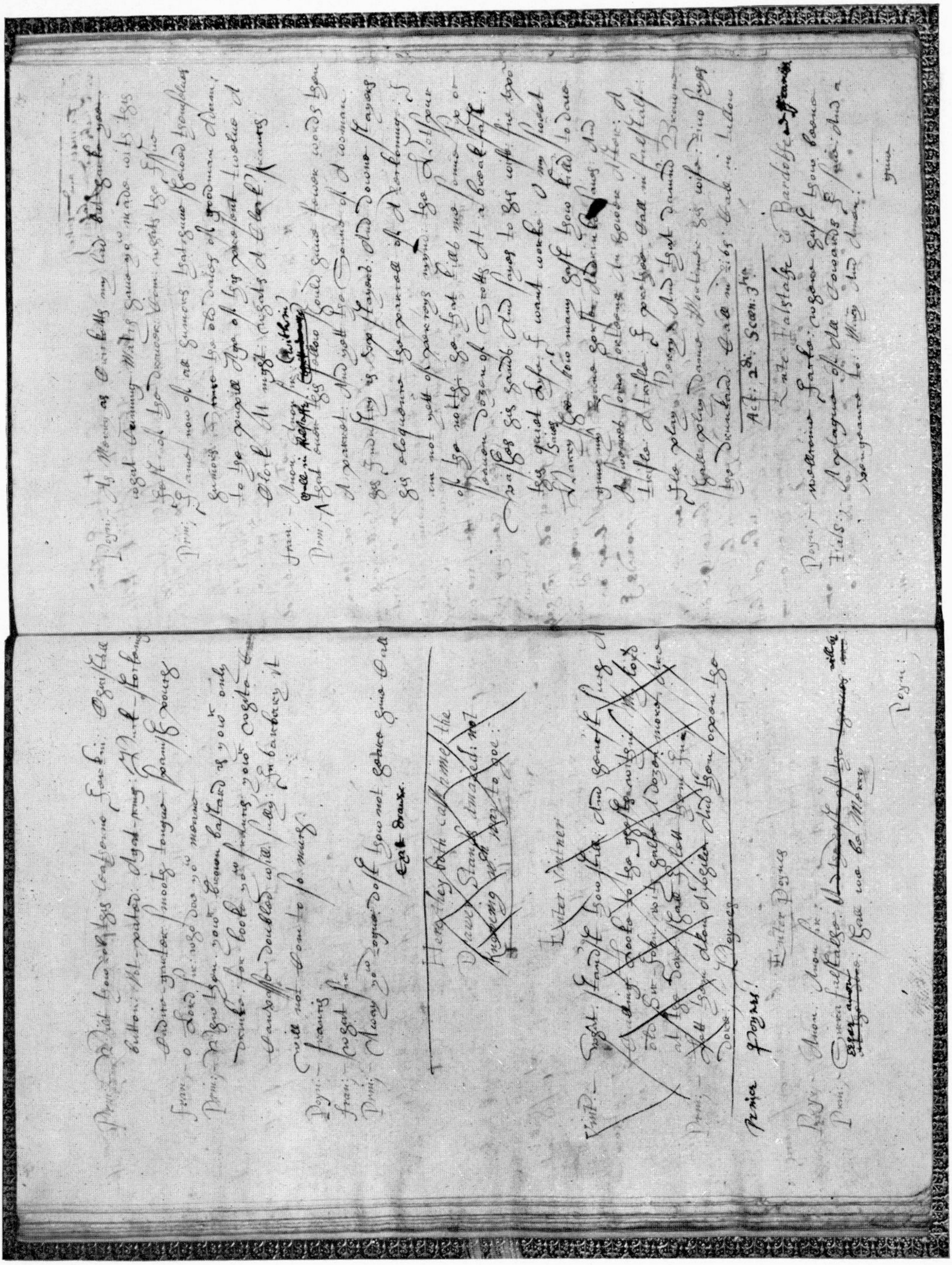

PLATE XVII

Henry IV. Two pages from the Dering Manuscript
(Folger Shakespeare Library)

PLATE XVIII

A. SHAKESPEARE'S BIRTHPLACE. Earliest known representation
of the Birthplace: engraving by R. GREENE
(British Museum)

B. SHAKESPEARE'S BIRTHPLACE, 1856. Water-colour by C. J. PHIPPS

PLATE XIX

A. SHAKESPEARE'S BIRTHPLACE, 1858. Restoration in progress

B. SHAKESPEARE'S BIRTHPLACE, 1864

PLATE XX

The Merchant of Venice. Gate Theatre, Dublin, 1946

Love's Labour's Lost. Shakespeare Memorial Theatre, Stratford, 1946–7

PLATE XXI

A. *King Lear*. Old Vic Production, 1946

B. *King Lear*. West Riding Production, 1946

PLATE XXII

A. *Twelfth Night.* Shakespeare Memorial Theatre, Stratford, 1947

B. *Pericles.* Shakespeare Memorial Theatre, Stratford, 1947

PLATE XXIII

Richard II. Shakespeare Memorial Theatre, Stratford, 1947

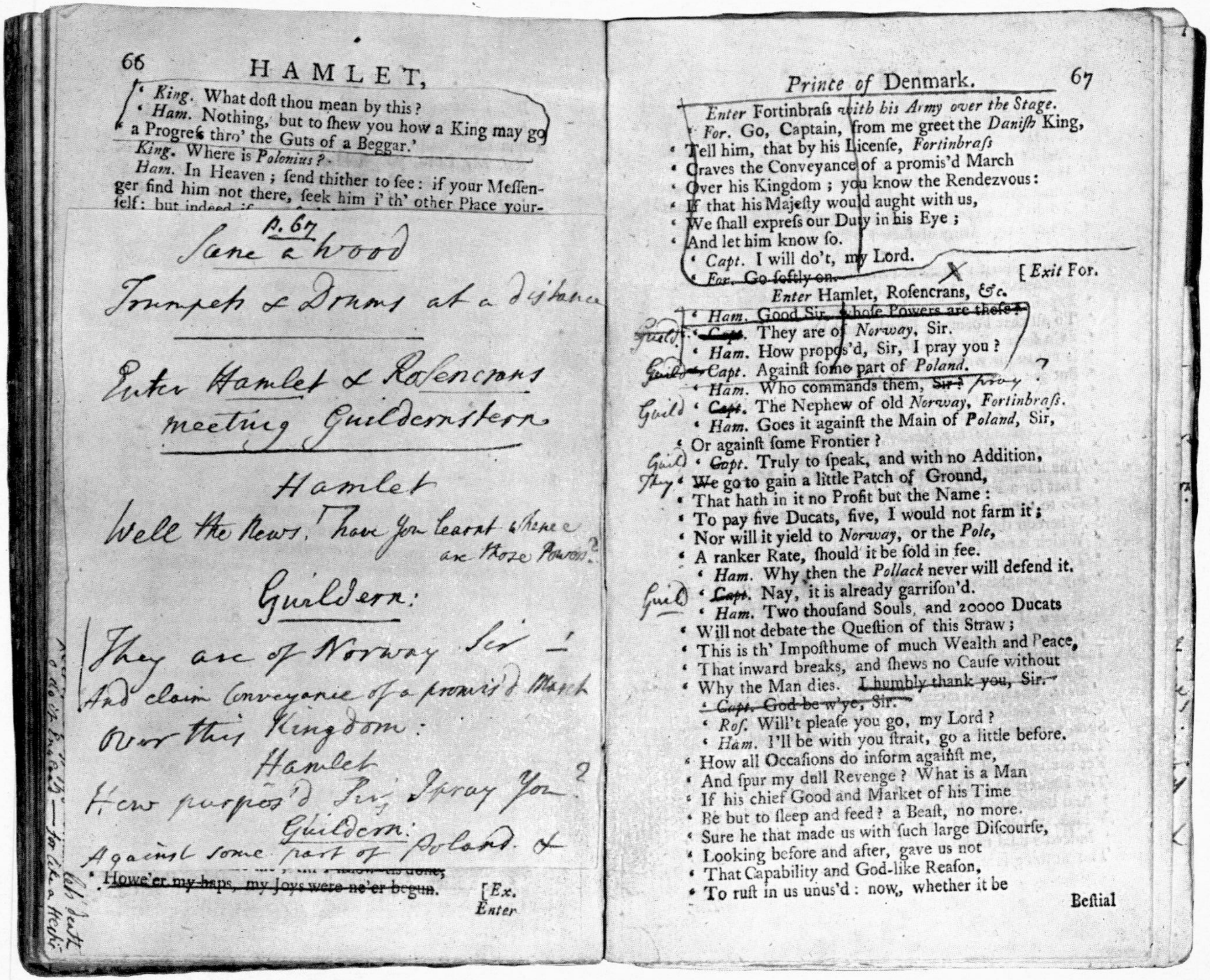

PLATE XXIV

67 Prince of Denmark.

Enter Fortinbras *with his Army over the Stage.*
For. Go, Captain, from me greet the *Danish* King,
Tell him, that by his Licence, *Fortinbras*
Craves the Conveyance of a promis'd March
Over his Kingdom ; you know the Rendezvous:
If that his Majesty would aught with us,
We shall express our Duty in his Eye ;
And let him know so.
Capt. I will do't, my Lord.
For. Go softly on.   [*Exit For.*

Enter Hamlet, Rosencrans, &c.
Ham. Good Sir, whose Powers are these?
Capt. They are of *Norway,* Sir.
Ham. How propos'd, Sir, I pray you ?
Capt. Against some part of *Poland.*
Ham. Who commands them, Sir?
Capt. The Nephew of old *Norway, Fortinbras.*
Ham. Goes it against the Main of *Poland,* Sir,
   Or against some Frontier ?
Capt. Truly to speak, and with no Addition,
   We go to gain a little Patch of Ground,
   That hath in it no Profit but the Name:
   To pay five Ducats, five, I would not farm it ;
   Nor will it yield to *Norway,* or the *Pole,*
   A ranker Rate, should it be sold in fee.
Ham. Why, then the *Pollack* never will defend it.
Capt. Nay, 'tis already garrison'd.
Ham. Two thousand Souls, and 2000 Ducats
   Will not debate the Question of this Straw ;
   This is th' Imposthume of much Wealth and Peace,
   That inward breaks, and shews no Cause without
   Why the Man dies. I humbly thank you, Sir.
Capt. God be w'ye, Sir.
Ros. Will't please you go, my Lord ?
Ham. I'll be with you strait, go a little before.
   How all Occasions do inform against me,
   And spur my dull Revenge ? What is a Man
   If his chief Good and Market of his Time
   Be but to sleep and feed ? a Beast, no more.
   Sure he that made us with such large Discourse,
   Looking before and after, gave us not
   That Capability and God-like Reason,
   To rust in us unus'd : now, whether it be

Bestial

66   HAMLET,

King. What dost thou mean by this?
Ham. Nothing, but to shew you how a King may go
   a Progress thro' the Guts of a Beggar.
King. Where is *Polonius* ?
Ham. In Heaven ; send thither to see : if your Messen-
   ger find him not there, seek him i' th' other Place yourself. but indeed if...

[handwritten annotations]

Same P. 67 (wood)

Trumpets & Drums at a distance

Enter Hamlet & Rosencrans
meeting Guildenstern

Hamlet

Well the news, Then you learnt whene
are those Powers?

Guild:ern:

They are of Norway Sir —
And claim Conveyance of a promis'd March
over this Kingdom
How propos'd Sir, I pray you ?
How prosper'd
Guilden. part of Poland &
Against some part of Poland &

How ... my hope ... now ... ne'er begin.   [Ex. Enter

TWO PAGES FROM DAVID GARRICK'S PROMPT-BOOK OF *Hamlet*
(Folger Shakespeare Library)

The production was in a formalized setting conforming to the elegance of this pleasant theatre. Rostrums, staircases, pillars, were slightly varied in different scenes; the appropriate use of dignified traverse curtains all ensured smoothness of action. The *décor* had the same simplicity as that of the West Riding, although it lacked the suggestion of adventure which prevailed at Huddersfield.

Much the same could be said of the production. In fairness, however, to the producer, John Fernald, it should be stated at once that any lack of boldness was obviously the result of a determination to present the play as he conceived it, in a straightforward manner, devoid of frills. The supporting cast all had that same air of competence, and if any of them had been inclined to break away, I feel that they would have received short shrift from Fernald.

Abraham Sofaer's Lear was an individualistic performance, and one could see that Fernald had given him his rein, whilst carefully building up the production around him—which, I think, is the correct method. This Lear had no point of comparison with its rivals. Where they stormed, he was quiet. Where they tore at the agony of the heart, he pleaded only for the moistened eye. Where he raved, they had been subdued.

Initially there seemed much to criticize in this performance. Although, according to the reference books, Sofaer is the oldest of the four actors who have this year grappled with Lear, I felt at first that he was the least successful in presenting age. Later I realized that this was deliberate. This Lear was to be old in body, but youngish in mind, youngish even in voice, so that all the great wealth of eloquence which gushes like a fountain from his brain should not bear the mark of senility. "I will do such things", thunders Lear, and Sofaer means to have no half-measures about it. He proceeds to do them.

The storm scene he played with gusto—there is no other word for it. He attacked and mastered the storm. His concentration as he speaks the line "I will talk with this philosopher" was a beautiful piece of work. The argument of the spirit is all that matters at that moment, and lightning, tempest, thunder, bodily anguish are all immaterial. Throughout this scene the raging of the elements was only incidental to the raging of Lear, even though his soul is already wandering. Some critics may feel this to be utterly wrong; Sofaer made it seem completely right. For the first time I felt that I understood Shakespeare's analogy between the tempest beating without, and the tempest within the royal mind.

His "Every inch a king" came as a fine piece of bravura, for a moment arresting the mental decay which had set in at the beginning of the 'Sweet Marjoram' scene; and coming only now in force, that madness touched the heart far more than if it had been given full rein in the earlier scenes. The modulations of Sofaer's voice are well known to our radio listeners, and his final "Howl, howl, howl, howl" reached the heights of poetry and of satisfaction. Would it be wrong to suggest that some self-satisfaction lurked in Sofaer's mind; that, from first to last, he knew exactly what he wanted to do, and was happily satisfied that he had done it?

The Repertory cast was, on the whole, of a higher standard than that of the West Riding. The Regan of Lorna Whitehouse was worth far more than a second glance. It did not have the vital arresting power of Margaret Leighton's performance, but it had decisiveness, together with an individualistic and well-regulated note of subdued hysteria, which gave a completeness to the character. Anne McGrath gave Cordelia the refreshing qualities of honesty and simplicity (but I am sad that I missed her first scene). Cyril Luckham was a sympathetic Gloucester, though at times he erred a little into sentimentality; whilst in Eric Berry, who played Edgar, we obviously have a young romantic actor of great possibilities. In voice and manner he is a little reminiscent of Alec Clunes, although, as yet, he lacks the same vitality.

It has become clear to me that *Lear* is not unactable, but that neither to actor nor onlooker is it understandable from one production. My appetite has grown with each performance I have seen. Now I would like to see a fresh attempt with Gabriel Toyne (West Riding) as producer. For *décor* he should have Guy Shephard, not bringing with him his over-elaborate setting from Bristol, but a semi-barbaric formalized design which this play demands, and which, having seen Shephard's recent work in *Tess*, I know that he can so well execute. Five of the principal parts are easy to cast. First and foremost, Rosalie Crutchley (Bristol) as Goneril—on consideration I think this is the most important performance in all the four productions. Next, Alec Guiness (Old Vic) as the Fool and Margaret Leighton (Old Vic) as Regan, though for this part Lorna Whitehouse (Liverpool) should be retained as a deputy. Robert Eddison (Bristol) as Edmund and Leon Quartermaine (Bristol) as Kent pass unchallenged. I would not complain if the producer were to include Cyril Luckham (Liverpool) or George Relph (Old Vic) as Gloucester, Ninka Dolega (West Riding) or Anne McGrath (Liverpool) as Cordelia, and Eric Berry (Liverpool) as Edgar; although I think in all these cases it might still be possible to do better.

And this leaves us looking for a Lear. Well, all we need is a man who, in addition to his own sense of poetry, will embrace within himself the magnetism and quicksilver brilliance of Olivier, the unspoilt honesty of Morant, the four-square solidity of Devlin, the self-assurance of Sofaer. I do not despair.

LONDON PRODUCTIONS

This season has seen some interesting groups of productions, both of Shakespeare's plays and of the Elizabethan or Jacobean drama closely associated with Shakespeare, by several London companies. Shakespeare seasons were given by the Old Vic Company, the Advance Players Association, and the Regent's Park Outdoor Theatre, covering between them a fair proportion of the plays and reaching out to include contemporary drama such as *The Alchemist, Volpone* and *The White Devil*.

A surprising feature of the season has been the coincidence of four performances of *Lear*. Clearly these could best be studied by grouping them together—such an opportunity for close and immediate comparison of various techniques and interpretations rarely arises—and this subject has been treated separately by Charles Landstone, as a single unit (see pp. 98–102). A large part of the Old Vic's work has, in the same way, been dealt with by George Rylands in a general survey, while a short note on the Advance Players' series and on the later Old Vic *Richard II* will be found at the end of this notice.

ELIZABETHAN DRAMA IN THE WEST END

reviewed by GEORGE RYLANDS

During the war and since, the Old Vic has undergone a complete transformation. The ideals of Miss Bayliss were directed towards the straightforward presentation of Shakespeare at a reasonable cost, the training of young actors, the orchestral rather than the virtuoso performance. These ideals have faded. More has been lost than has been gained and instead of the veterans and tyros of the Waterloo Road we have had a company whose work is very showy, somewhat superficial, and highly successful. It was inevitable that under the conditions of war the public and the critics should become quite undiscriminating. The inherent weaknesses and inequalities of most of the productions and the abandonment of the old tradition and of proper standards within certain necessary limitations have escaped the notice of eyes blinded by the glamour of a few bright particular stars. On the credit side we readily allow that certain individual performances have made theatrical history. Sir Laurence Olivier as Richard III, as Hotspur, as Justice Shallow: Sir Ralph Richardson as Falstaff; Alec Guiness as Lear's Fool. For these creations much may be forgiven. We are grateful for *Peer Gynt* and for *Oedipus Tyrannus*; and it was right that the Old Vic should make a shot, however misdirected, at one of Jonson's comic masterpieces. But when generous praise has been given where it is due, the fact remains that little justice has been done to Shakespeare and that the Governors of the Old Vic have a crisis to face. They may replace the stars who are shooting to distant spheres with others no less shining but what is needed is a firmament for them to sail in.

Messrs H. M. Tennent, under the auspices of the Arts Council, have also popularized Shakespeare in the West End and have had their own galaxy of stars and have been no less lavish in their dressing and designing. On the whole they have commanded better team-work and have been less inclined to sacrifice the play to the parts. With these must be named an effort perhaps more gallant than anything to the Old Vic's credit in this kind—Webster's *White Devil* with Robert

Helpmann as Flamineo. But when we attempt a cool and clear-headed estimate of all that the last five years or so have given us, we find that the Elizabethan productions suffer from the same fundamental and fatal defect. Producers and players have no feeling for style and no ear for blank verse. It was impossible to detect any difference between verse and prose in *The White Devil* or indeed to realize that Webster wrote metrically at all. *Antony and Cleopatra* was delivered evenly and rapidly as *Julius Caesar* should be delivered; but stylistically the two Roman tragedies are poles apart. Two or three minor examples will indicate the carelessness with which the professional stage studies Shakespeare's text. When Lear in the storm says "You houseless poverty...", it is the beginning of the prayer which he is to utter in full a moment later—"Poor naked wretches, wheresoe'er you are": it is not a vague aside. Brachiano's words, "Quite lost, Flamineo!" as he gazes entranced upon the dazzling Vittoria must not be dropped with casual indifference and telescoped into the sentence which follows. No habit is more pernicious than the modern practice in verse-speaking of 'jumping the points', of accelerating at the full stop and leaping the line-endings on the supposition that such licence counterfeits natural speech. A more grave disregard of Shakespeare's intention in the handling of words and movement was exemplified in Laurence Olivier's delivery of the speech in which Lear curses Goneril's unborn child. This is a formal invocation, as the pattern of the first line shows. The speech is built up line upon line except where the suspension of Nature's purpose is pointed by a half-line; monosyllables are set against trochaic dissyllables, the native and Latin elements are blended, the pace is measured until the outburst and relief of the final cry, "Away! Away!". Goneril in the Olivier production was fixed in a central chair while the King circled aimlessly about her.

"Comparatively few of Shakespeare's admirers are at all conscious that they are listening to music as they hear his phrases turn and his lines fall so fascinatingly and memorably." So wrote Bernard Shaw fifty years ago; and in his reviews of the Irving-Terry and other Shakespeare productions he takes as his text "the Shakespearian music", remarking that the players and playgoers of the time are as deaf as adders. They are so still. Shaw praised Miss Rehan for "her beauty of tone, grace of measure, delicacy of articulation, all the technical qualities of verse music, along with the rich feeling and fine intelligence without which these technical qualities would soon become monotonous". Of the part of Othello he wrote: "Tested by the brain it is ridiculous; tested by the ear it is sublime. The words do not convey ideas; they are streaming ensigns and tossing branches to make the tempest of passion visible." And elsewhere: "For the most part one has to listen to the music of Shakespeare—in which music, I repeat, the whole worth and charm of these early plays lies—as one might listen to a symphony of Beethoven's with all the parts played on the bones, the big drum and the Jew's harp." His words fell unheeded. One can only hope that the pupils of the new Old Vic School have engraved above the portals of their class-room the words of Paul Valéry: "L'oreille parle".

The rhetoric of Ben Jonson makes demands upon the speaker no less exacting than the poetry of Shakespeare, but of a rather different kind. The Old Vic Company ignored or evaded them by turning comedy in the grand style into knock-about farce. The language was frankly treated as gibberish and a good time was had by all. Despite the ingenious and effective doll's house setting the play would not translate from the age of Ben to that of Samuel Johnson, from Elizabethan to Hogarth's London. Sir Epicure Mammon is an Elizabethan obsessed with Renaissance Italy—with the literature and art no less than with the sensual delights. Ananias is a true Puritan, not a burlesque. Pertinax is the Elizabethan idea of a Spanish Grandee. Face is not a guardsman but a 'gentleman's gentleman'. Although Ralph Richardson's stature is too great for the role, we could at least hear and understand what he said and Alec Guiness as Abel Drugger did much to redeem a sad travesty.

We will pass over briefly other grave defects in these productions. Soloists cannot carry off Elizabethan plays. Edgar in *King Lear*, the King in 2 *Henry IV*, Enobarbus in *Antony and Cleopatra*—these are the corner-stones; and only Anthony Quayle in the last of the three did something to steady the play, although he played Enobarbus as a Brigade Major rather than a Sergeant Major. The setting of *Antony and Cleopatra* was so pretentious and uncomfortable that the tragedy never had a chance, from the great processional opening which was muddled away to nothing until the hauling up of the hero with pulleys and a fishing-net on to the platform surmounting what appeared to be an air-raid shelter or an elevator with sliding doors. The stage was so cluttered with permanent solids that the essential contrast of the juxtaposed scenes in Rome and Alexandria was quite lost. In *King Lear* and *Richard II* the settings were only a little less disastrous, but in *The White Devil* scenery, costume and lighting combined in a rich, strange, imaginative picture which suited the play and the players admirably.

That these lavish productions have revealed much talent no one will deny. There have been memorable and creative moments, flashes of insight into character and a few illuminating performances. They have succeeded with the public far beyond their deserts. For their vitality was largely spurious. The life of an Elizabethan play—*a fortiori* of a Shakespeare play—springs from the poetry; that is, from the lyrical, the rhetorical and the dramatic writing; the tropes and imagery, the counterpointing of syntax and scansion, the variations in tempo, the crescendos and climaxes, the quiet close and the dying fall. If a producer has at his command a histrionic personality as vigorous and magnetic as that of Laurence Olivier or a vocal instrument as trained as that of Edith Evans, and has not poetry, it profiteth him nothing. The play is as sounding brass or a tinkling cymbal. The Elizabethan and Jacobean writer was, as often as not, a musician, and their public were trained listeners. They possessed what T. S. Eliot has called in a pregnant passage "the auditory imagination". We have lost that instinct and we must look to the B.B.C. to recreate it. The Third Programme is believed to be raising our standard of musical appreciation, but we have as yet no ear for verbal music and we care nothing that Shakespeare is habitually spoken out of time and out of tune. Here, then, is another opportunity, an imperative duty, confronting the British Broadcasting Corporation.

SOME OTHER LONDON PRODUCTIONS

reviewed by UNA ELLIS-FERMOR

The Advance Players' season of productions by Donald Wolfit included *As You Like It*, *Hamlet*, *Lear*, *The Merchant of Venice*, *Othello*, *Twelfth Night* and *Volpone*. Characteristic of these productions was the rapid and easy transition from scene to scene, the smoothness of the changes achieved by the free use of permanent or semi-permanent sets and of small conversation scenes played before the curtains. This was perhaps specially noticeable in the *Hamlet* and the *Lear*, plays in which hitches in transition often mar the production. The stylized settings of *Twelfth*

Night and *As You Like It* (with the use of reversible sets) offered the corresponding point of interest in the comedies and helped to make plausible certain crucial passages such as the confusion of Viola and Sebastian. The general impression from this series of plays was that their merit lay in effectiveness of setting, in the care and attention given to the mechanics of production and in the resulting gain in tempo and unification. But in the acting there was too often a tendency to over-emphasis; in the tragedies (particularly, perhaps, in *Hamlet*) towards melodrama, to overweighting and underlining of points; in the comedies towards a corresponding broadening or over-pointing that turned to farce.

One production from the Old Vic season, Ralph Richardson's *King Richard II*, fell too late for inclusion in the general survey. There was something noteworthy in certain aspects of this performance, the symbolic setting and the corresponding use of *décor*, costume and lighting, the rendering offered by the production, and sometimes the acting itself. There was aesthetic economy, as well as symbolic significance, in the use of the central pillar framework with the adjustable combinations of curtains; costume, lighting and grouping achieved simultaneously beauty and emphasis.

Alec Guiness gave a reading of the character of Richard which will not easily be forgotten; intelligent, restrained, penetrating; a rendering which allowed him wider range than might be expected and those variations of mood and fantasy without which the character of Richard cannot be intelligibly presented. Harry Andrews as Bolingbroke and Richardson himself as Gaunt were in harmony with the whole effect, and Sir Lewis Casson's Duke of York was, as was to be expected, a little masterpiece in its kind.

But a disquieting feature in much modern production is a tendency to revert to the emphasis upon setting which characterized some of the work of the late nineteenth and early twentieth centuries. Once-famous sets of Reinhardt and Tree and a long line of their descendants represent a theatre in which elaboration of realism or fantasy in *décor* and lighting overwhelmed the play, distracting audiences, critics, actors and producers from bare and fundamental necessities: the play's coherence of thought and action, profundity and subtlety of character and articulate verse-music. This was followed by a movement (in France, Sweden, America and elsewhere) towards simplification and economy, a spareness of effect which, used with discrimination and imagination, threw the emphasis back again upon the playwright's words and laid upon producer and actor the responsibility for its rendering in terms of action and speech.

It is perhaps too much to say that we, to-day, are throwing away these hard-won gains and the astringent discipline they give to audience, critic and theatre-artist alike, but the frequency with which we are led to dwell primarily upon beauty or significance of setting or lighting is symptomatic of a trend which may re-establish habits from which we had painfully fought ourselves clear.

STRATFORD PRODUCTIONS

reviewed by H. S. BENNETT *and* GEORGE RYLANDS

The new regime at the Shakespeare Memorial Theatre, inaugurated by the Executive Council of the Governors of the Shakespeare Memorial Theatre under the chairmanship of Lieut.-Col. Fordham Flower, and directed by Sir Barry Jackson, has two seasons to its credit, so that one can distinguish the main changes in policy and attempt an estimate of what has been achieved. The most significant innovation has been the employment of a diversity of producers. Sir Barry has thrown his net wide—from Norwich to Yale, the old hand and the new, actor and academic, age and youth, ingenious experiment and sturdy tradition. This has been a great stimulus to all members of the company, and a valuable education hardly to be gained elsewhere. At the same time the method has its drawbacks. The players are constantly being called on to respond to a new producer and to accommodate themselves to very different views. This prevents stagnation, but is a severe tax on players who are asked to present a full series of plays each week as well as to rehearse the forthcoming productions.

The next notable change in policy is revealed in the lavish and sometimes extravagant expenditure on scenery and costume. While there have been some comparatively simple settings, such as that of Otis Riggs for *Measure for Measure*, or that of Sir Barry Jackson for *Pericles*, others have been more ambitious and less successful. Take, for example, the elaborate sets designed by Hal Burton for *Richard II*. These undoubtedly pleased the eye, but at times necessitated groupings and movements which lacked significance, or even militated against the realization of Shakespeare's ideas. The Deposition scene, which is the heart of the play, had none of the formal beauty of grouping and utterance which were clearly intended. Richard was too restless, and certainly the throne of contention should be set in the middle of the stage, as indeed must Richard be in the prison scene for the complicated soliloquy which expresses the Hamlet element in him—an element that Robert Harris or Walter Hudd failed, or perhaps did not desire, to convey. It must be freely admitted, however, that in general much taste and thought have been devoted to grouping, lighting and pictorial effect, so that a number of delightful scenes linger in the memory—the ever-changing, ever-enchanting Watteau-like effects of the groupings in Peter Brook's *Love's Labour's Lost*, or the ballet-like entrance of the Prince of Morocco and his train in Michael Benthall's *The Merchant of Venice*. The influence of the ballet was constantly felt in the productions, often endowing them with grace and with vivid rhythmical movement. It may be said that we have seen a number of Shakespeare's plays in these two years beautifully *illustrated* at Stratford.

Producers and designers then have much for which to thank Sir Barry; he has given them every chance and in return they have 'done him proud'. But what of the players and the plays? Has the cart preceded the horse? The players, according to general opinion, have found it hard to stand up to their settings, trappings and costumes. They have also had to battle with the uncertain acoustics of the Memorial Theatre, with its wide open spaces beyond the wings which absorb their speech, and a great gulf yawning between stage and stalls when the apron is not in use. Despite these difficulties, the general standard of performance has been commendable and even, for although there has been a tendency to indulge in too much animation for its own sake, at times to the detriment of the words, the players move well and are technically accomplished. What is lacking is power and personality. We have had grace and gaiety, but little that was passionate and profound—more sweetness than strength. Even in comedy, drama should not be turned to favour and to prettiness; in more serious plays such treatment, however brilliant in invention, is disastrous.

The company has been led for two seasons by Robert Harris, a mature and experienced actor who has been seen more in serious contemporary drama than in the costume play. He is thoughtful and sensitive, with dignity and control of movement and gesture, lucid in diction, at ease in poetry although uncertain in rhetoric. In these productions his performances lacked spontaneity, warmth and personal magnetism, so that he failed to unify those plays in which he was the central figure or focussing point. Paul Scofield, as Harris's second, won golden opinions in his first season as Armado, Malcolm, Lucio and Henry V. He has not had such good opportunities this season, but his creations of Pericles, of Mercutio and of Sir Andrew Aguecheek were full of interest and understanding. He is a gifted actor, with a more immediately compelling personality than anyone else at Stratford at present. But he is sometimes tempted to rejoice in the possibilities of his vocal resources, and the frequent echoes of Olivier's idiosyncracies in his intonations are tiresome. It is to be hoped that he will not be misled by the public into catching at an easy reputation through exploiting his surface abilities and indulging in mannerisms.

Shakespeare's women are not easy to cast for repertory purposes and the Director has not yet solved this problem completely. Valerie Taylor's Imogen was memorable for its intelligence and truth, and her Princess of France in *Love's Labour's Lost* was highly stylized and suited Peter Brook's stylized production. This season Beatrix Lehmann has taken such important parts as those of the Nurse, Portia and Viola. As Viola, she divided her audience into strongly opposed camps. We succumbed at once to the intelligent playing of the part which followed Shakespeare's meaning so admirably. At the same time it was clear that the peculiar quality of her voice, with its unusual intonations, was as unpleasing to some as it was acceptable to us. But as Viola, and even more as Portia, the quality of finish, the perfection of movement, the ability to suggest so much were everywhere present, and not to be gainsaid. Lastly, the second season witnessed the efflorescence of Daphne Slater—a young actress of promise, not yet ripe for the greatest moments (witness her Juliet), but already capable of conveying the virginal charm of Marina and Miranda. Her delightfully fresh rendering of Olivia as an emotionally adolescent girl revealed a more interesting and individual talent.

To see a Shakespeare play for the first time is a rare excitement, and if few have read *Pericles, Prince of Tyre*, even fewer can have had the chance of seeing it played. Nugent Monck jettisoned the first act which treats of the incest of Antiochus, and showed himself a confectioner with a light hand for pastry—which is what the play requires. With *Pericles* we enter the world of the final period, of shipwrecks and cruel stepmothers and bandits and lost princesses, of sounds and sweet airs, delicate cadences and verbal melody. More than this it brings us with a new imaginative vision to the three more familiar romances with which Shakespeare catered for the sophisticated Blackfriars audience, while at the same time returning to his first love, poetry. Paul Scofield as the Prince Charming was a little too elegant and epicene. The great anagnorisis of the fifth act missed its emotional effect as the climax of a fairy tale through being too measured and deliberate in tempo and elocution. Daphne Slater was charming and genuine as Marina and John Blatchley as Boult stamped the brothel scenes as Shakespeare at his most characteristic. Gower's hobbling archaisms were solved by the singing of Dudley Jones, one of the most accomplished actors in the company. He is a true Shakespearian and has the root of the matter in him. *Nullum quoa tetigit non ornavit.*

After seeing this production, *The Tempest* was a disappointment. Originally produced by Eric Crozier last year, it was re-produced by Norman Wright, using the same *décor* and costumes. Here he was unlucky, for nothing he could do could alter the gloomy setting, and for the most part the play resolutely refused to come to life. Can Prospero ever succeed in gaining our affections? Certainly Robert Harris's Prospero could not do so, and one wearied of the irritable, school-masterish series of outbursts and declamations which did nothing to prepare for the mercy and mansuetude of the final scenes. The most successful moments of the production were when Caliban (well played by John Blatchley) and Trinculo (Douglas Seale) came into collision.

It was wise policy to brigade these two late plays with the two earlier masterpieces of comedy, *The Merchant of Venice* and *Twelfth Night*. By this means something of the gains and losses of Shakespeare's art occasioned by the passage of years could be estimated in terms of the theatre. No greater praise can be given to Michael Benthall's production of *The Merchant of Venice* than to say that, despite our too great familiarity with the play, after the first few minutes of the exposition, which were unnecessarily fidgety, it ran easily, and even excitingly on its well-known course. Benthall's inventive fancy played about every incident, generally effectively, with humour and with dramatic point that was most refreshing. He was greatly helped by the simple but adequate set designed by Sophie Fedorovitch, who was also responsible for the costumes, which made a gay show against the unrelieved background. Benthall's production treated Shylock as an unsympathetic figure throughout, and never allowed him to steal the interest from the rest of the play. Despite this, the authoritative playing of John Ruddock was most convincing. Since so much emphasis was placed on the love theme, it was a pleasure to watch a Bassanio (Laurence Payne) and a Gratiano (Myles Eason) both played as gentlemen and not as raffish tailor's dummies. Portia is a great Renaissance lady and would not have been won by a lucky nincompoop. Beatrix Lehmann's Portia had that quality of style that denotes the artist. Her movements, gestures, and still more, the nuances of her inflections pointed the comedy delightfully and never failed to express the underlying seriousness of the play.

Shakespeare's other comedy of this period, *Twelfth Night*, produced by Walter Hudd, failed to reach the same level as *The Merchant of Venice*, largely because the producer would not let the play speak for itself, but obscured much of its poetry and meaning by overtaxing it with tiresome and frivolous 'business'. The whole key of the play is set by Orsino's opening lines: "If music be the food of love, play on"—but Hudd preferred to open with Viola's arrival on the coast of Illyria, and then to turn to Orsino's soliloquy, which was spoken in a brisk manner with a pause or two for musical diversion. After that, there was little enough left of Shakespeare's sentimental duke.

The more serious plays, *Richard II* and *Romeo and Juliet*, occasioned most disappointment. Those who came to Stratford for spectacle only had spectacle in full measure; those who came for Shakespeare's early poetry at its finest went away unsatisfied. Some reasons why this was so in *Richard II* have already been suggested. After his success with *Love's Labour's Lost* last year,

Peter Brook's production of *Romeo and Juliet* was eagerly awaited. Unfortunately, while he displayed great vigour and inventiveness, he did not show sufficient respect for the play as Shakespeare wrote it. His ability to make good use of the full stage, to keep a significant and highly coloured picture always before the audience, to make the Capulet-Montague feud always exciting was a joy to watch. Surely no more thrilling or dramatically inevitable sword combat has ever been seen in a performance of the play. Peter Brook's talents are so great that one is the more irritated by his wilfulness. In a play built so completely on the headlong rush of events it is preposterous that the performance should last for three hours and thirteen minutes (including three intervals), and that with cuts of more than 300 lines. It is arrogant to cut the entire scene between Juliet and Friar Lawrence (IV, i) for the sake of a huge piece of stage carpentry, however effectively that structure may be used in the preceding and succeeding scenes. In comparison with these major presumptions, it was only eccentric to play Peter as a blackamoor, to fill the piazza at Verona with exotic citizens, to alter the lines of the Prince for a spectacular entrance and to cut the last 140 lines of the play.

Romeo and Juliet is one of the best cast of the series. Paul Scofield's magnetic Mercutio and Myles Eason's superbly feline Tybalt were outstanding. John Ruddock's Friar Lawrence was beautifully keyed into the headlong violence of the young people of Verona. Beatrix Lehmann's Nurse was a striking performance, sufficiently vulgar and sentimental to provide a proper background for Juliet without stealing her scenes. Lawrence Payne's Romeo was virile, even violent, but it lacked variety and subtlety. He was notably better in his scenes with Mercutio and Benvolio than in those with Juliet. Daphne Slater's Juliet was young and fresh, and she was successful in conveying the pathos of the role, but she has not yet the resources for the highest moments, and her big scenes lacked variety.

To sum up, there has been much throwing about of brains and a generous expenditure of money. But the producers have been too anxious to display their virtuosity and to suppose that the familiar in Shakespeare must at all costs and even beyond recognition be made new. May we hope in the future for less illustration, more illumination?

Timon of Athens. Sir Barry Jackson and the Birmingham Repertory Theatre Company were generous enough to stage a private performance of *Timon of Athens* in the Conference Hall for the education and entertainment of the delegates to the 1947 Shakespeare Conference. The handicaps were great—Mediterranean heat, baffling acoustics and a complicated and inconvenient stage. Producer and actors, however, adapted themselves to the physical conditions with extreme skill and ingenuity, turning the upper level and inner-stage to Elizabethan account and timing their movements on the two long curving staircases with accuracy. Grouping and lighting were simple and effective and, as often before, one felt Shakespeare's independence of the painted scene.

The fatal flaw in *Timon of Athens* is the disparity between the first and second movements. The first is a social drama, almost as complete in itself as the first three acts of *Julius Caesar*, and it gains enormously from performance, and particularly from performance in modern dress. Shakespeare's mastery of minor character and of the give and take of dialogue is clearly shown. But this movement, which is essentially a tragi-comedy of manners, has as its sequel a rhetorical indictment of man as a social animal in which Shakespearian idiom and versification are strained to breaking-point and the result is closet drama ranking at its best moments with the *Prometheus* of Aeschylus or Shelley. The second movement is clearly an unfinished draft—the molten metal out of which Shakespeare was to strike lasting coin for the heath scenes in *King Lear*. But Lear is not a megaphone; he has with him the Fool and Edgar and Gloucester; from his madness and from his relations with them pity springs to stride the blast. In Acts IV and V of *Timon* pity is shouted down by wrath.

John Phillips played Timon under the direction of Willard Stoker. He is an actor of authority who did as much as could be done to unite the two Timons. Phillips's voice has great range and flexibility and in the magnificent tirades he revealed a power of acceleration, of changing gear, of taking a hairpin bend, worthy of a champion motor-cyclist in a cross-country trial. As Timon the First his speed and ease brought out the modernity or timelessness of the play, but in the second part his virtuosity was a handicap, concealing argument and dissipating passion. He neither moved nor persuaded, although his wonderful energy kept the play going and sometimes made the audience forget that they could hear very little of what was said and understand even less. The part of Apemantus is difficult. The Elizabethans found the deformed body and the warped mind more comical than we do, but Shakespeare, who had succeeded with Thersites, failed with Apemantus. The character was portrayed on this occasion as an out-at-elbows Bohemian of the Aldous Huxley period—a discharged reporter, insolvent artist or ham actor. Although such a self-styled critic of society is usually a vain and morbid egoist, Roy Malcolm exploited his opportunities with too evident a relish and his highly professional impersonation was embarrassing and painful. Alan MacNaughton, as the just steward, struck the note of pity which was sorely needed, and he was in many ways the most genuine of the players. His performance was memorable.

INTERNATIONAL NEWS

As has been noted above, no attempt is made by Shakespeare Survey to provide either a complete bibliography of recent writings on Shakespeare or a catalogue of his plays in production. In the following pages selection has been made—chiefly from the reports of our correspondents—with the object of presenting a general picture of the Shakespearian scene and of stressing what appear to be the most interesting and noteworthy trends.

Audiences in Great Britain have had an opportunity of seeing numerous Shakespearian dramas presented on the boards, and it is encouraging to observe how widely spread these performances have been—thanks largely to the Arts Council's sponsorship of local repertory and touring companies. Not only have many among the better-known plays thus been brought before audiences outside of London: these audiences have on occasion had the privilege of witnessing performances of works rarely given on the stage. Although it is impossible to review all of these productions, some indication of their scope is given elsewhere in this volume. The one fact that England has had four presentations of *King Lear* may be taken as a symbol of recent activities in this direction.

If the theatrical record here is encouraging, a dash of disappointment must be felt when Shakespeare's fortunes in other parts of the English-speaking world are brought under review. Perhaps no surprise need be experienced when we note the rarity of his appearance on the stage in the rest of the Commonwealth, since we fully appreciate with what peculiar difficulties theatrical endeavour in Canada, Australia, New Zealand and South Africa has to contend. Although interest in Shakespeare is strong in all these countries, the paucity of professional companies offers but few chances for more than occasional performances of the plays. Indeed, the only production of this kind that has been reported by our correspondents is that of *Hamlet*—and that was an Afrikaans version by L. I. Coertze, given at Johannesburg by the African Consolidated Theatres in May 1947.

'Henry VIII' on Broadway

Knowledge and appreciation of Shakespeare has been nobly enriched during recent years by the devoted and inspired efforts of many scholars in the United States of America, and it might have been expected that these efforts would have been accompanied there by an equally imposing array of professional productions. Unfortunately, however, although there have been numerous interesting amateur performances, Shakespeare's recent fate on the commercial boards has not been a very happy one.

Miss Rosamond Gilder observes that the appearance of but one new production of Shakespeare on Broadway during the season 1946-7 marks "an all-time low" and that this "is the inevitable result of the law of diminishing returns as applied to actors competent in the field of the classic repertoire". "Since the United States", she remarks, "has today no professional stock companies where young actors might get their basic training in the classics, and since fewer and fewer of our leading players care to risk the challenge of the great Shakespearian roles, the New York public is being deprived of the pleasures and excitements that Shakespeare offers.

"The opening of the first season of the American Repertory Theatre (a new organization headed by Eva Le Gallienne, Margaret Webster and Cheryl Crawford) with an elaborate production of *Henry VIII* was therefore hailed with great enthusiasm. It was hoped that this would prove to be the first step in the establishment of that much-needed permanent theatre. The fact that a play not seen in New York in this century was used as an opening guy seemed most hopeful. Indeed the production itself was a fine one. Designed by David Ffolkes and directed by Margaret Webster it had the benefit of the skills of two artists trained in the English theatre. Mr Ffolkes's setting and his costumes as well were a delight in themselves, vividly coloured, rich and bold. Margaret Webster introduced a pageant of Anne Boleyn's coronation: a screen which depicted the solid walls of Westminster Abbey became transparent and the Queen with her attendants appeared on an inner stage in all their glory, going through the Coronation Ceremony step by step as the description unrolls.

"By devices such as this, and by eliminating much of the plotting and counterplotting, Miss Webster presented a vivid and smooth-running production full of colour and pageantry with the great scenes so dear to Shakespearian actors—the trial scene and the scene of the fall of Wolsey—as the high points of an evening

more addressed to the eye than the heart. Miss Le
Gallienne played the Queen with considerable effect,
and Walter Hampden was a Lord Cardinal in the
honourable tradition. But the performance reached no
memorable heights and failed to arouse more than respectful interest. It was played through the winter as
part of a repertory which included Shaw, Barrie and
Ibsen. At the end of the season the American Repertory
Theatre found it necessary to suspend activities for the
time being, and those who hoped for a classic theatre
which would bring Shakespeare's plays in living form to
young playgoers in New York were again disappointed.

"The most active proponent of Shakespeare in
America during the past season was Maurice Evans
who toured his so-called G.I. *Hamlet* through the country
with enormous success. Maurice Evans, then a major in
the American Army, had played *Hamlet* in a cut version
to the troops in Hawaii during the war. He then gave
the play, re-costumed and re-set, in New York in 1945–6
and during the following year 1946–7 took it on a
gigantic swing across the country. It is authoritatively
reported that he grossed one million dollars in the two
seasons he played this, his third production of *Hamlet* in
America. The fact that he entirely omitted the grave-
yard scene and took other liberties with the text was
received quite calmly by all but a very few critics and
theatre-goers. Maurice Evans, being an Englishman and
trained in the English theatre, can read verse agreeably.
He gives an uncomplex if uninspired interpretation of
the part which has proved highly acceptable to audiences
that have all too little opportunity to see *Hamlet* at all.
His success as an interpreter of Shakespeare to the
American people is unquestionable. He follows in the
tradition of Sothern, Mantell and Hampden, and has
become a popular star on Broadway and in the country
at large."

A Shakespeare Festival in Poland

When we turn to Europe, the picture becomes
strangely variegated: fervent interest and endeavour in
some areas contrasts markedly with apathy in others.

For many countries, of course, the resumption of
unrestricted theatrical activities and of academic studies
has had to be carried out amid travail and occasionally in
face of almost unbelievable obstacles, both physical and
spiritual. Nazi occupation meant for many lands a violent
disintegration of cultural life and it left behind it a vast
tract of material destruction.

Perhaps the record of Poland may be taken here first,
both because that country suffered a peculiarly cruel fate
during the war and because its endeavours to achieve

cultural recovery are so closely associated with interest
in Shakespeare.

During the long nightmare of German domination
Poland's theatres and universities suffered almost incredible losses. The leaders of cultural life were deci-
mated: even the most elementary needs were rendered
unavailable to those who had been left. "For five years",
writes Professor Borowy, "no new books of a serious
character were allowed to appear in Poland; large
numbers of books were destroyed or turned into pulp....
In 1945, former actors, producers and stage-designers—
those whose lives had been spared—returned to the old
theatre premises—those that had escaped destruction.
Yet even in the best preserved buildings all interior
installations, scenery, costumes, stage-properties and
libraries were missing."

With courage and vigour, however, a new start in the
theatre was made, and it is significant that this new start
has associated itself largely with a revived enthusiasm for
Shakespeare. Hardly anything could serve to demonstrate more clearly his power and enduring inspiration
than the fact that, amid the ruins that were the bright
city of Warsaw, the Ministry of Fine Arts organized, in
the summer of 1947, a great 'Konkurs Szekspirowski'—
a Shakespeare Festival in which twenty-three Polish
theatres participated, with performances of *Much Ado*,
Twelfth Night, *As You Like It*, *The Merry Wives*, *The
Winter's Tale*, *A Midsummer-Night's Dream*, *The Tempest*,
The Two Gentlemen of Verona, *Hamlet* and *Othello*.

Along with this, noteworthy is another fact—the very
considerable space devoted to Shakespeare in Poland's
new, and excellently edited, theatrical magazine, *Teatr
miesięcznik*. To this journal Mieczysław Rulikowski con-
tributes an informative survey of Shakespeare on the
Polish stage ("Szekspir na ziemiach polskich"), Wiktor
Hahn surveys the Shakespearian influence in Polish
dramatic literature ("Wpływ Szekspira na polską litera-
turę dramatyczną") and also discusses an early production of *Hamlet* at Lwów in 1797 ("Prapremiera 'Hamleta'
we Lwowie w r. 1797"); *Timon of Athens* is analysed by
Ludwik Morstin, Bolesława Hajdukowicz stresses the
importance of Shakespeare for our times ("Szekspir a
widownia współczesna"), while many shorter notices
refer to various aspects of the dramatist's work.

Particular attention, moreover, is being paid in these
years of revival to the question of translation. The publication of Professor Tarnawski's new version of all the
plays has, it is true, been delayed by printing problems,
but active plans are being made not only for the appearance of this work but also for the preparing of still further
renderings of the most famous dramas.

Shakespeare in the U.S.S.R. and Eastern Europe

So far as the U.S.S.R. is concerned, there is no need here to cover again the ground so effectively dealt with by Mikhail M. Morozov in his recently published booklet, *Shakespeare on the Soviet Stage*, issued by *Soviet News* in 1947 with an introduction by J. Dover Wilson. Russia's extraordinary interest in the plays is amply revealed here, and Morozov rightly emphasizes the very great importance of the new translations now being made by that very distinguished poet, Boris Pasternak. It would have been a delight to have discussed more fully the Soviet achievements in this realm, but no useful purpose would be served by repeating here what has been accomplished so well in Morozov's study. Sufficient is it to underline the fact that since 1939 the U.S.S.R. has had its own annual Shakespeare Conference, at the last meeting of which Boris Pasternak read from his recently completed rendering of *Henry IV*, and that hardly any other dramatist than Shakespeare has proved so popular on the boards of Russia's hundreds of theatres.

In another Slavonic country, Bulgaria, the picture is not quite so rich in colour, although here too officially sponsored activities have been devoted to Shakespeare's honour. In 1946 the Ministry of Information and Arts inspired a belated celebration, held at the National Theatre, on the occasion of his three hundred and thirtieth anniversary. On this Marco Mincoff sends an interesting note:

"The programme consisted of selected scenes and monologues from his plays, speeches, and music— Elizabethan settings of his songs, arias based on his plays and orchestral pieces similarly based on his works. Kissimov's very theatrical and ranting delivery of the monologue from *Richard III*, which brought the house down, while it left one despairing of the audience's critical insight, also left one with the uncomfortable feeling that that was probably how it was meant to be spoken and that it was much nearer Burbage's interpretation than anything one would hear in Western Europe."

As yet no complete translation of Shakespeare exists in Bulgarian, but Lyubomir Ognyanov, whose version of *The Two Gentlemen* is being used by the National Theatre in a forthcoming production, is actively engaged in bringing to a conclusion a rendering of all the comedies. Mincoff's *Macbeth*, which will be closer to the original than any of the existing six versions, is due to appear towards the close of the year 1947. "The greatest difficulty", he comments, "is to adapt Shakespeare's sovereign freedom of style to a language that has formed itself on the French ideal of academic correctness." In 1946 appeared this author's biographical and critical study of Shakespeare's life and works—the first volume of its kind in Bulgarian.

From France to Austria

Owing to unforeseen circumstances no report has been received from our French correspondent, and as a consequence only one or two matters of interest may be recorded. Two important translations have appeared in the course of the year—André Gide's long awaited *Hamlet* and J. Lavelle's *Henry V*. Like his *Antoine et Cléopâtre*, Gide's *Hamlet* is unquestionably a brilliant piece of work in which the great writer's pure and limpid prose is turned to the best account in rendering with meticulous exactitude the text of Shakespeare. Unfortunately, however, Gide is not a poet, and his version, fine though it is, becomes something strangely different from the play as we know it. Instead of an often puzzling atmosphere, wrapped in Elsinore's fogs, the actors are set in a clear air, illuminated by a light that is hard and metallic. Lavelle's *Henry V* is a scholarly, conscientious piece of work, designed to aid students in their study of the drama and its value is increased by the translator's sound and elaborate introduction. With this version may be noted the appearance in *La revue théâtrale* of a rendering of *Der bestrafte Brudermord*, introduced by a preface from the pen of Gaston Baty, who expresses his conviction that the German text is a rough rendering of Kyd's early drama.

From both Belgium and Switzerland have come other translations into French. Our Belgian correspondent, Robert de Smet, comments on the enthusiasm that greeted the completion of Pierre Messiaen's complete rendering of the whole works, while Georges Bonnard stresses the significance of Pierre-Louis Matthey's *Romeo and Juliet*. Matthey's powers had already been shown in his version of *The Tempest* and here again his poetic imagination has served him well. In addition to these, Belgium has seen the appearance of a Flemish version of *Julius Caesar*, prepared by R. M. S. van den Raevensbusch, while in the Netherlands Burgerdijk's Dutch translation of the works, originally issued in the eighties, is being reissued with fresh prefaces to meet a public demand.

In Belgium and the Netherlands general interest in Shakespeare's plays grew markedly during the war years and is continuing. In these countries the theatres have recently presented, in Dutch and French versions, productions of *Othello*, *Hamlet*, *Romeo and Juliet*, *All's Well*, *Much Ado*, *A Midsummer-Night's Dream* and *Twelfth Night*. It is of interest to note that when the two last-mentioned comedies were performed at Rotterdam, The

Hague and Utrecht they played either to full or to almost full capacity.

The theatrical record is less ample in Switzerland, where, apart from the Arts Council's touring *Hamlet* and *Othello*, presented by Alec Clunes and Jack Hawkins, the only plays given during 1946–7 were *Macbeth* and *A Midsummer-Night's Dream*, acted in German by the Zürich Repertory Company. Vienna's stage has to report an almost equally meagre Shakespearian repertoire. None of the plays has appeared at the Burgtheater, although a new production of *As You Like It* opened at the Kammerspiele towards the end of 1945 and *The Two Gentlemen* was given the following season at Erich Ziegel's progressive playhouse, Die Insel. The provincial theatres in Austria have been somewhat more enterprising. The Linz Landestheater presented *Twelfth Night*, *Hamlet* and an open-air *Midsummer-Night's Dream*; Salzburg saw a good performance of *Twelfth Night* and Innsbruck had an interesting *Macbeth*.

Probably the most important Shakespearian event in Austria was the exhibition organized by the Nationalbibliothek under the direction of Josef Gregor. This comprehensive array of illustrative material was eagerly attended and its success demonstrates the keen general demand for Shakespeare which Karl Brunner reports from his country. Another sign of this interest is the fact that Brunner's own annotated edition of *Hamlet* was completely sold out within a few days of issue.

Shakespeare in Scandinavia

The tradition of inviting a foreign company to perform *Hamlet* at the Castle of Kronberg at Elsinore is being continued: in June 1946 the guests were the members of the National Theatre of Oslo. Norway had already seen this production, staged by Hans Jacob Nilsen (who also took the part of Hamlet). Both Norwegian and Danish critics have testified to the importance and success of this performance: what so often has been said in the past is now being repeated there: "No generation has been better able to understand Hamlet than the one now living."

The Oslo National Theatre also saw a production of *Much Ado*, in December 1946, with scenery by Helge Refn. His permanent set, which offered opportunities for light suggestions of change in locale, gained much praise for the aid it gave towards clarity and concentration in the presenting of the comedy.

Apart from the annual event at Elsinore, Denmark appears to be displaying less interest in Shakespeare than other ex-occupied countries. Dr Henriques deplores this "sad fact"—particularly sad in view of the "astonishingly great number" of Danish Shakespeare enthusiasts and critics during the past two hundred years: he suggests that Denmark's enforced isolation during the war years has led to the exploration of the latest in dramatic literature rather than to a renewed interest in classical authors. There have been no fresh translations, and criticism has been confined to articles and essays. Among these attention may be drawn to Alex Garde's review of the diverse interpretations of *Hamlet* on Danish stages during the past hundred years (*Hamlet i Generationernes Spejl*) and to Paul V. Rubow's lengthy discussion of the *Sonnets*, with an interpretation of their puzzling dedication (*Orbis Litterarum*, IV, 1–2).

In Sweden, according to the report of our correspondent, Agne Beijer, the new production of a Shakespearian drama is considered the principal event of the theatrical season, while, with the exception of Strindberg, no classic or modern author so frequently appears on the playbill. Although perhaps there has been a tendency of late to overstress the spectacular, undoubtedly the public is being presented now with a Shakespeare livelier in spirit, more powerfully dramatic, than had appeared in the respectfully academic performances of earlier years.

The new style in production was inaugurated in 1939 by Alf Sjöberg when he presented *As You Like It* at the Stadsteater in Göteborg. Here the background of the play was set in the style of Watteau and Boucher. Sjöberg followed this with his lively *Much Ado* at the Dramatiska Teatern in 1940 and with his *Merchant of Venice*, inspired by Tiepolo and Guardi, in 1944. In the presentation of *Twelfth Night* the influence of a pictorial artist again was evident. For this drama the producer turned to a modern surrealist painter, Stellan Mörner, and although in general the public had not been disposed to welcome this style in art, the application of the style to the theatre was instantly greeted with acclaim. Sjöberg's latest production is that of *Richard III* (1947): here a single permanent set was employed in association with the skilful handling of a 'light organ'.

All these productions were notable, and they have been associated with several others, such as the plays directed at Göteborg by Knut Ström and those at Malmö's magnificent Stadsteater presented by Sandro Malmquist. Equally notable is the influence of the theatrical interest thus aroused upon the work of critics and scholars. There has been a marked recrudescence of discussion relating to Shakespeare's plays both in newspapers and in periodicals.

A correspondingly vivid response to Shakespeare is reported from Finland by Rafael Koskimies. Recently,

Helsinki had *As You Like It* at the Suomen Kansallist-teatteri (January 1947), under the direction of Wilho Ilmari, and *The Taming of the Shrew* at the People's Theatre (Spring 1946). Provincial stages saw perform-ances of *The Tempest, Much Ado, Romeo and Juliet, Two Gentlemen of Verona, Othello* and *A Midsummer-Night's Dream.*

Shakespeare in Italy and Spain

The peculiar variation in Shakespearian interest from country to country is nowhere more clearly exemplified than by the Latin lands. In Italy, for instance, there has been little of Shakespeare seen on the stage, while at the same time translators have been active and critical studies are flourishing: in Spain Shakespeare has inspired no literary activity, while performances have been numerous. Our Spanish correspondent, Luis Astrana Marín, reports that for the stage many of the texts used are versions concocted by the actors from translations already suf-ficiently inaccurate: at the same time, the Secretary-General of the Spanish Society of Authors lists 270 performances of various productions of *The Taming of the Shrew, Merchant of Venice, Othello, Romeo and Juliet, Midsummer-Night's Dream* and *Hamlet.* In spite of the mangled texts, these have, in general, proved widely popular.

When we turn to Italy, we find a picture in reverse. The second volume of the complete *Shakespeare Teatro* edited by Mario Praz appeared in 1946—the most scholarly endeavour of its kind yet attempted in Italy. These volumes include versions already published, to-gether with others rendered by Praz himself, by the poet Eugenio Montale and other associates. At the same time Vincenzo Errante, the distinguished scholar-translator of Goethe and Rilke, has issued new versions of five Shake-spearian tragedies, while the poet Giuseppe Ungaretti has essayed the unexpectedly difficult task of bringing Shakespeare's *Sonnets* into an appropriate Italian form. Associated with such endeavours are those of the scholars, among whom our correspondent, Napoleone Orsini, is one of the chief. His vigorous and penetrating contribu-tions to the critical study of the dramatist are discussed elsewhere in this volume.

Little can be reported from Portugal during the year, save that the Faculty of Letters at the University of Coimbra (where a "Semana de Shakespeare" was organized in 1947) are continuing their work on a complete translation of the plays. In Greece one new translation was published—*Henry V*, by V. Rotas (1947): the National Theatre at Athens saw a production of

Much Ado, described by our correspondent, George Theotokas, as "in the traditional academic manner", and a more modernistic staging of *The Merchant of Venice* at the Piraeus Municipal Theatre.

Shakespeare and the Modern World

This survey of the more noteworthy events recorded by our correspondents presents a varied picture. Particu-larly interesting are the endeavours now being made in diverse countries to produce more fitting versions of the plays: it is significant that from Pasternak in the U.S.S.R. to Matthey in Switzerland modern poets are finding their own imaginations fired by converse with Shakespeare's scenes. In some of the reports interesting comment is made relating to the peculiar difficulties faced by those who seek to bring the English words into another tongue. Some of these difficulties are particular—for example, the impossibility in Italian of conveying the full meaning of a Shakespearian line in a single line of translation, because of the greater number of syllables in Italian words. Other difficulties are more general, such as those to which Georges Bonnard refers when he observes that, in order to render the spirit of Shakespeare into another speech, a poet-translator must allow his own imagination to be kindled by the glow in the verses before him and yet in this very process of kindling must inevitably find himself carried away by his own enthusiasm into realms not strictly akin to those by which he has been inspired. This is a subject which it would be inappropriate to discuss here; but it is one which, we hope, may later find adequate scope in the pages of *Shakespeare Survey.*

A second point of interest is the appearance in several countries of Shakespeare festivals, exhibitions and con-ferences. These are obviously inspired both by general and scholarly attention to Shakespeare's work and seem to indicate a trend towards more co-operative activity in the study and appreciation of his plays.

Although few truly great productions appear to have been given within the year, the list of performances is an impressive one and perhaps we shall not err in deducing from this list that Shakespeare's plays have the quality of appealing the more powerfully the more intense is the emotional spirit of a time or a land: his genius seems most to be appreciated when men's minds are stirred and life is uneasy. Poland's Shakespeare Festival may stand as a symbol of this, and with it we may associate the fact that during the days of pitiless bombing in England Shake-speare's works took a fresh hold on the public imagina-tion in this country. Perhaps the last word here should, however, be that of Mikhail Morozov:

"How direct Shakespeare's influence was so far as those who took an active part in the war were concerned, is shown by the following incident. The Germans were on the outskirts of Moscow. A unit of Soviet airmen, many of whom had just come back from an operational flight, was holding a meeting. One of the airmen was speaking. Suddenly he interrupted his speech, opened a book and began to read extracts from *Macbeth*. The impression created by this reading was tremendous. The blood-stained characters of this tragedy involuntarily merged in the imagination of the listeners with that frightful nightmare which the Hitlerite hordes were bringing with them....

"It was during the war that our readers and playgoers realized clearly that Shakespeare was no 'academic' writer who was held in reverence and read with enjoyment only by a few literary experts.

"Shakespeare is alive though he is three hundred and eighty years old. In the darkest days of the war, he, like a real friend, was with us. Shakespeare, the immortal, forms one of the cultural bonds between two peoples who share in common their veneration and love for his great genius."

THE YEAR'S CONTRIBUTIONS TO SHAKESPEARIAN STUDY

1. CRITICAL STUDIES

reviewed by UNA ELLIS-FERMOR

Setting aside bibliographical and biographical studies, which are treated in other parts of this section, and considering the year's work on one side only, that of interpretative and philosophical criticism, it is possible to discern already certain tendencies which may prove to be characteristic of the post-war revaluation. It is dangerous to force this too far and doubly so in this year's review, as, though there has been a relatively large output of books and articles, many have been extremely difficult to obtain and some impossible.[1] With this caution in mind, we can attempt to indicate certain trends, naming in each instance a few volumes which seem representative. It is clear that many writers, even when engaged with some different topic, are turning back to the contemplation of Shakespeare as an artist and as a poet, believing that the essence of Shakespeare studies is the study of the poetic content of the plays; in one article at least this is proclaimed as a principle. Almost equally clear, and in close relation to this, is the increasing recognition now given again to certain forms of interpretation which had fallen out of repute as 'old-fashioned'. Chief among them is the analysis and elucidation of character; this, coming back into its own in terms of modern experience, is no longer necessarily regarded as folly. Closely akin again to these two is the growing tendency to consider and appraise afresh the value of certain special advances made within the last quarter of a century, many of which are now strongly enough established for their character to be recognized and their relation to their background sketched.

The returning realization that the critic's primary concern is with the artist and the poet, implicit in much of this work and incidentally touched in some places, finds explicit statement in at least one article. So clearly is it stated that this[2] may stand as representative of the underlying idea of much modern Shakespearian criticism. Orsini considers that the recently prevailing tendencies in modern Shakespearian criticism have been hitherto the philological, the learned and the historical, and that they result in a 'Shakespeare' who is the product of his age, of his theatre, of his public, of current religious, philosophic or psychological thought, of the events of his personal life or of contemporary politics—of everything, in fact, except his own genius. This tendency Swinburne resisted in his day, and, later, Emile Legouis and Lascelles Abercrombie, but "the rights of aesthetic criticism" have still to be restored. The essence is the poetry itself; all other aspects are accessory: "Quindi, lo studio dell' opera Shakespeariana in quanto opera d' arte non sta nel cercare ciò che essa può avere di comune con altre opere, ma ciò che essa ha di individuale e di proprio."

---

[1] To this, one of the results of the present condition of the book-trade to which we are now becoming accustomed, must be attributed certain omissions which will be observed in this article. There is good reason to hope that this difficulty will not be so grave in other years, but I should like to take this opportunity of apologizing for it in the present.

[2] N. Orsini: "La Critica Shakespeariana" (*Anglica*, I, nos. 1–3; cf. also "La Lingua Poetica di Shakespeare", *ibid.* I, no. 6).

It is interesting to find that the critical principle so clearly declared by Orsini is in fact illustrated or endorsed by the works of several Englishmen. Wilson Knight, in *The Crown of Life*,[1] adds a critical interpretation of the late plays to the series of his studies of Shakespeare's art and thought. At no time has Wilson Knight been drawn aside from the line of criticism, original, imaginative, and interpretative, that he made for himself some twenty years ago, and, true to his own tradition, he here studies and justifies the last five plays as works of art, as drama and as poetic thought; as, indeed, the 'crown' of the foregoing tragic period and not a decline from it. This defence of the artistic status of the central group, *Cymbeline*, *Winter's Tale*, and *The Tempest*, will find a ready hearing, I imagine, with most readers. The cases for the earlier *Pericles* and the later *Henry VIII* are less easy to make, but Wilson Knight elucidates the artistic relation of the dubious first two acts to the rest of *Pericles* and advances a challenging claim for *Henry VIII* as a wholly Shakespearian play on an aesthetic argument.

E. A. Armstrong's *Shakespeare's Imagination*[2] is again in essence a study of Shakespeare's art in one specific branch, that of his imagery, its sources and functions. The author's preoccupation with the psychological aspect of his subject introduces an element not always germane to that of artistic achievement, but reference to and consideration of the artistic process is frequent, and the book, which belongs properly to a later section of this summary, is symptomatic of the return of criticism to the essential Shakespeare, Shakespeare the poet. Characteristic also are the implications or undertones of Alfred Harbage's *As They Liked It*[3] and A. P. Rossiter's introduction to his edition of *Woodstock*.[4] Both of these, though one is occupied primarily with the moral aspects of Shakespeare's work and the other with the historical, indicate by asides and incidental references the preponderating significance of the poetic or artistic values. This is revealed again in various articles, such as "The Golden World of *King Lear*",[5] where, with Sidney's distinction between 'brazen' and 'golden' worlds in mind, Geoffrey Bickersteth examines, in a close and subtle argument, the process by which the tragic artist transmutes his material into form, so that what was "ugly, irrational and wicked" ends by compelling us "to accept without question its beauty, its reasonableness and its moral worth". To these may be added others such as J. M. Nosworthy's "The Structural Experiment in *Hamlet*";[6] and the apt, provocative title of L. C. Turner Forest's "A Caveat for Critics Against Invoking Elizabethan Psychology"[7] might serve as a summary of the more critically conscious position of several writers such as Orsini himself. A timely reminder of the misleading effects of seeking to interpret the inner life of the artist too closely in terms of the conditions of his outward life comes in George Sampson's "Shakespeare and Bach".[8]

In close relation, as has been said, to this tendency, this orientation towards the findings of the

---

[1] *The Crown of Life. Essays in Interpretation of Shakespeare's Final Plays* (Oxford University Press, 1947).

[2] *Shakespeare's Imagination. A Study of the Psychology of Association and Inspiration* (Lindsay Drummond, 1946).

[3] *As They Liked It. An Essay on Shakespeare and Morality* (New York, Macmillan, 1947).

[4] *Woodstock. A Moral History* (Chatto and Windus, 1946). For a further comment on these two works, see the section on "Life and Times".

[5] Geoffrey Bickersteth, "The Golden World of *King Lear*". Annual Shakespeare Lecture of the British Academy, 1946.

[6] *Review of English Studies*, XXII (October 1946), 282–8.

[7] *Publications of the Modern Language Association of America*, LXI (September 1946), 651–72.

[8] Reprinted in *Seven Essays*, by George Sampson (Cambridge University Press, 1946). To the articles mentioned above might be added certain of the papers in *The Shakespeare Association Bulletin*, XXI, 4.

older aesthetic criticism at its best, comes the revival of a special branch of 'interpretation', that of character. John Palmer's *Comic Characters of Shakespeare*[1] proclaims without evasion what its material will be and Hermann Sinsheimer makes a full-length investigation of the character of Shylock[2] and of the place occupied by Shakespeare's study in the development of a traditional myth. This he traces through medieval history, fantasy and literature to the drama of Marlowe and Shakespeare. Harbage's *As They Liked It* is a detailed study first of the nature of moral stimulus and response in the plays and then of the concept of Justice. But the author is not preoccupied with abstract ethical questions; the actual nature and just interpretation of the characters concerns him equally, albeit primarily in their moral aspects, and at certain points he defends this seemingly outmoded type of criticism against the twentieth century's condemnation: "All criticism that has had a respectful hearing resides safely within the limits of Shakespeare's meaning." There are, moreover, numerous dramatic theories suggested, of which time alone prevents a further discussion here.

It is interesting to find that several articles or lectures are frank interpretations, reinterpretations or evaluations of individual characters from the plays. W. M. T. Dodds makes an acute and careful analysis of the character of Angelo;[3] one peculiarly close to the interests of the modern world, whose appraisal has long been overdue. She draws out with care and precision the implications of habitual self-discipline and self-awareness which deepen the significance of Angelo's conflict and make of his situation "the diagram of a tragedy sketched in in a comedy". J. R. Moore makes the straightforward yet novel suggestion that there is little mystery about Iago[4] except for the artistic masterliness of this study of a common type, an unintelligent, resentful subordinate officer, the military counterpart of a 'stickit minister'. (This conclusion the author owes in part to his students of the United States Army University. It had not, apparently, occurred to criticism hitherto to collect the testimony of professional soldiers on this study of a soldier.) Professor Salvador de Madariaga again makes a study of a character, this time of Hamlet[5] in an unwonted setting, as "one of the great Europeans of the spirit" to be grouped with Faust, Don Quixote and Don Juan. He indicates the relations and differences of these four characters, who embody among them the imaginative ideals of three of the greatest European civilizations, revealing thus, without destroying the artistic significance of the character itself, the relation of Shakespeare's figure to a body of thought diffused far beyond the limits of the play. Finally, Miss L. B. Campbell's "Bradley Revisited"[6] offers us the very title under which o contemplate this new-old trend of modern Shakespearian criticism which, while respecting the main direction of Bradley's thought, is willing to expose interpretations which have "focused attention upon misleading issues".

This tendency to revert to what is old and plain, acknowledging in it a sanity and a wisdom, a centring down of criticism upon the essentials, goes naturally with a tendency to examine and

[1] This volume was unfortunately not available for more detailed description. It is to be hoped that it can be included in a later issue.

[2] *Shylock. The History of a Character or the Myth of the Jew* (Gollancz, 1947).

[3] "The Character of Angelo in *Measure for Measure*" (*Modern Language Review*, XLI (July 1946), 246–55).

[4] "The Character of Iago" (*Studies in Honor of A. H. R. Fairchild*, ed. C. T. Prouty; University of Missouri Studies, 1946).

[5] "Don Juan as a European Figure" (Nottingham University College, Byron Foundation Lecture, 1946).

[6] "Bradley Revisited: Forty Years After" (*Studies in Philology*, XLIV (April 1947), 174–94).

place the findings of more recent criticism. We are near the middle of a century whose early years saw the development, if not the actual beginning, of many new lines of investigation whose fruitfulness in Shakespearian studies sometimes momentarily blinded criticism to the value of what was familiar. There is a tendency at the present day to reconsider, but not as yet to underestimate, these findings. Many of the most important of them, the palaeographical, bibliographical and textual studies that are refounding our texts, the antiquarian studies that have given us back the Elizabethan stage, lie outside the scope of this section. But within the field of strictly critical studies certain lines of exploration have opened up which have increased our understanding of the content of Shakespeare's plays and the findings from these are now being collected and codified. The studies of the history plays as keys to Shakespeare's political thought; of the late plays in their relation to his art and poetry; of his imagery, its nature and functions; which we owe, in the last three decades, to the work of Murry, Tillyard, Charlton, Spurgeon, Clemen, Wilson Knight and others, are producing a succession of studies to this day, some of them still by the very men who initiated the investigations.

Studies of the once-neglected history plays are, with a few exceptions, on specific aspects or plays. But L. B. Campbell treats *Shakespeare's Histories*[1] as what they most clearly and significantly are, "Mirrors of Elizabethan Policy", and A. P. Rossiter makes the valuable contribution of the idea and term 'Moral History' to distinguish the Shakespearian group and a few others, like *Woodstock*, that are akin to it. In both these studies the nature of the thought and material of which the Histories were made and the nature of the resulting works of art, of the art-form, in fact, which they illustrate, is clearly examined. Other volumes and articles in various places support these longer studies, R. Speaight writing on *Shakespeare and Politics*, W. A. Armstrong on "The Elizabethan Conception of the Tyrant",[2] John Laird on "Shakespeare on the Wars of England".[3]

The 'late plays' that once needed the advocacy of H. B. Charlton and E. M. W. Tillyard, are now, thanks to their interpretations, centres of critical interest. Of G. Wilson Knight's illuminating analyses mention has already been made in this section. At the opposite extreme stands G. B. Shaw's *Cymbeline Refinished*,[4] the preface to which also indicates the increasing modern preoccupation with these plays.

The criticism of imagery, which has for nearly twenty years been associated with the name of Caroline Spurgeon, is still attracting scholars, English and Continental. E. A. Armstrong's *Shakespeare's Imagination*[5] carries this exploration in a specific direction (never before so thoroughly investigated), its psychological basis and indications. Modifying rather than following Spurgeon's theory of 'image-clusters', Armstrong lays bare some extremely interesting image-sequences and patterns. The weakness of these critical methods which set recent psychological assumptions in authority over the art and wisdom of the ages is one upon which C. S. Lewis neatly put his finger a few years ago. But the habit remains, to bewilder those of us who find that when all has been

[1] *Shakespeare's 'Histories', Mirrors of Elizabethan Policy* (San Marino, California, Huntington Library, 1947). This and the following volume are both treated more fully in the section on "Life and Times".

[2] *Review of English Studies*, XXII (July 1946), 161–81.

[3] In *Philosophical Incursions into English Literature* (Cambridge University Press, 1947).

[4] In *Geneva, Cymbeline Refinished and Good King Charles* (Constable, 1947).

[5] See above, p. 119 and footnote.

explained away there still remains the original mystery—the work of art itself. (It is perhaps only fair to admit that Armstrong acknowledges this from time to time himself.)

It is, moreover, noticeable that the study of Shakespeare's sources tends more and more to concern itself with the transmutation of the raw source-material into art and that even notes on details treat their evidence in this way. Among various recent contributions in this field may be cited Ethel Seaton's "*Antony and Cleopatra* and the *Book of Revelation*".[1]

Finally, there is a group of essays and articles for which F. P. Wilson's "Shakespeare Today"[2] might serve as introduction, those that are concerned, like his, with surveying the present position of Shakespeare studies or with examining special aspects of the living Shakespeare: "Shakespeare and American Scholarship" (R. A. Law);[3] "Shakespeare on the Soviet Stage"[4] (Mikhail Morozov's analysis of recent Soviet interpretations of some of the plays most popular in Russia); "Verse and Speech in *Coriolanus*"[5] (H. Granville-Barker's study of a specific aspect). This group and this survey may fitly be closed with mention of Kenneth Muir's "The Future of Shakespeare",[6] which surveys not so much the position of Shakespeare studies to-day as the lines along which they might or should develop tomorrow.

As I suggested at the beginning of this brief and inadequate notice, we are, it would seem, at a pausing place in critical studies. Certainly a revaluation of the critical habits and tendencies of the last half-century was to be expected about now. The war made it certain. Shakespeare's readers all over the world will watch with increased interest to see what the next few years produce, and will await, almost with impatience, what we may soon expect—the harvest from the reviving Continental Shakespeare studies.

2. SHAKESPEARE'S LIFE AND TIMES

reviewed by CLIFFORD LEECH

The period under review has been made notable by the appearance of Sir Edmund Chambers's *Sources for a Biography of Shakespeare*.[7] This short book "records the substance and often preserves the language of a course of lectures given to students working for the Bachelorship of Letters at Oxford during 1929 to 1938". The aim is to treat Shakespeare as a typical subject for biographical research in the sixteenth and seventeenth centuries, and Chambers briefly surveys the variety of historical records (Tenurial, Ecclesiastical, Municipal, Occupational, Court, National and Personal) and other, less reliable, sources of information. There is, of course, no intention of bringing together here the sum-total of knowledge and conjecture that the exploration of Shakespeare's life has produced, but rather to indicate how biographers of his contemporaries may apply to their tasks the methods which have been found useful in Shakespearian research.

---

[1] *Review of English Studies*, XXII (July 1946), 219–24.
[2] In *Britain Today* (no. 131, March 1947), 24–9.
[3] In *Twentieth Century English* (New York, Philosophical Library, 1947).
[4] Translated by David Magarshak (*Soviet News*, 1947).
[5] *Review of English Studies*, XXIII (January 1947), 1–15.
[6] *Penguin New Writing* (no. 28, 1946).
[7] *Sources for a Biography of Shakespeare* (Oxford, Clarendon Press, 1946).

The less professional reader, however, might find the book's usefulness increased if references to Chambers's longer works were given: these would indicate what results had been achieved through the use of the sources here surveyed, and would bring out the typical character of the facts and speculations concerning Shakespeare's life which find a place in the present volume.

John Henry de Groot in *The Shakespeares and 'The Old Faith'*[1] has considered the available evidence for the religion of Shakespeare's parents and has argued that no conclusion on this matter could be reached without the help of John Shakespeare's "Spiritual Last Will and Testament". This document, wholly Catholic in spirit and phrasing, is shown to be authentic in all but its opening sentences, being a translation from an Italian form of profession which exists to-day in Italian, Spanish and Romansch versions. The original was the work of St Charles Borromeo, Archbishop of Milan, who made contact with the Parsons-Campion mission to England when it visited Milan in May 1580. De Groot has drawn on the work of Herbert Thurston and the Countess de Chambrun, but has related their discoveries to the problem as a whole and has satisfactorily answered objections that from time to time have been made.

He is on less certain ground, inevitably, when considering to what extent William Shakespeare was influenced by his father's religion. Chambers, reviewing de Groot's book,[2] has emphasized that Shakespeare has left us in the plays no evidence of his religious outlook: this is a salutary warning against rash assumptions, but it is difficult to believe that Shakespeare's imagery and his handling of theme have remained uninfluenced by his attitude to religious ideas. De Groot gives a number of examples of Catholic feeling in imagery, and at some length demonstrates that *King John* modifies the strong Protestantism of *The Troublesome Raigne*; perhaps wisely, however, he does not attempt minutely to explore Shakespeare's intellectual position, which would demand a consideration of the attitudes of mind implied by the problem plays, the tragedies and the romances. Kenneth Muir, in an article on "*Timon of Athens* and the Cash-nexus",[3] has drawn our attention to the way in which the plays after 1600 reflect a change in the implied attitude to political order: the treatment of political themes becomes more critical, less of a straightforward exposition of the Tudor idea: so, in the matter of religion, one might conclude that Shakespeare's earliest environment left him with an attachment to the old faith, but that from *Hamlet* to *Timon* his view of things became increasingly anthropocentric.

The strange variety of comment provoked by the Shakespeare plays is forcibly illustrated when one turns from the works of scholarship just noted to William Bliss's *The Real Shakespeare*[4] or to Miss Barbara A. Mackenzie's *Shakespeare's Sonnets: Their Relation to his Life*.[5] Bliss calls his book "A Counterblast to Commentators", and exhorts us to turn our back on speculation and to accept the Folio text as the authenticated work of "the sanest and most equable-minded of men, the most crystal-clear in thought and expression". He does, however, himself enjoy a modicum of speculation, averring that Shakespeare as a boy sailed round the world with Drake, and as a young man made a voyage to the Levant and knew shipwreck on the sea-coast of Bohemia. Despite the evidence of the 'actors' lists' we are told that Shakespeare was never

---

[1] *The Shakespeares and 'The Old Faith'* (New York, King's Crown Press, 1946).
[2] *The Review of English Studies*, XXIII (April 1947), 161-2.
[3] *The Modern Quarterly Miscellany* (no. 1, 1947).
[4] *The Real Shakespeare. A Counterblast to Commentators* (Sidgwick and Jackson, 1947).
[5] *Shakespeare's Sonnets: Their Relation to his Life* (Cape Town, Maskew Miller, 1946).

an actor. Anxious to satisfy himself that Shakespeare was a Catholic, Bliss assigns parts of *Henry VIII* to another playwright, yet elsewhere assures us that the First Folio is his canon. In his rejection of contemporary scholarship he is able to put forward a remarkable view of the provenance of the Folio text, believing apparently that each of its plays is independent of the earlier Quartos. Bliss might have checked a few of his incidental statements, such as that Shakespeare was his father's first child and that the Chamberlain's Men were the same company as Her Majesty's Players. *The Spanish Revenge*, mentioned on p. 237, is apparently Kyd's play. The book makes free with some famous names in Shakespearian scholarship: their possessors will not mind, but the general public should not be bemused by these gusty frolics.

Barbara A. Mackenzie weaves a sentimental story round the *Sonnets*, as many have done before her. She finds reference to three rivals with Shakespeare for Southampton's regard, and would have us believe that the poet and the patron came to a final breach in 1596. There is much strained interpretation offered us, a tear-sprinkled image of the poet, and a strenuous denial of homosexual leanings despite the hysteria here found in the poems and the identification of Shakespeare with the deserted mistress of *A Lover's Complaint*. This is novelette-writing which rashly employs a famous name. In the weaving of her small tapestry of tears, Miss Mackenzie overlooks the performance of *Love's Labour's Lost* at Southampton's house in 1605, after the Earl's release from prison.

The considerable though heterodox scholarship of M. Abel Lefranc is displayed in *A la Découverte de Shakespeare*,[1] which was published in 1945 but has only now arrived for review. In this volume Lefranc brings together the results of his researches on the plays and their authorship since the publication of *Sous le Masque de William Shakespeare* in 1919. He is, of course, intent on seeing William Stanley, sixth Earl of Derby, as the author, and repeats many of the well-worn arguments (John Shakespeare's illiteracy, the unlikelihood that a Stratford boy should come to have a strongly latinized vocabulary, the alleged mysteries of the Droeshout engraving and the Stratford bust) without a consideration of recent inquiries into the conditions of sixteenth-century Stratford. When, however, he draws attention to the poet's knowledge of falconry, of warfare, of magic, of the ways of princes, he at least underlines once more the astonishing receptivity of the poet's mind. He makes us think too that the author of the plays must assuredly have reached Italy. But it is particularly necessary that the setting forth of Lefranc's thesis should have no appearance of disingenuousness, and one is therefore disconcerted by his reference to Robert Parsons's *A Conference about the Next Succession to the Crown of England* (1594): he states that Parsons concluded his treatise by favourably considering William Stanley's claim to be Elizabeth's heir, but he does not point out, as he should, that the *Conference* surveyed the claims of many others and in particular that of the Infanta of Spain. The greater part of Lefranc's work on this occasion is, however, devoted to speculation concerning the origins and implications of *Hamlet* and *A Midsummer-Night's Dream*. He believes, with Miss Winstanley, that the Darnley murder was much in the poet's mind when he wrote *Hamlet* and that he was making through the play a political comment on the royal succession. Lefranc has indeed brought together a remarkable series of parallels between the murders of Darnley and Hamlet's father, and has even traced the names 'Rosenkrandtz' and 'Gullenstarne' among those whom Bothwell knew after his flight from Scotland.

[1] *A la Découverte de Shakespeare* (Paris, Editions Albin Michel, 1945).

We need, however, to distinguish between the experiences which go to the making of a play and the 'message' it contains. It is by no means impossible that Shakespeare's knowledge of the Darnley murder was among the formative influences on *Hamlet*, but it is difficult to believe that one can simultaneously and successfully write a tragedy and a political utterance: a tragedy makes a statement about the human situation as a whole, perhaps using contemporary themes as symbolic of a universal and abiding state of affairs; a political play urges a particular line of conduct upon its audience and is essentially dependent on a notion of free choice. Indeed, Lefranc defeats his own purpose when he sees Hamlet as simultaneously William Stanley and James VI, and when at the end of the play James VI is identified with Fortinbras: with such transformations taking place, *Hamlet* could not effectively convey a political message. At one point Lefranc goes so far as to suggest that *The Spanish Tragedy*, the *Ur-Hamlet* and other sixteenth-century revenge-plays were similarly related to the Darnley murder, but he leaves this theme hurriedly, half-conscious perhaps that it spells disaster for his argument concerning authorship: if Thomas Kyd could use the Darnley affair, so might the man of Stratford. *The Spanish Tragedy*, indeed, has close parallels with the matter of Scotland: the garden in which Horatio is murdered, the love-scene which immediately precedes the murder, the very name of Bel-Imperia, her earlier betrothal to Andrea and her wooing by Balthazar, the picture spoken of in the added 'Painter's Scene'—all these cohere strangely with details in the Darnley story. We must remain grateful to Lefranc for continuing to extend our knowledge of the world of thought and experience from which the plays came, but we are likely to feel that his obsession with William Stanley makes him regard as assured fact what is only ingenious speculation.

It is interesting to find points of contact with Lefranc's methods in Lily B. Campbell's study of the history plays.[1] Miss Campbell finds that the history plays use the stories of past kings to comment on the political problems of Shakespeare's own time: both she and Lefranc, for example, believe that John's behaviour in the matter of Prince Arthur's death is a reflection of Elizabeth's hesitation over Mary Stuart and her anger with Secretary Davison when she found that the execution had been carried out. Again a caveat is necessary. There can be little doubt that the politics of his time were a consuming interest with the Shakespeare who wrote the histories and that more or less consciously he was aware of parallels between the chronicle-material he handled and the affairs of great ones in later years. But it is difficult to credit that he would habitually make overt reference to matters of high policy; it is surely unthinkable that, in the scene between John and Hubert when Arthur's death is reported to the King (IV, ii), he would wish his audience to see it as "a dialogue that in essence did take place between Queen Elizabeth and Secretary Davison".

But Miss Campbell has very considerably enriched our understanding of the 'history' as a dramatic form. She has demonstrated how history won remarkable popularity in the sixteenth century, being used and admired by both humanists and reformers, and she has differentiated between tragedy and historical drama by her assertion that the former has to do with ethics, the latter with politics. In many places she is able to correct hitherto current views, as when she shows that the distortion of Machiavelli's doctrines can be found earlier than Gentillet's *Contre-Machiavel* (1576): in 1572 an anonymous writer of *A Treatise of Treasons against Queen Elizabeth*

---

[1] *Shakespeare's 'Histories', Mirrors of Elizabethan Policy* (see p. 121, above).

attacked Burghley and Sir Nicholas Bacon as Machiavels and Catilines and drew a picture of a "Machiavellian State and Regiment" that is thoroughly in keeping with later popular notions.

Miss Campbell did not see Tillyard's *Shakespeare's History Plays* until her book was completed; a detailed comparison of the views put forward by these two scholars would be an illuminating exercise. One notes, too, that Miss Campbell still regards *The Famous Victories* as a source-play for *Henry V*.

History is also partly the concern of A. P. Rossiter in the 'Preface' to his edition of *Woodstock*.[1] He links the histories with the moralities, justly emphasizing the moral (and non-tragic) nature of *Gorboduc*, and throws yet more light on the Elizabethan conception of order in the universe and the state. He is able to show that the author of *Woodstock* is unconventional in his political implications, being far readier than Shakespeare to believe that subjects may check a king. The influence of Tillyard, evident here, is seen also in several recent articles: Kenneth Muir's mentioned above, C. H. Hobday's on "The Social Background of *King Lear*",[2] and W. A. Armstrong's on "The Elizabethan Conception of the Tyrant".[3] Hobday sees in *Lear* Shakespeare's horrified reaction to "bourgeois individualism". There is, of course, something in this view, for no one can read the plays of the early seventeenth century without knowing that the Renaissance cult of the individual had become suspect, but this article suffers markedly from over-simplification: we read of "the healthy robustness of Marlowe, Shakespeare and Jonson", the "increasing decadence and preciousness" of the playwrights that followed; there is no realization of the peculiar complexity of Marlowe's thought, and he is made simply a believer in the cult of individualism; we are told that Lear dies in order to show that neither the new bourgeois order nor a return to feudalism will solve society's problems; and the paper concludes with a sentimental picture of the last plays as an expression of Shakespeare's fond hope for a better way of life. Armstrong gives a workmanlike account of Elizabethan portraits of tyrants, but rather neglects the spirit of scepticism that enabled Marlowe to delight with Tamburlaine and Shakespeare to see humanity in Macbeth.

In his latest volume[4] T. W. Baldwin is concerned with many things, including the dating of Shakespeare's early plays, but his principal theme is the Renaissance inheritance of act-division from the commentators on Terence and the development of the principles governing it. He hardly demonstrates that the late sixteenth-century dramatists in England worked with consciously held structural principles always in view, but he does throw additional light on their classical inheritance. His theories would be more cogently presented if he concentrated on the significant things that his arduous researches have brought to light, instead of describing every step of so long a journey.

We are in debt to Louise C. Turner Forest for her article "A Caveat for Critics Against Invoking Elizabethan Psychology",[5] in which she forces us to recognize that Elizabethan psychology was no more uniform than the psychological writings of our own day should

[1] *Woodstock. A Moral History* (Chatto and Windus, 1946).
[2] *The Modern Quarterly Miscellany* (no. 1, 1947).
[3] *Review of English Studies*, XXII (July 1946), 161–81.
[4] *William Shakspere's Five-Act Structure. Shakspere's Early Plays on the Background of Renaissance Theories of Five-Act Structure from 1470* (Urbana, University of Illinois Press, 1947).
[5] *Publications of the Modern Language Association of America*, LXI (September 1946), 651–72.

lead us to expect. She admits that a dramatist might fix upon a particular notion and apply it strictly to a particular character (as Ford does in *The Lover's Melancholy*), but we should not therefore see every character as a case-history. Lawrence Babb, in a review of Professor Draper's *The Humors and Shakespeare's Characters*,[1] utters a similar warning. Miss Forest's article should dispose of the belief that there was a single 'psychological' theory to be grasped. One wonders whether an article on "Elizabethan Chiromancy", by Carroll Camden,[2] sufficiently allows for a similar vagueness in Elizabethan thought.

3. TEXTUAL STUDIES

reviewed by JAMES G. McMANAWAY

Any year in which three volumes of the New Cambridge Shakespeare are published can be accounted profitable for the students of Shakespeare's text. Perhaps the choice of titles (*1 and 2 Henry IV* and *Henry V*) was fortuitous, but a careful reading of these plays is peculiarly appropriate in these post-war years, and their publication has the same timeliness that John Dover Wilson discovers in Shakespeare's composition of *Henry V*.

In a word [he writes], *Henry V*, so apposite in theme and spirit, as I and many others discovered, to the dispatch of a great expeditionary force in 1914, was actually written for a similar occasion in 1599 [the invasion of Ireland under the Earl of Essex]. Yet it would have been written in any case about this time, and the occasion was for Shakespeare a stroke of luck....For the zenith of the play is not the victory—that is lightly passed over, and (in itself miraculous) is ascribed to God alone—but the King's speeches before the battle is joined, the battle which all but the King think already lost. Every line of what Henry then says breathes the English temper, but one above all—

We happy few, we band of brothers.

If History never repeats itself, the human spirit often does: Henry's words before Agincourt, and Churchill's after the Battle of Britain, come from the same national mint.

The choice of subject by E. M. W. Tillyard for his most recent contribution to the interpretation of Shakespeare may have followed naturally upon his publication of *The Elizabethan World Picture*, but it is as likely to have been dictated by his own unquiet of mind about the place of Britain in a chaotic world. In his erudite and provocative book entitled *Shakespeare's History Plays*, Tillyard pleads for the reading of these plays as two tetralogies and argues with particular effectiveness that the later series, *Richard II* to *Henry V*, can only be understood textually and aesthetically if it be granted that *Henry IV*, though in two parts, is one play, and that Shakespeare had *Henry V* in mind when he began writing *Richard II*. In this he and Dover Wilson are in substantial agreement. [Venturing into the field of bibliography Tillyard guesses (pp. 216–17) that the two parts of *The Troublesome Raigne* (1591) may be bad quartos of an early play by Shakespeare which he later revised as the F text of *King John*.]

The New Cambridge volumes should be read in conjunction with Tillyard's volume and

---

[1] *Modern Language Notes*, LXII (January 1947), 56–7.
[2] *Ibid.* 1–7.

with the editor's own *The Fortunes of Falstaff*, which appeared in 1943, and his article, "The Origins and Development of Shakespeare's *Henry IV*".[1] In the latter, Wilson rejects Tillyard's admittedly "hazardous and revolutionary" suggestion that Shakespeare "may well have written early versions of the plays of the second tetralogy, *Richard II*, *Henry IV*, and *Henry V*, now lost but recast in the plays we have. Further, the *Famous Victories of Henry V* [entered in the Stationers' Register in 1594; earliest surviving Q dated 1598] may well be an abridgement of Shakespeare's plays on the reigns of Henry IV and Henry V", for the reason that both 1588, when Tarleton was acting in a play about Henry V at the Red Bull, and 1592, when Nashe refers to a play on this subject, are incredibly early dates. He also argues that the Lord Cobham who protested the debasement of Oldcastle's name was William Brooke, who became Lord Chamberlain on 8 August 1596 and died on 6 March 1597. This was suggested by H. N. Paul in Hemingway's Variorum edition (p. 355) and would be easy to accept if Professor Hotson is correct in his belief[2] that "the two parts of *Henry IV* must be pushed back into the season of 1596–7".

There is general agreement that Shakespeare's foul sheets served as copy for the First Quarto of 1 *Henry IV*. This survives in a single sheet, sig C, which came to light in the binding of a copy of Thomas's *Rules of Italian Grammar* and passed into the hands of Halliwell-Phillipps. His note, dated 25 May 1867, records that it was found "some years ago". Because F reads 'President' at II, iv, 32, where Q has 'present', Wilson insists that Q6 (1613), which was used in printing F, must have been collated with the prompt-book, but the emendation is required by the context and is hardly beyond the powers of whoever purged the text of oaths.

The explanation of Hal's jest with Francis (II, iv, 33–99) wins the approval of the anonymous reviewer of the edition in the *Times Literary Supplement*,[3] but Janet Spens disagrees[4] on the ground that nothing in the text indicates the drawer imagined the Prince was about to offer him a place in his household. Dr Spens is entirely justified in her objection to Wilson's stage direction at the beginning of II, iv and his notes on II, iv, 96–9 and 108, which describe Hal as "unsteady", "a little tipsy", and "not quite sober", for there is no indication whatever that the Prince's physical or intellectual powers are impaired. She rejects, too, the paraphrasing of II, iv, 90: "Now I am of all humours..." as "I am ready for any sort of fun that ever was." Instead, she echoes the interpretation given earlier by Tillyard, that while Francis has one parrot-like humour, of "Anon, anon, Sir", and Hotspur the one humour of Honour, the Prince has urbanity and versatility and is composed of *all* humours.

In 2 *Henry IV*, Wilson has made extensive use of Shaaber's admirable Variorum edition. Q was set from Shakespeare's foul papers, and F from a literary transcript of the prompt-book, possibly in the hand of Ralph Crane. At some time unknown to us, Shakespeare's intention of having two royal processions in v, v was abandoned, as is shown by F's shortened stage direction at l. 5, though with no change in the second speech of the first Groome; Wilson follows Q in retaining all of Shakespeare's pageantry. This pious gesture is a dramatic reminder that a Shakespeare drama is not one, but many plays: the ideal play as the author conceived it; the text as written; the tidied up fair copy, later marked and perhaps abridged for representation; the im-

[1] *The Library*, 4th ser., XXVI (June 1945), 2–16.
[2] 2 *Henry IV*, Variorum ed. pp. 354–5.
[3] "The True Prince", *Times Literary Supplement*, 24 August 1946.
[4] In a letter to the same issue.

perfect rendition on the stage; and the printed text or texts, that may represent one or more of these versions, either "maimed, and deformed", or "perfect in their limbes".

The first textual problem in the play is the presence in many copies of Q of a cancel sheet (not a half-sheet, as stated by Wilson) with the text of a scene (III, i) that had at first been omitted. In an article entitled, "The Cancel in the Quarto of 2 *Henry IV*"[1] the present writer concluded from the evidence of paper, typography, punctuation, and spelling that the cancel was printed by Simmes shortly after Q was first put on sale and suggested that if the publishers did not voluntarily prepare the cancel, Shakespeare or a representative of his company may have procured its insertion. Wilson conjectures with great plausibility that the scene was omitted because the single leaf containing it had been accidentally left behind at the playhouse; thus it was not part of the manuscript licensed for printing, and when the cancel was inserted, the content of the scene proved to be so dangerous that Q was not reprinted.

The second textual problem is to account for the omission in Q of about 170 lines of text preserved in F. Since these all relate to the deposing of Richard, modern writers have agreed that the censor or the publishers deleted them to avoid trouble with the authorities. Editors usually reprint Q, restoring the excised passages from F. Hitherto no one has explained satisfactorily how III, i, containing the most explicit references to Richard, escaped the censor's pencil. Wilson's brilliant conjecture that the leaf with this scene was never seen by the censor is probably the final word on the subject.

In *Henry the Fifth*, his third and latest volume to be considered, Wilson dismisses the Bad Quarto of 1600 with a brief characterization of it as "a 'reported' version, probably supplied by traitor-actors, of performances—perhaps in a shortened form for provincial audiences—of the play as acted by Shakespeare's company", and refers his readers to detailed discussions by H. T. Price, E. K. Chambers, W. W. Greg, and G. I. Duthie. The Folio text is accepted as a reprint of "the manuscript exactly as Shakespeare handed it to his company...in 1599", i.e. Shakespeare's foul papers, not the fair copy prepared from them for use as a prompt-book.

Starting with the concluding couplet in II, Prologue,

> But till the king come forth, and not till then,
> Unto Southampton do we shift our scene,

Wilson and Duthie, who is associated with him in the preparation and annotation of the text, construct the hypothesis that originally Shakespeare kept his promise to continue the story of Falstaff but that the absence of Will Kempe from 1599–1602 left the company without a suitable actor and necessitated the excision of the role of Falstaff and the recasting of portions of the play before it was ever produced. With considerable plausibility they argue that II, i and iii, which are located not in Southampton and France but in London, are interpolations, written to prepare for and recount the death of Falstaff, and that the Jamy-Macmorris episode at III, ii, 63ff. and Henry's long soliloquy after the departure of Erpingham at IV, i, 34 are additional fillers to replace the lost matter of Falstaff. In some of the episodes, for example that of the leeks, they suppose Pistol was substituted for the Fat Knight, and they cite as proof Pistol's lines, "News have I that my Doll is dead i' th' spital Of malady of France", rejecting the usual emendation of

---

[1] *Studies in Honor of A. H. R. Fairchild*, University of Missouri Studies, 1946, pp. 67–80.

'Doll' to 'Nell' on the ground that Shakespeare failed to bring this speech into accord with the revised text.

In an almost exactly contemporaneous study entitled "With Sir John in It"[1] J. H. Walter advances the same hypothesis, adds the Boy's soliloquy (III, ii, 28–53) to the list of interpolations, and supplies many details overlooked by Wilson and Duthie. He observes that the absence of Kempe did not prevent the Chamberlain's Men from performing "Sir John Old Castell", i.e. Part 1 or 2 of *Henry IV*, on 6 March 1600 and could hardly have kept Shakespeare from introducing Falstaff in *Henry V*. Instead, Walter supposes that the Master of the Revels deleted the Falstaff scenes out of deference to Lord Cobham and that Shakespeare was enforced to alter his play accordingly.

The survival of irregularly distributed 'Shakespearian' spellings, as in II, iii, the textual disorder of such passages as II, i, 27–31 and 105–6 and III, i, 22–5, and the difficulties in nearly all the scenes in which Pistol and Fluellen appear suggest to Walter that there has been extensive revision and that, though the copy for F was in general in a scribal hand, the passages cited, and others, were printed from Shakespeare's MS.

If it was Cobham's protest, instead of the temporary defection of Kempe that necessitated the excision of Falstaff, it is possible that Shakespeare took the unlicensed fair copy and interpolated his revisions in the margins or on loose leaves of paper. In that case, this manuscript, a fair copy of which was afterwards licensed for acting and marked for prompt use, and not Shakespeare's original foul sheets, served as copy for F. It was not a consistently revised text, as Walter points out: Pistol's recommendation to Nym to marry Doll Tearsheet (II, i, 74–9) ignores Falstaff's claim to her; and his reference to Doll and his advancing years (V, i, 79 ff.) would be more appropriate to Falstaff than to Pistol; again, one of the speeches assigned to Pistol, "Master Fer ! I'll fer him, and firk him, and ferret him" (IV, iv, 29–30), has a definitely Falstaffian ring. Walter suggests plausibly that the reversed order of IV, iv and v in Q is correct and that F errs because of the confused state of the copy. Doubtless some of the inconsistencies and defects were eliminated in the preparation of the prompt-book.

The volume of *Studies in Honor of A. H. R. Fairchild*, referred to above, contains two other studies of direct interest to Shakespearians. The first (pp. 9–35) is an admirable exposition by Giles E. Dawson of the nature of Elizabethan copyright and a summary of the sometimes tempestuous history of "The Copyright of Shakespeare's Dramatic Works" to the death of perpetual copyright in 1774. He shows that there never was a copyright of the collected Works and that each successive publisher of the Works, whether an individual or a syndicate, owned a majority of the separate plays.

The second essay (pp. 119–32) is an acute and closely reasoned study by Harry R. Hoppe of "*John of Bordeux*: A Bad Quarto that never Reached Print", based on Renwick's edition of the manuscript for the Malone Society. Hoppe is clearly right in his insistence that the text results from the combined efforts of reporter-dictators and a scribe, rather than of a reader-dictator and a scribe, as Renwick suggested. Other 'bad' texts are available only in printed versions; Hoppe's observations and conclusions are important because the play under examination is a manuscript, in which the mental and physical processes of the compilers frequently reveal themselves.

---

[1] *Modern Language Review*, XLI (July 1946), 237–46.

The stage directions in the F text of *Lear* led W. W. Greg to the conclusion that a prompt-book was its basis, but his correspondence with John Berryman has resulted in a modification[1] of some of his earlier opinions. Bearing in mind the fact that in Act II the Bastard's soliloquy should be printed as a separate scene, he now suggests (1) that the editor of F may have introduced act and scene divisions, working from an undivided Q and an undivided prompt-book, or (2) that "the manuscript used for the Folio *Lear* may have been altered to fit it for a late provincial performance"—Berryman inclines to the latter alternative.

The survival of proof sheets in early editions of Shakespeare has generally been attributed to accident. A new and more plausible explanation is offered by Francis R. Johnson in "Printers' 'Copy Books' and the Black Market in the Elizabethan Book Trade",[2] namely that the sheets are found in 'copy' books, one or more of which were allowed to workmen in Elizabethan printing shops. Starting with the litigation that followed the printing of Dowland's *Second Book of Songs or Ayres* in 1600, Johnson traces the recorded history of the "ancient custom" of allowing 'copy' books and produces a short but valuable chapter on a neglected phase of early printing, illustrated by references to the proof sheets in the First Folio and other dramatic texts and to the remarkable Folger Library fragment of the first edition of the *Passionate Pilgrim*.

The perplexities arising out of Renaissance punctuation are little appreciated except by editors of early books, and even these, in my opinion, are frequently too confident of the authority of their texts. It is now generally conceded that 'Elizabethan' spellings are much more apt to originate with the compositor than with the author, except in rare cases where unfamiliar or poorly written words are painfully reproduced *literatim*. Frequently it has been possible to assign pages of a book to one or another of the compositors who worked on it on the basis of their preferential spellings, and on occasion data have been compiled that seemed to warrant belief that some compositors may be identified by their characteristic habits of punctuation. If these things be true, it is not surprising that Dover Wilson is driven to confess[3] his bewilderment at the variety in the early editions of the twenty-one plays he has edited and to agree with W. W. Greg that "We can probably rely on [the punctuation] of the early editions even less than we can on their spelling". Like Peter Alexander, whose British Academy lecture on "Shakespeare's Punctuation" Wilson is reviewing, I too have long been fond of the F pointing of Hamlet's "What a piece of worke is a man!", but, while denying that the punctuation in either Q2 or F can be proved to be as Shakespeare set it down, I confess that Wilson's eloquent use of quotations from Hooker's *Ecclesiastical Polity* and Pico della Mirandola's *Oratio de Hominis Dignitate* almost persuades me to accept the reading of this aria as it is scored in Q2.

[1] *Review of English Studies*, XXII (July 1946), 229.
[2] *The Library*, 5th ser., I (September 1946), 97–105.
[3] *Review of English Studies*, XXIII (January 1947), 70–8.

BOOKS RECEIVED

*Inclusion in this list does not preclude review, though certain reviews
are held over for the next volume*

ARMSTRONG, E. A.. *Shakespeare's Imagination. A Study of the Psychology of Association and Inspiration* (London: Lindsay Drummond, 1946).

BALDWIN, T. W. *William Shakspere's Five-Act Structure. Shakspere's Early Plays on the Background of Renaissance Theories of Five-Act Structure from* 1470 (Urbana: University of Illinois Press, 1947).

BERSTL, JULIUS. *The Sun's Bright Child. The Imaginary Memoirs of Edmund Kean* (London: Hammond, Hammond, 1946).

BICKERSTETH, G. L. "The Golden World of *King Lear*". Annual Shakespeare Lecture of the British Academy, 1946. From the *Proceedings of the British Academy*, vol. XXXII (London: Geoffrey Cumberlege, 1947).

BLISS, WILLIAM. *The Real Shakespeare. A Counterblast to Commentators* (London: Sidgwick and Jackson, 1947).

BRISCOE, E. E. and SWINYARD, LAURENCE. *Shakespeare's Stratford-on-Avon* (London: Charles F. Kimble, n.d.).

CAMPBELL, LILY B. *Shakespeare's 'Histories.' Mirrors of Elizabethan Policy* (San Marino, California: The Huntington Library. London: Cambridge University Press, 1947).

DE GROOT, J. H. *The Shakespeares and 'The Old Faith'* (New York: King's Crown Press. London: Geoffrey Cumberlege, 1946).

ELLIS, OLIVER C. DE C. *Cleopatra in the Tide of Time* (The Poetry Lovers' Fellowship with the International Fellowship of Literature. London: Williams and Norgate, 1947).

GUNDRY, W. G. C. *Was Shakespeare Educated?* (London: Lapworth, 1946).

HARBAGE, ALFRED. *As They Liked It. An Essay on Shakespeare and Morality* (New York: Macmillan, 1947).

KNIGHT, G. WILSON. *The Crown of Life. Essays in Interpretation of Shakespeare's Final Plays* (Oxford University Press, 1947).

KNIGHTS, L. C. *Explorations. Essays in Criticism Mainly on the Literature of the Seventeenth Century* (London: Chatto and Windus, 1946).

MACKENZIE, B. A. *Shakespeare's Sonnets: Their Relation to his Life* (Cape Town: Maskew Miller, 1946).

MADARIAGA, SALVADOR DE. *Don Juan as a European Figure*, Byron Foundation Lecture, 1946 (Nottingham University College).

MELSOME, W. S. *The Bacon-Shakespeare Anatomy* (London: Lapworth, 1945).

MOROZOV, MIKHAIL M. *Shakespeare on the Soviet Stage*, translated by David Magarshak, with an Introduction by J. Dover Wilson (London: *Soviet News*, 1947).

POLAK, A. LAURENCE. *More Legal Fictions. A Series of Cases from Shakespeare* (London: Stevens, 1946).

PROUTY, C. T. (ed.). *Studies in Honor of A. H. R. Fairchild* (University of Missouri Studies, vol. XXI, no. 1. Columbia: University of Missouri, 1946).

ROSSITER, A. P. (ed.). *Woodstock. A Moral History* (London: Chatto and Windus, 1946).

SAMPSON, GEORGE. *Seven Essays* (Cambridge University Press, 1947).

SEMPER, I. J. *Hamlet Without Tears* (Dubuque, Iowa: Loras College Press, 1946).

BOOKS RECEIVED

SHAKESPEARE, WILLIAM. *Macbeth.* Illustrated by Salvador Dali (New York: Doubleday, 1946).

SHAW, BERNARD. *Geneva, Cymbeline Refinished, and Good King Charles* (London: Constable, 1946).

SINSHEIMER, HERMANN. *Shylock. The History of a Character or the Myth of the Jew* (London: Gollancz, 1947).

STEVENSON, D. L. *The Love-Game Comedy* (New York: Columbia University Press. London: Geoffrey Cumberlege, 1946).

VENABLE, EMERSON. *The Hamlet Problem and Its Solution. An Interpretative Study* (Cincinatti: John G. Kidd, 1946).

WATKINS, RONALD. *Moonlight at the Globe. An Essay in Shakespeare Production* (London: Michael Joseph, 1946).

WILSON, J. DOVER (ed.). *The New Shakespeare. Henry V* (Cambridge University Press, 1947).

INDEX

INDEX

Blatchley, John, 109

Bliss, William, *The Real Shakespeare* reviewed, 123–4

Blount, Edward, 57

Boccaccio, Giovanni, 68

Filocopo, 69

Bond, R. W., 11

Booth, Edwin, 61

Borcherdt, H. H., 11

Borromeo, St Charles, 123

Boy Companies, *see* Theatre, Elizabethan

Boyle, Roger, Earl of Orrery:

Mustapha, 66

Henry the Fifth, 66

Bradbrook, M. C., 4

Bradley, A. C., 14, 120

Braines, W. W., 6, 30, 34, 36 n.

Brandt, Sebastian, 68

Ship of Folys, 67

Braun and Hohenberg, 26, 30, 31

Civitates Orbis Terrarum, 26

Breuning, P. S., 23

Bridewell Dock, 30

Bridges, Robert, 7

Bristol Old Vic, 99–100

Brodmeier, Carl, 3

Brook, Peter, 107, 108, 110

Brooke, Ralph, 61

Brooke, William, Lord Cobham, 128, 130

Brotanek, R., 11

Brown, Christopher, 28

Brown, Pamela, 98

Brown, Ralph, 72

Brunner, Karl, 115

Buc, Sir George, 44

Buchel, Arend van, 23

Bulgaria, 114

Burbage, Cuthbert, 41, 42, 65

Burbage, Richard, 8, 25, 38, 39, 41, 42, 43, 46, 50 n., 62, 65

Burdett-Coutts, Baroness, 59

Burghley, Lord, 126

Burton, Hal, 107

Burton, Robert, *Philosophaster*, 65

Butler, Charles, *Principles of Musik*, 70

Byrd, William:

Mass for Three Voices, 69

Psalms, Sonnets, Songs, 70

Songs of Sundrie Natures, 70

Calvin, John, 67

Camden, Carroll, 127

Camden, William, *Britannia*, 27; Gough's edition, 81

Campbell, L. B., 11

"Bradley Revisited" reviewed, 120

Shakespeare's 'Histories' reviewed, 121, 125–6

Campbell, Oscar J., 9

Campbell, Mrs Patrick, 92

Campion, Thomas:

Ayres, 70

Lords Masque, 54

Songs of Mourning, 70

Canada, 112

Carleton, Sir Dudley, 44

Carmichael, Coralie, 94

Carnegie, Andrew, 87

Cartier, Jacques, *Two Navigations to New France*, 69

Cartigny, Jean de, *The Wandering Knight*, 62

Cartwright, William, *Royal Slave*, 65

Casson, Sir Lewis, 106

Castiglione, Balthasar, 68

Castle of Perseverance, 64

Cawardine, Sir Thomas, 65

Caxton, William, 67

Cervantes, Miguel de, 68

Don Quixote, 70

Chamberlain, John, 44

Chambers, Sir Edmund, 3, 4, 5, 9, 10, 17 ff., 49 n., 54, 55, 80, 129

Sources for a Biography of Shakespeare reviewed, 122–3

Chambrun, Countess de, 71, 123

Chandos portrait of Shakespeare, 62

Chapman, George, 52, 71

Gentleman Usher, 64

Masque of the Inner Temple, 64

Masque of the Middle Temple, 54

Charles Pratt and Co., 57

Charlton, H. B., 121

Chaucer, Geoffrey, *Canterbury Tales*, 67

Chew, S. C., 76

Children of the Queen's Revels, 42

Churchill, Winston, 127

Cicero, *Foure Severall Treatises* (1577), 69

Civitas Londini, 28 ff.

Clarke, Roger, 28

Clifford Family, 71

Clunes, Alec, 115

Cobham, Lord, *see* Brooke, William

Cocteau, Jean, 97

Coertze, L. I., 112

Coffin, Martyn, 67

Cole, B., 81

Colet, John, 68

Collier, Constance, 92

INDEX

INDEX

Hahn, W., 113

Hajdukowicz, B., 113

Halliwell-Phillipps, J. O., 1, 57, 59, 62, 70, 73, 83, 86, 87 nn., 128

Hampden, Walter, 113

Handlyng Sin, 71

Harbage, Alfred, 4, 6, 7, 8
   As They Liked It reviewed, 119, 120

Harcourt, Robert, *Relation of a Voyage to Guiana*, 68

Harington, Sir John, 72

Hariot, Thomas, *New Found Land of Virginia*, 69

Harmsworth, Sir Leicester, 58, 67–8

Harris, Robert, 107, 108, 109

Harrison's Description of England, 29

Hart, Alfred, 13

Hart Family of Stratford, 80, 82, 87

Hartmann, Georg, 8

Harvard "47 Workshop", 13

Harvey, Gabriel, 71

Hathaway, Anne, *see* Stratford-upon-Avon

Hawkins, Jack, 115

Helpmann, Robert, 104

Heminges, John, 25, 38, 41, 42, 46, 57

Henry VIII, 71

Henry, Prince, 72

Henslowe, Philip, 9, 25
   'Diary', 71

Herbert, Philip, Earl of Pembroke, 71

Herford, C. H., 3

Hertford, John, 67

Heywood, Thomas, 38, 70, 75
   A Curtaine Lecture, 70
   Fair Maid of the Exchange, 64
   Four Prentices, 64
   If You Know Not Me, 64
   Marriage Triumph, 64

Higden, Ranulf, *Polychronicon*, 67

Hillebrand, H. N., 7, 10

Hilton, John, *Ayres*, 70

Hind, A. M., 37 n.

Hinman, Charlton, 77 n.

Hobday, C. H., 126

Hoefnagel, Georg, 26

Hohenberg, *see* Braun

Holinshed, Ralph, 38

Holland, Henry, *Herωologia Anglica*, 33

Hollar, Wenceslas, 26, 34–5, 37 n.
   'Long View', 34–5

Holtom, William, 85

Hondius, Ludovicus, 35 n., 36 n.
   'View of London', 31–2, 33, 37 n.

Hood, Thomas, *Regiment of the Sea*, 68

Hooker, Richard, *Ecclesiastical Polity*, 131

Hope Theatre, 44

Hoppe, H. R., "*John of Bordeaux*" reviewed, 130

Horace, 51

Hornby, Mrs, 81, 87 n.

Horneby family of Stratford, 86

Hotson, Leslie, 9, 76, 128

Houghton, Arthur Amory, 70, 71

Hudd, Walter, 107

Hulshof, A., 23

Humphrey, Ozias, 62

Huntington, Henry E., 58, 66

Hunt, H. O., 86

Hunt, Hugh, 100

Ibsen, Henrik, *Peer Gynt*, 103

Ilmari, Wilho, 116

Immermann, Karl, 2

Inglis, Esther:
   Les C. L. Pseaumes de David, 72
   Octonaries, 72

Insatiate Countess, 64

Ireland, S., 82, 87 n.

Irving, Sir Henry, 61, 72

Irving, Washington, 81, 82

Isaacs, J., 10

Italy, 116

Izod, Mrs, 83

Jacke Jugeler, 64

Jackson, Sir Barry, 107

Jaggard, William, 57, 59, 75

James I, 21, 32, 71, 82, 125
   Basilikon Doron, 21
   Daemonologie, 71

Janssen portrait of Shakespeare, 62

Johnson, F. R., "Printers' 'Copy Books'" reviewed, 131

Johnson, Dr Samuel, 60

Johnston, Denis, 97

Jones, Dudley, 109

Jones, George, 83

Jones, Inigo, 11; drawings of Bankside, 33–4

Jones, Robert, manuscript poem of, 71

Jonson, Ben, 29, 54, 61, 71, 82, 103, 126
   and the King's Men, 43–4
   and the respectability of the theatre, 40
   and the 'War of the Theatres', 41
   greater popularity than Shakespeare, 44
   plays written for Blackfriars, 44
   Works:
     Alchemist, 44, 104
     Bartholomew Fair, 44

INDEX

INDEX

INDEX